Engaged Neutrality

Engaged Neutrality

An Evolved Approach to the Cold War

Edited by
Heinz Gärtner

LEXINGTON BOOKS
Lanham • Boulder • New York • London

Published by Lexington Books
An imprint of The Rowman & Littlefield Publishing Group, Inc.
4501 Forbes Boulevard, Suite 200, Lanham, Maryland 20706
www.rowman.com

Unit A, Whitacre Mews, 26-34 Stannary Street, London SE11 4AB

British Library Cataloguing in Publication Information Available

Library of Congress Cataloging-in-Publication Data

Names: Gärtner, Heinz, 1954- editor.
Title: Engaged neutrality : an evolved approach to the Cold War / edited by
    Heinz Gärtner.
Description: Lanham : Lexington Books, [2016] | Includes bibliographical references
    and index.
Identifiers: LCCN 2016050835 (print) | LCCN 2017001689 (ebook) | ISBN
    9781498546188 (cloth : alk. paper) | ISBN 9781498546195 (Electronic)
Subjects: LCSH: Neutrality. | Security, International.
Classification: LCC JZ6422 .E54 2016 (print) | LCC JZ6422 (ebook) | DDC
    327.1—dc23
LC record available at https://lccn.loc.gov/2016050835

♾ ™ The paper used in this publication meets the minimum requirements of American National Standard for Information Sciences—Permanence of Paper for Printed Library Materials, ANSI/NISO Z39.48-1992.

Printed in the United States of America

Contents

Acknowledgments

In fall 2015, the Austrian Institute of International Affairs organized, together with the Austrian Ministry of Defense and Sports, a conference on "Neutrality from the Cold War to Engaged Neutrality" at the National Defense Academy. We also wish to thank the following sponsoring institutes: the Austrian Study Centre for Peace and Conflict Resolution, the International Institute for Peace, the Department of Political Science at the University of Vienna, the US Embassy (Vienna), the Chumir Foundation (Canada), and the Swiss Embassy (Vienna).

We owe deepest respect and gratitude to the former Federal President of Austria Heinz Fischer for his opening statement in a video message. We are greatly indebted to the keynote speakers Gerald Klug (former Austrian Minister of Defense) and Bundesrat Ueli Maurer (Swiss Minister of Defense). We are thankful to Caspar Einem (president of the Austrian Institute for International Affairs) for the introductory remarks.

It goes without saying that the project would not have been possible if the authors had not agreed to contribute to the book. Furthermore, we want to thank Petra Podesser, member of the administration of the Austrian Institute for International Affairs, who contacted the authors with kindness, energy, and persistence. Special thanks go to Katharina Hämmerle and Stefan Pfalzer, who spent many hours and days copyediting the incoming texts.

Foreword

A Plea for an Interest-Driven Policy of Neutrality

GenMjr Dr. Johann Frank

Today's predominant understanding of neutrality in Austria is a result of a long-standing critical debate about the concept of neutrality, including an attempt to trade neutrality for NATO membership in the 1990s and, within the framework of the Security and Defense Doctrine of 2001, an EU defense alliance. At least since the development of the Austrian Security Strategy of 2013 (ÖSS), however, neutrality has once again been accorded the political importance it had never lost among many circles of society. In the light of the return of armed conflicts to Europe, the lack of a common European peace framework and the increase in international conflicts, in Minister Doskozil's view, neutrality has gained importance in the recent past.

This statement only seems contradictory at first. Instead, it represents the understanding of the Austrian population that an interest-driven policy of neutrality and lived multilateralism are complimentary instead of contradictory.

Since at least the adoption of the new Austrian Security Strategy, Austrian neutrality has been understood not as limiting, but as an extended policy option in the sense of an engaged policy of neutrality.

In my view, the added foreign and security policy value of neutrality for Austria, for Europe, and for the international community is self-evident. We must not base our understanding of neutrality on what we cannot and should not do. Instead, the last few years' policy of creating and implementing chances and opportunities from an active policy of neutrality should be pursued.

Our status as a neutral country does not only entail rights, but also places us under the obligation to pursue a situation-specific national military defense policy based on the Swiss model. A pre-effect, that must be taken into account when determining the focus of national security policy regarding likely operational tasks.

Austrian neutrality is not a given. The country must have the possibility to defend it by military means in order for the concept to remain credible.

Legally, there are two derogations to neutrality:

The recognition of the higher order of obligations resulting from the Charter of the United Nations.

Art.23j of Federal Constitutional Law (BVG), which allows for comprehensive Austrian participation in the European Union's Common Foreign and Security Policy.

The legal core of Austria's military neutrality did not change with the accession to the European Union. The "3 Noes" apply: Austria still doesn't join a military alliance, doesn't allow the establishment of military bases on its territory, and doesn't participate in any wars. These core pillars of our security policy constitute important guiding principles of the Austrian foreign and security policy.

Within the European Union, neutral states have been granted special legal status. Article 42(7) of the Treaty of the European Union (TEU), also called "Irish clause," explicitly stipulates that the policies of the European Union "shall not prejudice the specific character of the security and defence policy of certain Member States." In practice, this means that even within the framework of CSDP, there is no automatic contribution- or assistance obligation.

Unlike at the time of the Cold War, the Austrian policy of neutrality is no longer primarily oriented towards remaining neutral in a war between states. Austrian neutrality is no longer defined by nonparticipation in wars, but instead by an active foreign and peace policy.

Taking into consideration the added security policy value of neutrality and the critical environment in and around Europe, an active Austrian policy of neutrality fulfils three functions:

- It supports Austria in building bridges and offering good services,
- It enhances Austria's profile as a contributor to international crisis management and comprehensive conflict prevention,
- It is oriented towards an autonomous EU Common Security and Defense.

Illustrated by a few examples, the three security policy functions of neutrality can be explained as follows:

Quite a few people might see neutrality as a limiting factor for our actions. However, the fact that neutral Austria is not bound by a commitment to any military alliances is actually not a limitation, but gives us a greater room for maneuvre, both in terms of foreign and security policy.

As a result, Austria has been able to stay out of costly and unsuccessful international interventions. Good examples are Iraq and Afghanistan, but also Libya. Additionally, we have been able to be proactive on our own, for example, with regard to the EU weapons embargo in Syria, where Austria was able to push through its initiative in spite of opposition. Other example is the destruction of the Assad regime's chemical weapons, where Austria was proactive in Washington, as well as within the framework of OPCW.

Figuratively speaking, neutrality gives us the political opportunity to build bridges. A very fitting example in this regard are the West Balkans. Austria is very active in the region as well as the biggest provider of troops. In cooperation with other countries, Austria is very proactive in building bridges from countries in the West Balkans to the EU. However, it is their responsibility to implement reforms and cross those bridges.

With regard to the still unsolved conflicts in Ukraine and the behavior of Russia, Austria could try to act as a facilitator in the course of the OSCE chairmanship in 2017. Moldova und Serbia might be further examples where Austria's neutral status as an EU member and Partnership for Peace (PfP) country might serve as a role model. From the perspective of a neutral country, the concept of neutrality is still viable and important as long as no inclusive European security architecture involving Eastern Europe and Russia exists.

Because of its status of neutrality, Austria has been able to establish itself as a host to both international negotiations and international organizations. For instance, Austria hosts the third UN headquarters, the International Atomic Energy Agency, several UN specialized agencies, the OPEC secretariat, as well as the OSCE secretariat. In addition, the negotiations on the Iran Deal or the Syria peace negotiations are current examples of Austria being a place of mediation.

The second important task of a proactive neutrality policy is international crisis management. Since the beginning of our contribution in the 1960s, more than 100,000 Austrian solders and civil aides have participated in over 100 peacebuilding and humanitarian missions. In this context, the focus is on an enhanced coordination of civil and military measures, as well as a good coordination of security and development policy.

The precondition for the international deployment of the Austrian Army remains the existence of a mandate by the UN Security Council. It, however, doesn't mean that we automatically participate in UN-mandated missions. As outlined in the Austrian Security Strategy (ÖSS), further criteria, like the probability of success and feasibility, have to be met in order to allow for participation.

A credible contribution to international peace management, however, is not limited to military means. It also includes contributions to civil crisis management, measures to strengthen multilateral structures, as well as arms control and disarmament initiatives.

With regard to the latter, Austria has been actively involved in the prohibition of cruel and indiscriminate weapons, for instance antipersonnel mines and cluster munitions. Currently, Austria is very active within the framework of the concept of human security, primarily in the area of the humanitarian consequences of nuclear weapons, where it was able to get 159 countries on board.

There is a bit of backlog in the civil crisis management sector, however. In EU operations, Austria is among the biggest providers of troops, appropriating 9,75 percent, of a total of 3,866 personnel (August 2016), but its contribution of 2 percent out of 1,284 experts to EU civil missions is below average.

Also with regard to the implementation of the EU Global Strategy on Foreign and Security Policy (EGS), presented by High Representative Mogherini in June 2016, alliance-free and neutral countries are accorded a very important role. Among other things, the task of counties like Austria will be to claim the necessary autonomy to take and implement military decisions, identified in the EGS, in order to be able to act independently, if necessary.

A common security and defense policy independent of decisions taken by NATO is of key importance for neutral countries. The EGS explicitly takes this factor into account by stipulating that "EU-NATO relations shall not prejudice the security and defence policy of those Members which are not in NATO."

In order to "act autonomously if and when necessary," as specified in the EGS, the EU has to be able to generate its own situational analysis of international developments, define its own interests, and, building on the latter, establish its own European policy approach in coordination with strategic partners. Neutral countries like Austria should, if necessary, demand this autonomy to act and take independent decisions in order to ensure a development and strengthening of CSDP.

The creation of a European Army is probably too ambitious for the near future. Even Germany, which continuously advocates for a greater degree of interconnectedness and the intensification of military cooperation within the EU, only conceptualizes the project of a "European Army" as a European defense pillar within the framework of NATO.

A stronger military cooperation among like-minded states with the aim of protecting Austrian neutrality and sovereignty is, in my view, both sensible and, in light of the many challenge facing Austria and Europe, also increasingly necessary.

To sum up, today's understanding of neutrality has to be reflected in our foreign and security policy: as a builder of bridges and as a convincing facilitator, as a high-profile actor in international crisis management and as a partner in the shaping of an independent common security and defense policy of the EU. As a result of the many challenges in Austria and within the EU, an active, dedicated policy of neutrality cannot be taken for granted. We have to act in a dedicated and courageous fashion, using political, diplomatic, and—if legally and factually possible—also military means.

Neutrality is a central pillar of Austria's identity and sovereignty. For many Austrians, it is associated with a high guarantee for security. The awareness that neutrality also requires independent capabilities for national military defense, as well as an adequate defense budget, has to be raised. In reference to international politics and the current security policy challenges, neutrality should be interpreted in terms of an interest-driven active policy of peace.

Introduction

Engaged Neutrality

Heinz Gärtner

The concept of neutrality has proven time and again that it can adapt to new situations. What are the big new challenges after the end of the Cold War? They are the Proliferation of weapons of mass destruction; terrorism, which potentially holds new dangerous dimensions in combination with proliferation; fragile and dysfunctional states, which can be breeding grounds for terrorism, a source of uncontrolled immigration and a source for the development and dissemination of organized crime. They also contribute to the loss of important economic areas. Neutral states are well suited (in many ways better than other states) for making an important contribution to the fight against these new dangers. Neutral states sometimes receive higher acceptance than members of alliances. Assistance for reconstruction and humanitarian aid efforts in war-torn countries can happen within the framework of the UN, the EU, the OSCE or the NATO partnerships. The possibility of participation in the foreign policy and crisis management of the EU is explicitly permitted. Neutral states are also part of robust deployments such as the ones within the NATO Partnership for Peace (PfP).

The concept of security has transformed from a geographic to a functional one, which is no longer primarily aimed at the defense or conquest of a specific territory, but rather at stabilization, prevention, crisis intervention, and humanitarian challenges. Civilian structures (humane living conditions, schools, a functioning police and justice system, and an intact administration) cannot be established and economic development cannot take place, if security is not ensured. Notwithstanding their own interests, neutral states have an obligation to make a contribution. The concept of "human security" means protection from existential threats such as hunger, epidemics, and oppression as well as protection from sudden and painful physical and psychological cuts into daily life—be it regarding living conditions, work, or

1

community. Neutral states must especially stand up for the protection and the security of every individual. Their armed forces have a particular importance for the concept of human security. The tasks for these forces lie within the fields of conflict prevention, peacekeeping, disaster relief and reconstruction of postwar and dysfunctional societies. These duties are also included in the Petersberg tasks of the EU.

The image of the solider has radically changed in this century compared to the last, when his main task was the eradication of his enemy. Today, his duties increasingly revolve around the protection of people and civilians. "Responsibility to Protect" (R2P) is the main task of states and international organizations, according to a report of an international commission.[1] The new challenges cannot primarily be resolved with artillery, heavy tanks, fighter jets, or even precision-guided ammunition. What is most important are well-trained soldiers and highly qualified specialists. Of course, this requires modern and appropriate equipment. There is a demand for adequate transport capabilities as well as modern communication, and reconnaissance systems. All the aforementioned activities are not an obstacle for small neutral states, but rather a necessity for showing international solidarity. It is not only necessary for neutral states, but also sensible for the international community of states to establish a broad legitimacy for coercive measures in the form of a mandate of the Security Council of the United Nations.

Civil-military cooperation is particularly important in these cases. Specific cases (e.g., Battle Groups or Rapid Reaction Forces) require the services of special forces. Within the spectrum of missions, small neutral states can develop important niche capabilities regarding evacuation, support for catastrophes, and humanitarian crises (e.g., construction of field hospitals), peacekeeping and reconstruction efforts (e.g., engineers), rescue and security deployments as well as prevention, stabilization, and combat missions. Neutral small states can perform central tasks particularly in the civil-military field because in many ways they enjoy more acceptance of International Organizations (IOs), NGOs and civil forces than allied countries. The neutral status also facilitates domestic cooperation between the military and NGOs.

The most important feature for any alliance are the mutual defense obligations. Neutrality and military alliances are negatively related. When the importance of collective defense obligations—which come into force in case of an attack on a member state's territory—increases, neutrality gets a different meaning. The consequence for neutrality would not be to engage but to keep out again. Conversely, when alliance obligations are no longer necessary, the status of neutrality is no longer in question in this regard. Neutrality means nonmembership in an alliance based on political convention, or on constitutional and international law.

NATO AND NEUTRALITY

Since the end of the Cold War, NATO has been redeveloping its basic structure: preparing for a collective defense was no longer the only or even primary item on its agenda and as a second-core task, its focus has since then included crisis management and expeditionary missions. NATO turned toward new tasks, which have only little to do with the collective defense of the alliance members: International crisis management—especially in regions outside defined alliance borders ("out of area"), like in the former Yugoslavia or Afghanistan ("out of continent"), and the inclusion of nonmembers within the framework of the Partnership for Peace (PfP) and of the Euro-Atlantic Partnership Council (EAPC).

On the one hand, NATO remained committed to collective defense. On the other hand, it was able to undertake new missions including contribution to effective conflict prevention, and active engagement in crisis management and crisis response operations. In addition to territorial defense (covered by Articles 5 and 6 of the Washington Treaty), the Alliance security also started to take the global context into account. Alliance security interests could be affected by risks of a wider nature, including acts of terrorism, sabotage, organized crime and by the disruption of vital resource supply (arrangements and consultations as responses to risks of this kind can be made under Article 4).

In addition to the existing "collective defense" and "crisis management" core tasks, the new Strategic Concept, adopted at the Lisbon Summit in November 2010, NATO introduced "cooperative security" as a new one. This core task is to coordinate the network of partner relationships with non-NATO countries and other international organizations around the globe. Cooperative Security should contribute to arms control, nonproliferation, and disarmament. It should provide a framework for political dialogue and regional cooperation, increase military interoperability, and prepare for operations and missions. Cooperative Security is not limited to the European partners, but includes a wide range of partners globally.

Indeed, in some cases non-NATO members may play an even more important role in the new operations than NATO members, for example in the field of peace operations, humanitarian assistance, and disaster relief (providing food, water, and medicine), Protection of Civilians (PoCs), reconstruction and crisis management. Non-NATO states could participate in those missions and cooperate with NATO while retaining their current defense profile. Other partners have regional priorities and niche capabilities. That means that there can be a division of labor not only between NATO members and partners but also among partners. Some partners will be committed to the crisis-management dimension, while others concentrate more on territorial defense. Some partners will look more to the East, others more to the South. The common basis should remain the concept of cooperative and common security. Within the concept of the "framework nations," interoperability can be tailored. Cooperation can be functionally oriented.

Naturally, the fundamental priority of a neutral security policy during security deployments and deployments abroad does not lie with alliance obligations. However, modern neutrality also does not exclude cooperation with alliance members or alliances, as long as they agree on the key issues. Neutral states share basic threat analyses and goals with NATO within the framework of the partnerships, which are not necessarily limited to the institution of PfP. In the partnership context, peace operations are well compatible with neutrality. However, neutral states—but not only them—consider a United Nations Security Council mandate necessary for their participation in any armed peacekeeping operation.

After the Ukraine crisis in 2014–2015, it appeared that NATO returned to traditional territorial and collective defense rather than concentrating on crisis management or cooperative security. NATO had never given up collective defense. It is rather a question of priorities. The Ukraine crisis refocused NATO's priorities on the East of Europe. The threats and challenges in the South have not disappeared, however. Human security, dysfunctional states, regional conflicts, refugee flows, natural disasters, terrorism and nuclear proliferation are here to stay. The emergence of the "Islamic State" is a case in point. It would be unfortunate for neutral states if crisis management were more and more replaced by collective defense. The disintegration of the Westphalian system in many states of the Middle East and in the Mediterranean will produce more dysfunctional states and more radical non-state actors. The state's monopoly of the use of force is being dissolved, which leads to the privatization of violence and a new medievalism. It will probably produce a much larger challenge than we know now.

In the wake of the Ukraine crisis, those parts within NATO, who support territorial and collective defense, once more prevailed. At the Wales Summit in 2014, NATO allies included the concept of a Very High Readiness Joint Task Force (VJTF) into the overall NATO Response Force (NRF) structure to enhance the capabilities of the NRF in order to respond to emerging security challenges posed by Russia. Although it should also counter the risks emanating from the Middle East and North Africa, it is mainly based on collective defense. Partners cannot be part of collective defense operations, therefore their possibilities for the participation is becoming more limited.

Focusing more and more on both the East and on collective defense would reduce both cooperative security and the role of partners. Moreover, the effort to define crisis management and missions in the South as collective defense would leave little room for partners to contribute. The Alliance should rather reinforce its common and cooperative security capabilities that include the interoperability, Connected Force Initiative, NATO Response Force, Civil-Military Relations, Counter Insurgency, and host-nation support.

The nonmembership in an alliance, anchored in neutrality law or political convention, is a clear characteristic of neutrality. The most important feature of an alliance are the mutual obligations of assistance, which are incompatible with neutrality. As long as NATO sees itself as a "military alliance," there can be no membership for neutral states in NATO. But within the framework of partnerships, crisis management, and cooperative security, they can provide capacities that are similar to those of the members of a transformed NATO.

THE EUROPEAN UNION AND NEUTRALITY

Enshrined in Treaty of Lisbon of European Union is a solidarity clause (Article 222), which requires member states to support other member states in case of man-made disasters (e.g., terrorist attacks) and natural disasters, should the state concerned request it. Contributions from member states are voluntary and happen upon request from the state concerned. European cooperation of police and justice take priority over military means. Behind the solidarity clause stands very much the idea of collective security. The concept of collective security aims at enhancing the security among its member states, while the concept of collective defense is aimed at an outside enemy.

However, this clause is not part of the Common Security and Defense Policy (CSDP) and must not be confused with assistance obligations (Article 42.7). According to this clause, member states must provide each other with "aid and assistance by all means in their power" in case of armed aggression towards a member state. This includes the promise to use military force. The so-called Irish Formula in the Treaty of Lisbon makes an exception for neutral and nonaligned states. It states that this article "shall not prejudice the specific character of the security and defense policy of certain member states." The formulation applies not only to the neutral and nonaligned states, but also to NATO members. They have to "be consistent with commitments under the North Atlantic Treaty Organisation, which . . . remains the foundation of their collective defence and the forum for its implementation." The Treaty therefore allows both neutral states and the NATO members of the EU to opt out. The Treaty of Lisbon indicates exceptions for these states resulting from their commitments to the NATO treaty. Therefore, exception clauses regarding this part of the treaty are valid for all EU member states, which puts its meaningfulness into question.

The solidarity clause does not go far enough, however, as it is limited to member states, even though references to global solidarity (Article 3) can be found in the treaty. The Treaty of Lisbon knows another solidarity clause that goes beyond the EU's member states. Article 3 states:

> In its relations with the wider world, the Union shall uphold and promote its values and interests and contribute to the protection of its citizens. It shall contribute to peace, security, the sustainable development of the Earth, solidarity and mutual respect among peoples, free and fair trade, eradication of poverty and the protection of human rights, in particular the rights of the child, as well as to the strict observance and the development of international law, including respect for the principles of the United Nations Charter.

If Europe does not play a critical role by addressing these and other challenges, it will lose its relevance. This concerns multilateral diplomacy in particular, but also the proportional involvement of civil and military contributions. During the last decades with its big natural disasters, some neutral states provided assistance for elementary events within and outside of Europe.

Neutral states cannot turn away from their responsibility to take part in the resolution of regional and global problems. Neutral states cannot let themselves be guided by interests, whether they are their own or European. It goes without saying that many of the new challenges, such as climate change, demographics, organized crime, proliferation and terrorism, have a direct impact on Europe. But aberrations in other parts of the world also have indirect negative global consequences. The genocide in Rwanda in 1994 shocked the entire UN system and was the reason why the "International Commission on Intervention and State Sovereignty" wrote the report on R2P. The Report reminds states and the United Nations of their responsibility to prevent genocide and severe human rights violations.

The general rules of the Lisbon Treaty emphasize that the national security "remains the sole responsibility of each member state" (Article 4). While this does not mean that states may not enter into obligations of alliances considering the presence of NATO member states in the EU, it means, however, that each EU member state remains free to make this decision. This implies that no obligations conflicting with their neutrality arise for the neutral states. This statement is valid from an international law perspective. The future of the EU does not lie in collective or territorial defense, but in crisis management and collective security:

> In broad terms, crisis management is about preventing a crisis from occurring, responding to an ongoing crisis, or assisting in the consolidation of peace (or order) once the acute phase of a crisis has passed. It is not necessarily per se

about conflict resolution. The purpose of crisis management is to respond to the immediate needs of a crisis and/or contribute to the strengthening of long-term peace in a situation of relative stability, at the request of the authorities of the recipient state. (Tardy 2015)

The Global Strategy for European Foreign and Security Policy[2] observes "fragile states breaking down in violent conflict." Therefore, the EU will "engage in a practical and principled way in peacebuilding" and concentrate on efforts in surrounding regions to the east and south, while considering engagement further afield on a case-by-case basis. The EU will foster human security through an integrated approach.

The "Global Strategy" leaves—similar to the Treaty of Lisbon—collective and territorial defense to NATO. At the same time it stresses the exception for neutral states: The "EU-NATO relations shall not prejudice the security and defence policy of those Members which are not in NATO."

The "Global Strategy" concentrates preemptive peacebuilding and diplomacy.

The Lisbon Treaty provides the basis for the strategy—According to Article 42.1:

> The common security and defense policy shall be an integral part of the common foreign and security policy. It shall provide the Union with an operational capacity drawing on civilian and military assets. The Union may use them on missions outside the Union for peace-keeping, conflict prevention and strengthening international security in accordance with the principles of the United Nations Charter. The performance of these tasks shall be undertaken using capabilities provided by the Member States.

A clear authorization of these missions by the United Nations Security Council would certainly increase acceptance of such campaigns. The argument that waiting for such a mandate is impossible during certain missions—such as evacuations for example—is spurious. The protection of civilian and mission personnel is always part of any mandate in conflict areas (e.g., in Mali, Central Africa, Congo, Darfur, Chad and others). Furthermore, evacuation measures do not imply support for a warring party, which is forbidden for neutral states. It is further wrong to claim that the UN Security Council works too slowly to react to crises in a timely manner. After the attacks of 9/11, the Security Council unanimously adopted Resolution 1368, which underlined the right to self-defense, within twenty-four hours. The second substantial Resolution 1373 was also ratified unanimously three weeks after the attacks. This resolution regulated in detail bans on the residence of terrorists, passport forgeries, and border controls and was binding not only for those states who ratified it but all 191 member states. Through the unanimous adoption of resolution 2170 (2014) and 2199 (2015) under the binding Chapter VII of the United Nations Charter, the Council condemned what it called "gross, systematic and widespread abuse" of human rights by the Islamic State in Iraq and the Levant (ISIL, also known as ISIS) and Al-Nusra Front.

EU's Rapid Reaction Forces or so-called "Battle Groups" could help with the preparation for missions ranging from humanitarian help and solidarity to robust missions, which may include armed combat due to safety require-ments. The latter missions should be legitimized through a UN Security council mandate. Because these Battle Groups would not be used as a last resort—as required by the doctrine of the just war—but rather in a timely manner or even preemptively, it is all the more important that they are autho-rized by a legitimate authority.

These Rapid Reaction Forces or Battle Groups are tailored towards the per-manent structured cooperation provided in the treaty. Member states, "whose military capabilities fulfil higher criteria and which have made more binding commitments in this area," may establish a structured cooperation. However, the "criteria and commitments on military capabilities" are established by the member states themselves. This means that participants themselves can decide with which capabilities they want to take part in the Battle Groups. For example, there is no obligation to provide troops for high-tech combat missions.

Battle Groups could be especially useful for UN missions. The Charter of the United Nations outlines common contingents for Chapter VII tasks under the command of the UN Security Council (Article 43–47). These have never been implemented because member states did not want to make them avail-able permanently. The protocol of the Treaty of Lisbon regarding the per-manent structured cooperation stresses specifically that the "United Nations Organisation may request the Union's assistance for the urgent implementa-tion of missions undertaken under Chapters VI and VII of the United Nations Charter."

ENGAGED NEUTRALITY

Neutral states can and should actively participate in crisis-management oper-ations and conflict avoidance. This entails among other things: preventive diplomacy, early detection and timely action, peaceful conflict settlement, but also threat of sanctions, disarmament, and military trust building. Mem-bership in a military alliance, like NATO, is not necessary for the preven-tion of violent conflict. Crisis management and conflict prevention can also be conducted within the framework of the EU, NATO Partnerships, or the

Organization for Security and Cooperation in Europe (OSCE). Neutral states can actively participate in the EU crisis-management tasks, as provided for by the Lisbon Treaty. As an EU member and a party to the Treaty, they are "full and equal partners" in the planning and decision-making process of these activities. Neutrality is no obstacle to the EU crisis-management operations, whatsoever. They closely cooperate with NATO in important and necessary areas, such as crisis management, humanitarian operations, or peacekeeping. Cooperative security and the concept of partners offer the possibility of co-decision for every operation with their participation. "Engaged neutrality" means active participation in international security policy in general and in international peace operations in particular.

Of course, there can be no neutrality between democracy and dictatorship, between a constitutional state and despotism, between the adherence to human rights and their violation. There can be no neutrality between the condemnation and the tolerance of human rights violations, between right and wrong or between democratic and authoritarian forms of government. There is no neutrality towards glaring human rights violations, tolerance of injustice, torture, or genocide. The obligations of neutral state are defined in negative terms as the nonmembership in a military alliance, nonparticipation in foreign wars, and the non-deployment of foreign troops on the territory of neutral states. Neutral states are not allowed to offer other states or alliances the prospect of entering into a war at their side.

Nonetheless, neutrality allows for a crucial advantage in the debate on these values. It releases from geopolitical and alliance-related considerations. Western democratic constitutional states need to detract from their values time and again due to pragmatic considerations. Small neutral states have no global geopolitical interest that would lead to establishing military bases in or delivering weapons to authoritarian states that neglect human rights and constitutional values (although there are exceptions). Neutral states are less limited by alliance obligations in their fight for democracy, human rights, and constitutional states everywhere. Neutrality does not allow double standards. However, a reassessment of neutrality is necessary. The old Swiss concept of "sitting still" should definitely become something of the past. False diplomatic caution has to be replaced by a courageous and aggressive advocacy of self-evident values.

Neutrality cannot mean "keeping out" anymore, but rather demands an intense involvement in international crisis management. Neutral states need to utilize these advantages and possibilities, which result from its engaged neutrality policy. The state of neutrality itself already implies that, from the outset, it does not maintain a hostile attitude during conflicts. Engaged neutrality means involvement whenever possible and staying out only when necessary.

THE BOOK

Johanna Rainio-Niemi underlines that the history of neutrality as a political thought and practice are older and broader than the Cold War. She asks what was distinctive to neutrality during the Cold War, or to "Cold War neutrality." Neutrality has been declared obsolete many times in its long and layered history. Yet a close companion to wars and conflicts throughout documented human history, and an inherently flexible concept, it has also made many comebacks in varying forms and contexts. Rainio-Niemi asks what the differences do tell about Finland's and Austria's Cold War neutrality and about these countries' relationship to the legacies of their erstwhile Cold War neutrality? As possible lessons to be learned from their Cold War neutrality, she draws attention to the nature of the institutionalization of neutrality and the way in which neutrality would be embedded in the overall context of the institutional commitments (international and/or bilateral) of an aspirant neutral.

The interrelationships between the Austrian and the German Question (1952–1955) often have been ignored in that scholarly debate especially by German historians. There was no broad and intensive scholarly discussion if Austria's attempts to sign a state treaty and to reach a status of neutrality (1952–1955) were examples for Germany. *Michael Gehler* shows how the Austrian State Treaty signed by the Four Powers and the status of permanent neutrality enacted by a constitutional law have been seen and could have served as a kind of model for a German Peace Treaty.

Liliane Stadler asks why neutral European states have remained neutral since the end of the Cold War. She finds this question puzzling, because most Cold War neutrals have de facto reduced their former policies of neutrality to military non-alliance. She traces the historical development of three diverse case studies: Switzerland, Sweden, and Austria. She applies two competing theoretical explanations for the ambiguous persistence of neutrality: path dependence and ontological security. What these tests reveal is that the former is inadequate to explain the research puzzle, while the latter is only applicable if it undergoes a slight refinement. While path dependence accounts for the persistence of neutrality by conceptualizing it as an institution, from which it would be costly to diverge, ontological security theory conceptualizes neutrality as a defining aspect of state identity. By applying these theoretical approaches, Liliane Stadler finds that neutral states respond to critical moments in their environment by pursuing reversible, rather than irreversible foreign policy options, because this allows them to balance between their competing needs for physical and ontological security.

For *Laurent Goetschel*, the concept of neutrality emerged at a time when wars regularly threatened the existence of small states. Some of these states saw abstention from military warfare as a survival strategy. At the same time, neutral states developed compensatory activities in the fields of humanitarian and peace policies. These two dimensions, of which the first one may be called realist and the second one idealist, have marked neutrality since its inception. Parts of their idealist dimension of neutrality became more relevant in international politics. So Laurent Goetschel assumes that neutral states can achieve a double gain as "middle powers."

Adrian Hyde-Price examines some of the key implications of the concept of neutrality for European security, particularly in the light of the changing geopolitics of the post–Cold War European security system. He focuses on the tension between neutrality, collective security, and solidarity, and draws primarily on the contrasting experiences of Sweden and Finland on the one hand, and Austria, Ireland, and Switzerland on the other. He also discusses the option of neutrality for Ukraine.

Terry Hopmann reminds us that the neutral and nonaligned states of Europe heavily influenced the content of the Helsinki Final Act of 1975 as the outcome of negotiations within the Conference on Security and Cooperation in Europe (CSCE). Many of these states saw in the CSCE an opportunity to break down barriers between the two dominant alliance systems in Europe, NATO, and the Warsaw Treaty Organization, and to try to override the Cold War divisions with a new normative structure to enhance security in a divided Europe. The CSCE held three major review conferences after the signature of the Helsinki Final Act, all in capitals of neutral or nonaligned countries, namely Madrid, Belgrade, and Vienna. With the end of the Cold War, as the major states tended to assign the CSCE and the OSCE, as it was renamed in 1995, a lesser role in European security, many of the neutral and non-aligned states continued to consider it as vehicle, in which their views about security issues could be discussed outside of the framework of an expanding NATO and a newly formed Central States Treaty Organization (CSTO). For the most part, the OSCE Chair-in-Office, the most important political post in the OSCE, has been held by neutral or nonaligned states as well as by middle powers that are aligned with a major power bloc. Furthermore, the normative underpinnings of the OSCE remain attractive to neutral and nonaligned states that tend to reject reliance on power politics in international relations that by and large leave less powerful states with little or no influence over matters that concern their vital security, as well as their economic and humanitarian interests. Thus, while NATO, the European Union and the CSTO have generally been dominated by the major states of Europe and North America, the OSCE remains a vehicle, in which the concerns of the neutral and non-aligned states may be addressed and in which their normative power may be advanced in contrast to the military and economic powers that otherwise dominate the international relations of Europe and the North Atlantic area.

For *Christian Nünlist* neutral Switzerland's foreign policy has received a modern face-lift: In the twenty-first century, an active and cooperative foreign policy flourished under Micheline Calmy-Rey and Didier Burkhalter. Switzerland's values are firmly anchored within the West, but its independent foreign policy often finds niches for providing useful good offices to the international community. Civilian peacebuilding, including at the interface with development policy, is a key element of today's Swiss "soft power," cleverly using neutrality for fighting global challenges in multilateral frameworks.

Since 1992, the European Union has been working on the ongoing development of a Common Foreign, Security, and Defense Policy. This framework facilitates the commitment to establish appropriate Rapid Reaction Forces, so-called "Battle Groups," in order to conduct demanding missions. The increased use of the "Permanent Structured Cooperation" instrument by member states willing to enhance their cooperation serves as a possible relief to strengthen the EU's capacity to act in the area of the Common Security and Defense Policy. The new EU Security Strategy assesses the threat posed by regional instability of failing states having a geographical proximity to the EU and provides solutions to assure Europe's security and to prevent refugee movements to Europe triggered by political instability or war. *Franz Leidenmühler* and *Sandra Grafeneder* stress that Austria's existing permanent neutrality does not hamper the country's participation in the EU's crisis management. On the contrary, a permanently neutral member state can play a vital role in enhancing the EU's Common Foreign, Security, and Defense Policy. They can improve the assessment of current challenges for and threats to the security of the Union.

NOTES

1. Report of the International Commission on Intervention and State Sovereignty: "The Responsibility To Protect," December 2001.
2. European External Action Service (EEAS), 2016. *Shared Vision, Common Action: A Stronger Europe, A Global Strategy for the European Union's Foreign and Security Policy*, June.

BIBLIOGRAPHY

Mearsheimer, John J. 1990. "Back to the Future: Instability in Europe after the Cold War." *International Security* 15(1): 5–56.

Tardy, Thierry. 2015. "CSDP in Action—What Contribution to International Security?" *Chaillot Papers.* Paris: European Union Institute for Security Studies, May 2015.

European External Action Service (EEAS). 2015. "The European Union in a changing global environment: A more connected, contested and complex world." *Strategic assessment of HR/VP in preparation of the 2016 EU Global Strategy on Foreign and Security Policy of June 2015.*

Waltz, Kenneth N. 1993. "The Emerging Structure of International Politics." *International Security* 18(2): 75–76.

Chapter 1

Cold War Neutrality in Europe

Lessons to be Learned?

Johanna Rainio-Niemi

In early 2014, soon after the escalation of the crisis in Ukraine, neutrality—a concept that had been practically forgotten by the international public for the past few decades—made an interesting comeback to Western public political debate. Among the initiators of the debate were respected senior policy advisers of the United States such as Zbigniew Brzezinski and Henry Kissinger, according to whom neutrality and the so-called "Finland option" could offer a model when the future of Ukraine was to be drafted (Brzezinski 2014; Kissinger 2014; Mearsheimer 2014; Cohen 2014).[1] Framed by increased discussion about the return of the age of geopolitics, hard power, and even a new Cold War, the ideas of neutrality and the "Finland-option" kept appearing in international public debates for a few months' time in the spring of 2014. This analogy was substantiated by three main points: Finland shares a long, territorial border with Russia; it has good relations with both East and West, and is militarily nonaligned.[2]

In Finland, the US veteran policy advisers' analogy-building caused discomfort. The reception varied from embarrassment to rejection: had the distinguished international commentators forgotten that the twenty-first-century Finland was politically fully aligned, a member of the European Union (since 1995), an integral part of the West instead of wavering in any "grey zone" between the East and West. On pages of the *Financial Times*, Finland's veteran diplomats reminded the international audience about the facts of Finland's history: being historically and societally one of the Nordic countries, having fought two major wars against the Soviet Union and, nowadays, being a fully committed EU member, the case of Finland was so different from Ukraine that it had nothing to offer for the latter or any other former Eastern bloc country for that matter.[3] In an interview by the German newspaper *Die Zeit*, the then prime minister of Finland, Jyrki Katainen, when asked about the

Finland model, emphasized that "Finland is not neutral" but is one of the fully commited EU member states with a strong "NATO-option," meaning that staying outside the military alliance is not based on any deeper values but is a pragmatic matter of affairs that prevails for the time being (Der Tagesspiegel 2014; YLE News 2014a).

While Finnish politicians and the general public appeared reluctant to talk about the "Finland-option," in Austria—another EU and Eurozone member state that has opted to remain outside military alliances—a lively domestic debate emerged on whether "Austria's model of neutrality" could be used as a guideline for Ukraine.[4] This discussion was not *literally* about the Austria of today or of yesterday but it, rather, provided an interpretation of Austria's history in the period of 1955–1995 and contemplated its value as potential guideline for Ukraine today. According to this interpretation, in 1955, Austria had been reestablished as a permanently sovereign state by the leading international powers and in that connection also made a unilateral declaration of permanent neutrality outside military alliances. From the 1950s to the late 1980s, Austria had strived for a closer association with the "core Europe" but had to wait for forty years, until 1995, before it, together with the two other "former neutrals" Sweden and Finland, was able to join the European Union.[5]

According to the Austrian model of neutrality as proposed in Austria, a "self-chosen," sovereignly governed decision on "non-alignment and even neutrality" would not prevent a country from adopting and developing (Western type of) the rule of law and strong democratic institutions. Further, it would not prevent a country from cultivating a free-market economy and cooperating on these terms with both West and East. Exactly this had been the case with Austria in 1955–1995 and the strategy had brought along economic prosperity, social equality, a stable political order and democracy. By adopting neutrality, Austria had grown into "a symbol of cooperation and not of conflict between the East and the West"[6] and had been able to find a niche as an internationally acknowledged bridge-builder and mediator across the divides in world politics and between the East and the West in the Cold War era.

This essay contemplates the differences in the Finnish and Austrian ways of dealing with and making use of the legacies of the countries' erstwhile neutrality in connection with the debates in the spring of 2014.[7] Whereas there was a wide-reaching wish to avoid the whole discussion on the Finland option in Finland, in Austria the ideas of a distinctive Austrian model of neutrality for Ukraine were self-initiated and received domestic political support as well. What do these differences tell us about Finland's versus Austria's relationship with their erstwhile neutrality? Further, considering the Finnish uneasiness with any recycling of the elements of its national neutrality history, what does the Finnish sensitivity tell about neutrality as experienced in the most fragile of the European Cold War neutrals?

The following text first takes a look at how neutrality has been given meanings in Austria versus Finland since 1995, and then turns to neutrality during the Cold War years. Asking what would be the possible lessons to be learned from the experiences of Cold War neutrality and the comparative reflections on Finland and Austria, attention is drawn to two aspects in particular. The first concerns the question of the degree and nature of the institutionalization of neutrality and the question of how neutrality (however defined) locates into the overall context of institutional commitments (international and bilateral) of the aspirant neutral. These, as Finland's Cold War neutrality tells us, can significantly facilitate or, alternatively, enfeeble ("*de jure* or *de facto*") a country's possibility to *exercise* its neutrality freely in practice.

This remark draws our attention to another aspect to be considered. Instead of merely asking what neutrality is when established, it also ought to be asked *what can be made* out of neutrality once it has been established. Considering the Cold War experiences of neutrality, it may be noted that in the most successful cases, neutrality was systematically made use of as an instrument of nation- and state-building. It was something much more comprehensive and all-encompassing than an official foreign, security, or military nonalignment policy. The idea of neutrality was carefully planted in domestic society and integrated with the collective and popular ways of thinking about the common identity of the state and nation. It was made into national identity.

NEUTRALITY IN POST–COLD WAR EUROPE: NORDIC AND CENTRAL EUROPEAN PATHS?

Austria, Finland, and Sweden joined the European Union in 1995. Austria was the first to hand in its membership application in July 1989. In this connection no changes were planned to the country's constitutionally anchored permanent neutrality, the prevailing interpretation being that neutrality should not limit a country's options to economic or other *non-military* types of European cooperation (Gehler 2012).

A few formative years later, when the Cold War had ended and the Soviet Union was about to dissolve, Sweden submitted its membership application in July 1991, followed by Finland in March 1992. These two former neutrals ended up with another type of interpretation concerning the compatibility of neutrality and EU membership: both viewed that the *political* type of neutrality that Sweden had pursued since the early nineteenth century and Finland since Second World War was not compatible with membership in the European Union, especially not in the form the EU would exist after the Maastricht Treaty (February 1992). The word neutrality was removed from both countries' official policy vocabularies after the submission of the membership applications.

As Sweden's prime minister stressed in 1992, the term neutrality no longer was an "adequate general designation" for the policy that Sweden wished to pursue in the new Europe where the country needed a "clear European identity."[8]

In Finland, the wish to break all ties with the past neutrality was the most total. References to neutrality were erased from official policy vocabularies by the mid-1990s. The dominant narrative was to be that in Finland neutrality had never had any identity political meanings whatsoever. This interpretation differed from the case of Sweden, where neutrality's meanings to the history of national identity remained acknowledged regardless of the announced loss of neutrality's present day relevance. According to the Finnish interpretation, in contrast, neutrality had always been a purely pragmatic choice that had been determined by the necessities of national survival in the Cold War world. With the end of the Cold War and the collapse of the Soviet Union, there was no need for this policy anymore and it could be dropped virtually overnight. With the EU membership application, Finland was back on to the "right" identity political track again, neutrality being seen to have represented a disguise of Finland's "true Western self" and a symbol for the country's "displaced identity political location" in a "grey zone" between the East and the West (Lipponen 2008, 212–213; Himanen 2003; Tarkka 2012; Railo and Laamanen 2010).[9]

These differences notwithstanding, all three former neutrals followed notably similar lines in their EU policies during the first decade of their membership (1995–2005). In all three countries, "the core of the erstwhile neutrality (Munro 2005)"—military nonalignment—was left intact while the concept of neutrality rapidly lost its day-to-day political relevance. This trend was visible also in Austria where neutrality, like in Sweden and Finland, lost its place in the active policy vocabularies being well on the way to turning into a relatively insignificant object of national nostalgia.[10] In all three former neutrals, the focus was on adaptation to EU membership in terms of the economy, politics, and public administration. The will to participate in international crisis-management cooperation under the NATO-EU-UN auspices modified the meanings of military nonalignment in order to allow active participation. All three countries reshaped their foreign and security political doctrines to meet the requirements of the emerging common European defence and security policy (launched during Finland's EU chairmanship in 1999) and to seize the options of deepening transatlantic cooperation. In the course of the 1990s and 2000s, the intensified interconnections between the national, the transatlantic, the common European, and, in the case of Finland and Sweden, the Nordic security networks, combined with many experts and politicians signaling their increased interest in the "NATO-option," encouraged many to ask whether the time had come for the former neutrals to let go of the rest of their "inherited inhibitions," that is, military nonalignment. Such debates were particularly intense at the turn of the millennium when

NATO was preparing for the 1999 and 2004 enlargement rounds. Yet, the two enlargement rounds came and went: most of the former Warsaw Pact countries joined the alliance but, in the end, none of the former neutrals did.

In all three countries, the decision for continued military nonalignment was explained by references to its exceptionally sound popular support and, in this way, by its key role in the former neutrals' national and state identity. This applies also to Finland where public support for military nonalignment has remained until today. Like in Sweden, in Finland also the weight of the NATO option has varied in the course of the years, but the idea as such has not lost its relevance. Quite the contrary: after 2014, the NATO option made a return to the center of public attention in both countries and has been an element integrated also into the debates on the planned, deeper bilateral military and defence cooperation between the two Nordic countries.[11]

During the past ten years, the development in Austria has taken a different path. Whereas the security policy strategy of 2001 had still predicted that Austria's neutrality would gradually narrow down to military nonalignment à la Sweden and Finland with a strong NATO-option, around the 50th anniversary celebrations of Austria's state treaty and neutrality declaration in 2005, the interest in the option seemed to be waning. At this point, all former Warsaw Bloc countries to the East of Austria were on their way to full NATO membership. In Austria, by contrast, attention was turning away from the NATO option. Little by little new types of meanings were reattached to neutrality, most notably ones related to regional and neighborhood stability policies and peace-enforcing measures.[12] In this renewing form, neutrality made an official comeback in the SPÖ-ÖVP coalition government program of 2011 (resonating to some extent with a similar type of renaissance of neutrality in Switzerland since ca. 2008).

These post–Cold War developments provide us with some obvious explanations to the divergent reactions and responses to the discussions regarding the model of Finland's/Austria's neutrality in connection with the Ukrainian crisis in the spring of 2014. While the concept of neutrality has made a comeback with revised contents to Austrian politics, nothing similar has happened in Finland. Further, whereas a sharp distinction is nowadays drawn between the concepts of neutrality and the still prevailing military nonalignment, most recently redefined in Finland as "staying outside military alliances,[13]" in Austria, a correspondingly strict separation has not been drawn after the Cold War.

FIRST LESSON: INSTITUTIONAL
EMBEDDING OF NEUTRALITY

Apart from the differences in the ways in which the interpretations of neutrality have evolved in the post–Cold War period, there were formal differences in Austria's and Finland's neutrality already during the Cold War. Yet it was exactly these two countries' policies of neutrality that were most directly shaped by the Cold War confrontation out of which their neutrality emerged.

Both countries were on the losing side of the Second World War. After 1945, Austria, which had been an integral part of the German Third Reich, remained under a four-power occupation (the United States, the USSR, Great Britain, and France) until 1955. Finland had fought its war against the Soviet Union in an alliance with Germany in 1941–1944, and the Soviet-led Allied Control Commission left the country in 1948 after the ratification of the Paris Peace Treaty (1947). In contrast to Finland's Peace Treaty, the Austrian postwar occupation ended with the reestablishment of the Austrian Second Republic, with a State Treaty (instead of a Peace Treaty) that was signed in May 1955.

In post-1945 Europe, Austria's and Finland's geopolitical location that bordered on the Iron Curtain was notably similar in relative terms. Although only Finland shared a border directly with the Soviet Union, in both countries the geopolitical and the other Cold War concerns resonated across politics and society in a notably straightforward manner. After 1955, both Austria and Finland, albeit on a different basis as will be discussed below, adopted neutrality, aiming thus to pursue their future policies—regardless of many domestic and international doubts regarding the viability, and credibility of their options to neutrality—within a broader policy framework where the models of the older European neutrals, Switzerland and Sweden, were important.

In retrospect, an aspect that was to have great significance to Austria's versus Finland's ability to pursue neutrality in practice went back to different formal status and the overall institutional embedding of the two countries' neutrality. This type of issues were to gain great relevance in the Cold War context where the prevailing modes of conflict in Europe were not openly military but entangled with much more multidimensional confrontations in the fields of politics, economy, and culture. Further, under the Cold War circumstances, the interpretation and the counterinterpretation of international law and all types of bilateral treaties grew into one of the key battle fields, opening a way also for exerting influence and pressure on the Cold War neutrals. In this context, the question of how a country's neutrality was institutionalized and how it fit together with the given country's other institutional, legal, and treaty-based commitments gained great weight in the shaping of the country's ability to pursue its neutrality in practice. Here Finland—especially in comparison to the other Cold War newcomer neutral, Austria—offers an illuminating case in point.

Finland's Desire for Neutrality and the Bilateral Security Pact with the Soviet Union (1948)

The history of Finland's Cold War neutrality is often traced back to the year 1948 and, somewhat paradoxically, to the signing of the Soviet-Finnish bilateral security pact (the Treaty of Friendship, Cooperation and Mutual Assistance, FCMA Treaty.).[14] The FCMA Treaty was to have a constitutive impact on how Finland was to pursue and was able to pursue its neutrality in the Cold War world. Yet, initially the two elements—neutrality and the bilateral security pact—were formally two separate issues—neutrality was initially desired primarily by Finland, and the security pact by the Soviet Union.

The idea of a bilateral security pact had been on the Soviet agenda many times in the 1920s and 1930s. Most recently, in 1939, Finland had gone to war, basically, to avoid such a pact and its potential repercussions. After the war, Soviet proposals for a security pact were rejected in Finland by referring to the unconcluded peace treaty. By the end of 1947, the peace treaty was signed, and in the meanwhile the Soviet Union had established bilateral security pacts with Romania, Bulgaria, Hungary, Yugoslavia, Czechoslovakia, and Poland. Finland was the missing link in the chain of treaties. Stalin's invitation to the treaty negotiations arrived in February 1948, almost concurrently with the communist takeover in Czechoslovakia. This led many, including George Kennan, to suspect that "Western democracy" had come to an end in its "northern outpost."[15]

Back in 1948 when the FCMA treaty was being negotiated and Finland wished to include a reference to its wish to stay outside great power conflicts, there was yet no clear picture of what neutrality would mean in the Cold War context. By the time that Austria was adopting its neutrality, the vision was clearer as it was between the years 1950–1955 that the first debates and battles on the meanings and worth of neutrality in the new post–Second World War world were undertaken internationally. In 1948, by contrast, neutrality as an idea and practice was still associated primarily with the type of prewar neutrality that many European small states—including Finland (but not Austria)—had tried to follow in the 1930s, mostly without success. Only Sweden and Switzerland had managed to maintain their neutrality—to a great annoyance of both the United States and the Soviet Union and not without concessions made to Nazi-Germany during the war. These experiences fresh in memory, in 1948 both sides of the emergent Cold War conflict—both being also in the middle of their post-war alliance-building—rejected the idea of neutrality as thoroughly unviable.[16]

However, regardless of the failure of Finland's last-minute neutrality in 1939, the wish to pursue neutrality according to the model of other small European countries, especially of neighboring Sweden, had not lost its appeal among a notable segment of Finnish policymakers. On an explicit request of the Finnish delegation at the FCMA negotiations in Moscow in 1948, a reference to the treaty parties' respect for Finland's wish to stay outside conflicts[17] was added to the treaty preamble. This reference, as pointed out above, was not made to Cold War neutrality as it would be known to national and international audiences later in the 1950s but, rather, to the European small-state neutrality of the interwar years. Further, the reference to noninvolvement was critically important for getting the FCMA Treaty ratified in Finland's parliament. Illustration for this aspect is provided by the broadcasted speech of President Juho Kusti Paasikivi on April 9, 1948, where he underlined that the notion of neutrality in the FCMA Treaty preamble gave public recognition to Finland's desire to stay out of great power confrontations. This was "a principle that is unanimously approved by the Finnish nation and a policy that most of the small states try to follow." Simultaneously, the president also recognized the rather particular conditions of Finland's neutrality desire: the lease of the "Porkkala" naval base to the Soviet Union for fifty years did lend Finland's "neutrality" a color which did "not quite fit with the handbooks of international law."[18]

Austrian State Treaty and Neutrality (1955)

Whereas in 1948, Finland's wish to stay outside conflicts—that is, its "neutrality"—was not given much credit in Soviet eyes,[19] by the early 1950s the Soviet Union was using neutrality as an instrument in the pursuit of its own policies. In 1952, Stalin had come out with an idea of "a belt of neutral countries" that would run from Finland in the North to Yugoslavia in the South, also including Germany and Austria in the middle. In all these countries, Soviet campaigns for neutrality-generated controversy and resistance: in Germany, Chancellor Konrad Adenauer in the front, equaled neutrality with "Sovietization." In Austria, Foreign Minister (1945–1953) Karl Gruber warned Austria of neutrality in the model of Finland as a way to Eastern dependence, also introducing in this connection the term "Finlandization" (Gruber 1953; Majander 1999; Auffermann 1992, 347–371; Matson 1998).

However, in 1953–1954, the mood in regard to Austria's (but not on Germany's) neutrality started to change rapidly and the willingness to compromises was growing on all sides.[20] The Austrian State Treaty in May 1955, which preceded the culmination of the first Cold War détente phase in the Geneva Conference later in the summer, restored Austria's full state sovereignty and territorial unity. It was to be followed by the declaration of Austria's permanent neutrality by parliament in October 1955. Regardless of the fact that the two issues were connected with one another in several ways in practice, formally, Austria's permanent neutrality was not written down in the State Treaty. It was not multilaterally or internationally guaranteed. Obviously, the fascination with the Swiss model that otherwise was in a key role in rendering Austria's neutrality acceptable to all sides, the virtues of the Swiss model—in Western or Austrian eyes—did not reside in the *international* legal guarantees that were a part and parcel of Swiss neutrality. And, indeed, under the Cold War circumstances, it can be argued, such an international or multilateral agreement could have easily led to a situation, whereby Austria's neutrality would have been a topic for continuous Cold War–spirited contestation and dispute between the parties to the agreement. At the same time, Austria's neutrality declaration remained free of linkages to any bilateral agreements such as was the FCMA Treaty between Finland and the Soviet Union. Austria's neutrality declaration was, instead, issued by the country's own parliament and given a status as a constitutional amendment.[21] In contrast to both Finland's and Sweden's neutrality, Austria's neutrality was thus legally based yet, unlike in the case of Switzerland, this legal basis did not relate to international but to national law. This neutrality was legally framed, yet unilateral and national which—in comparison to Finland—gave Austrians much better options to keep the interpretations over the meanings and implications of neutrality in strictly domestic hands (in practice in the hands of the two main parties in parliament, the SPÖ and the ÖVP).

Finland's Paradox Neutrality

The changing mood in the mid-1950s international relations and the Geneva spirit of détente opened new vistas also for Finland's neutrality. Quite paradoxically however, the consolidation of neutrality's position on the geopolitical map of Europe reinforced Finland's neutrality yet, at the same time, was to strengthen the linkages between Finland's neutrality and the FCMA Treaty in rhetoric and praxis. Since the mid-1950s Finland's neutrality—which had started out as a primarily national desire boiling down to the small state neutrality of the pre-war years and the model of the other Nordic countries, and, especially, the remaining neutral, Sweden—became more complexly entangled with Finland's bilateral Soviet relations and the FCMA treaty.

In 1955, the Soviet Union returned the "Porkkala" naval base to Finland, removing a major obstacle on the way to the "normalization" of Finland's neutrality. Yet, in exchange, the bilateral security pact between Finland and the Soviet Union was extended for twenty more years. In connection with this renewal, Finland's neutrality was lent explicit support by a separate mutual declaration which noted that the FCMA Treaty was based on the recognition of and respect for Finland's wish to follow a policy of neutrality (Hanhimäki 1997, 169–194). This declaration—which, for the first time, used the term neutrality—was rightly seen as a major recognition of Finland's neutrality. As a side effect, however, this declaration also established a more explicit de facto link between Finland's neutrality and the FCMA treaty commitments. With the continuation of the Cold War confrontation beyond Geneva, these connections made Finland's neutrality inherently vulnerable to the Cold War pressures. Especially the option to begin military consultations and, in fact, the mere raising of the question of whether there would be a need for bilateral Finnish-Soviet consultations over the possible need for military assistance from the Soviet Union to Finland proved to be a highly effective tool in influencing Finland's policies. The so-called "consultation card" never disappeared from the Finnish policymakers' horizon: the threat of the Soviet Union publicly raising the question of the need for mutual consultations hung over all major crises in Finnish-Soviet relations during the Cold War decades. After a series of crises in Finland's Soviet relations in 1958–1961—all related to Finland's attempts to integrate with Western European economic cooperation (on pace with the other European neutrals)—the wish to avoid the Soviet consultation calls evolved into a main priority of Finnish policy making. Under the even more all-encompassing Cold War circumstances, a widening sector of policy fields could be scrutinized by the Soviet Union in virtue of the FCMA treaty. In the course of the years, this avoidance gave ground to pre-anticipation of potentially negative Soviet reactions in several policy fields, and the need for a continuous and preemptive demonstration of Finland's "trustworthiness." In order to avoid its neutrality and sovereignty being discredited by consultation requests as defined in the FCMA treaty, Finland was ready (and pushed) to notably far-reaching compromises in regard to the very same elements—neutrality and sovereignty—it tried to safeguard. This pattern left its mark not only on Finland's foreign relations but also on domestic politics and political culture in the 1970s in particular.[22]

Finland's neutrality never ceased to be conditioned and also shadowed by the bilateral security pact. Towards the late 1960s, the inbuilt weaknesses became ever more evident. After the replacement of Nikita Khrushchev at the top of the Soviet state in late 1964, the Soviet leadership was keen to target trends of Europeanization in Finland's foreign relations and the increased Western biases of the public debate and opinion as well as in the ways in which neutrality was interpreted in Finland (i.e., in the model of Sweden, Switzerland, and, also, Austria). These trends, the Soviet Union argued, seemed to be risking Finland's commitment to the FCMA treaty obligations. As a result, the concept of neutrality was wiped away from all bilateral Soviet-Finnish diplomatic documents in the latter half of the 1960s. After the Prague crisis in 1968, the Soviet disapproval of neutrality grew ever more explicit—not least because of the fear for a spillover effect of Finland's model to the Eastern bloc countries (cf. also Hungary 1956). The FCMA treaty was to be prolonged twice more in 1973 and 1983 but Finland's neutrality was no longer mentioned in any official Soviet-Finnish documents or diplomatic connections until 1989. In 1989, neutrality made a sudden comeback onto the agenda of bilateral relations during Michael Gorbachev's visit to Helsinki at a point of time when the Cold War was already ending.[23]

The founding facts continued to frame the individual countries' policies of neutrality for many years to come. In terms of how neutrality was institutionalized, Austria proved to be better equipped from the beginning than was Finland where the linkages between the FCMA Treaty, the country's Soviet relations and its neutrality grew tighter and more complex during the course of the Cold War. Further, in terms of timing, the Austrians were in a position to learn a few more Cold War lessons—also by looking at the case of Finland and its postwar Soviet relations—before they embarked on the path of Cold War neutrality than had been the Finns in 1948.

Regardless of these formative elements, however, there also was some room for maneuvre and this room also changed over time. Neutrality, from this perspective, was not pre-fixed and monolithic but, rather, a fluid and flexible process, something that was rehearsed and modified in actual practice for many decades after its initial adoption. In this light, the key question is what was and what could be made of neutrality by the individual neutral countries under the national and international Cold War circumstances that they were faced with.

SECOND LESSON: MAKING A NATIONAL IDENTITY OUT OF NEUTRALITY

Neutrality has been widely seen and discussed as one of the main threads in Switzerland's and Sweden's national history since the nineteenth century, as one of the founding myths of these countries as modern states and nations. Yet, it has also been noted that it was only in the course of the twentieth century that neutrality truly changed "from being a pragmatic tool meant to serve national security to an all-encompassing dogma of a utopian republic situated between opposing blocs, well integrated domestically and admired around the world as the model of democratic statehood" (Wenger 2003, 23–24).[24] Considering the post–Cold War developments, the dimensions related to statehood and national identity appear to have been also among the most pertinent within the legacies that neutrality has left behind.

Further, a deep societal and politico-cultural embedding of neutrality into national and official identity seems to be characteristic especially of the "strongest" among the neutrals, the ones who proved most successful in putting through their narratives of neutrality at both the national and international level. This leads us to think about neutrality's role as an instrument of state- and nation-building, and in the production/re-production of the collective state and national identities. At its most successful neutrality seems to have been, and made into, something much wider than an official foreign or military nonalignment policy. Further, the use of neutrality as a vehicle of nation- and state-building and its domestic embedding was not a pre-given but resulting from systematic and conscious policies in all those countries that have exercised neutrality in the twentieth century, and perhaps especially important in those countries that practiced neutrality during the ideologically tense circumstances of the Cold War (Rainio-Niemi 2014).

During the Cold War, neutrality was a very elusive, varied, and politicized phenomenon. By the early 1960s, a long way had been taken from the understandings of neutrality as a wartime abstention from an open military conflict and, also, from the early postwar perceptions of neutrality simply as non-participation in military alliances. Simultaneously, the rapidly widening and politicizing scope of meanings and uses of neutrality on all sides ran the risk of obfuscating what exactly neutrality meant. To avoid neutrality being washed away by the ever more politicized Cold War and to retain the ownership over the national policies of neutrality, all European neutral countries—with Switzerland and Sweden in the forefront—adopted increasingly proactive roles in the articulation of their own policies of neutrality internationally and at home. Under the Cold War circumstances, more than perhaps ever before, "successful" and credible neutrality started requiring ever more capacity to create public image policies and skilful rhetoric. This indeed was no classical wartime neutrality but ever more clearly peacetime neutrality, or, more precisely, neutrality as pursued in the absence of an open war, during a "cold" war. It was to require an exceptional amount of argumentative capacity, reflexivity, and cognitive power. The small neutrals of Europe with their well-educated populations had many competitive advantages in these endeavors.

The two Cold War newcomer neutrals, Austria and Finland are cases in point. Both countries introduced their neutrality in relatively strained international circumstances. Neither Austria nor Finland had a well-established long-term history as a neutral country or could build upon sound domestic (or international) consensus in the matter of their neutrality. In both countries the idea of neutrality was inherently contested and this applies especially to Austria.

In Finland the domestic approval of the idea of neutrality (with also some prewar history) was broader to start with. Simultaneously, however, the proximity to the Soviet Union created particularly heavy external pressure regarding the "adequate" interpretations of neutrality and these pressures were also to divide domestic opinions. Regardless of these troubles, however, both countries very rapidly established, neutrality as a key element of the state and national identity—an aspect that the opinion surveys that were regularly conducted in both countries since the 1960s amply verify and a living proof for continued meanings of neutrality as a device of state and nation-building also in the Cold War context.

In a longer historical perspective, Austria in particular stands out as a case for neutrality's successful use as an instrument of state- and nation-building. Austria's choice for neutrality was strictly conditioned and shaped by the wider international and Cold War politics and originally divided opinions within the country. Yet, within a decade or so, neutrality had been systematically turned into a key element of Austria's state and national identity. In a previously conflict-ridden society with a minimal level of internal cohesion, no shared idea of what an Austrian state should be, the achievement is notable. By the late 1960s, neutrality had grown and been consciously turned into a key element of Austria's new stately and national existence and a symbol of its permanent separation from Germany.

Finland, on the other hand, offers a case where the domestic embedding of neutrality remained constrained, limited, or weak. Regardless of a wider domestic consensus on the desirability of neutrality in 1948, the vulnerability of Finland's neutrality to the Cold War pressures was to make it into a subject of deeper conflicts and controversies that divided also the domestic political field. Since the 1960s the growing Soviet criticism of Finland's neutrality was accompanied by deepening conflicts over the right type of interpretations regarding neutrality within Finland. These tensions were internal and external at once and rapidly polarized the political opinion landscape and limited Finland's ability to make use of neutrality as a tool of public diplomacy like the other European neutrals. Finland's neutrality remained fragile and politically more vulnerable than was the case with the other neutrals.

The picture, however, is not unequivocal. Staring from the late 1950s systematic efforts were taken by the key ministries and civil servants to model Finland's neutrality in accordance with the societally deeply embedded Swiss and Swedish models of neutrality. Results were soon to be seen in neutrality's high and also abiding popular support. Also in Cold War Finland, neutrality rapidly developed into something familiar and even cherished by the people, the majority of civil servants and other state elites. While the political groupings were engaged in the battles quarreled over the "right" meanings of neutrality and, simultaneously, over the meanings of the FCMA Treaty and the friendly Soviet relations to Finland, at a broader popular and societal level, the results of the efforts of the societal and identity political embedding of neutrality remained stable. By the mid-1980s, the deepest domestic polarizations were fading away on pace with the ending of the Cold War. At this point, the idea of Finland's neutrality had become deeply internalized at the

level of public opinion and the majority of decision makers. Also internationally Finland was without much reservation being counted among the European neutrals by the mid-1980s. Ironically, Finland's neutrality was most
widely approved both home and abroad just before it was to be abandoned
with the end of the Cold War.

NEW CONFRONTATIONS—NEW NEUTRALITY?

When the Cold War confrontation was reaching its end in 1980s Europe,
international relations scholars and experts of neutrality gathered to contem-
plate whether a conflict of one type or another was a prerequisite for meaningful neutrality. Some argued that this was the case. Others looked for new
contents for neutrality as a transformative policy that would alter the basic,
conflict-ridden logic of international relations towards a new type of peaceful
dialogue, cooperation, and stability.

The conflict-centered view seems to come out ahead as the stronger one.
In the early post–Cold War years' (relatively) optimist atmosphere, neutrality lost its day-to-day relevance (Austria/Switzerland) or was abandoned
altogether (Sweden/Finland). Without a major confrontation from whence a
neutral stance would derive its sense and significance, neutrality was becoming increasingly meaningless. Where it retained its meanings, these meanings
were associated much more with history and national identity than with day-
to-day politics.

Following a conflict-centered definition of neutrality, it can be asked
whether the most recent onset of a new age of confrontations in international
relations would bring along and/or create a need and desire for a new type
of neutrality. Recent years' trends in Switzerland and Austria seem to point
to this direction; to a revival and redefinition of the concept of neutrality in
accordance with the new type of confrontations in world politics and in the
regions around the European Union.

In two other former neutrals Sweden and Finland, on the other hand,
the increased polarization seems to have strengthened the longing for solid
national defense capacity, mirroring also the concerns regarding the increased
military tensions in the Baltic Sea area. So far, there has been no major interest in refashioned neutrality. This applies especially to Finland where the
NATO option has undergone a powerful renaissance regardless of a simultaneous, very pronounced emphasis on the wish to avoid any drastic moves in
this or any other security matters, at least for the time being.[25]

Both paths—the Nordic and the Central European—seem logical in a longer post–Cold War perspective: irrespective of the certain inflation of neutrality in the early post–Cold War years, Switzerland and also Austria did retain

their option to neutrality. Sweden and Finland, in contrast, abandoned neutrality in the 1990s, retaining the now very narrowly conceived component of military nonalignment. It will be interesting to see whether the Ukrainian crisis will be noted in history textbooks as the watershed when the four former Cold War neutrals' paths separated for good. Will Sweden and Finland proceed towards deeper bilateral cooperation? While the actual degree of cooperation still remains to be seen, it is also as yet unknown whether that development would take place with or without giving up the principle of military nonalignment.

The Cold War and the Cold War neutrality are history and will never return as such. This does not mean, however, that neutrality as an idea and practice whose histories reach way back beyond the Cold War would have reached the end of its history with the end of the Cold War. With the emergence of new conflicts and confrontations we will witness new forms of neutrality. These will not necessarily (or even likely) appear in the same places as before, but also the new forms of neutrality will in all likelihood be geared towards the basic functions and uses of keeping a region or a polity outside conflicts of the others. This aim can be initiated either by a country or by outside power(s) with an interest in a restoration and/or maintenance of a status quo in a certain geopolitically sensitive area. As the discussion of Finland's and Austria's cases of neutrality above suggests, in actual history these aims and desires often combine in complex, varying, and inherently flexible ways.

NOTES

1. Also see the *Financial Times* editorial on Febuary 24, 2014.

2. While "military non-alignment" often gets understood in international public debates as being more or less synonymous with "neutrality," in Finland and Sweden a distinction has been drawn between neutrality and military nonalignment since the end of the Cold War. These countries remain outside military alliances yet neither claim to be neutral or follow a policy of neutrality.

3. On Finland's veteran diplomats' responses to Brzezinski and Kissinger: Réne Nyberg, 2014. "Finland's History is so Different from Ukraine's," *Financial Times*, Febuary 25; Jaakko Iloniemi, 2014. "The Finnish Experience is very Difficult to Copy," *Financial Times,* March 11. On domestic reactions for example, YLE News. 2014b. *Kissinger: Suomi toimisi mallina Ukrainalle* [Kissinger Finland could be a model for Ukraine], March 18; Helsingin Sanomat, 2014. *Ukrainan suurvaltapelissä Suomi on tarjolla vaihtorahaksi* [In the Great Game over Ukraine, Finland is offered as a trade-off], Febuary 29.

4. In the spring 2014, the idea of an Austrian model for Ukraine received relatively wide domestic support across the party political lines from the coalition parties to the Green Party in the opposition. For the Austrian discussions see for example,

Alfred Gusenbauer, 2014. "Die Kampf um die Ukraine," *Format*, March 14; the Green Party's version on the party website www.gruene.at, *Krim-Krise: Grüne Prioritäten*; also see APA, 2014. Lunacek: Aktive Neutralitätspolitik statt pro-russischer Pseudo-Neutralität der Freiheitlichen, March 18. http://www.ots.at/presseaussendung/OTS_20140318_OTS0103/lunacek-aktive-neutralitaetspolitik-statt-pro-russischer-pseudo-neutralitaet-der-freiheitlichen; also see Die Presse, 2014a. *Kurz: Österreich schickt Neutralitätsexperten in die Ukraine*, March 27; Die Presse, 2014b. Krim-Krise: Wiener Vier-Punkte-Plan für die Ukraine, April 2. Only the Freedom Party (FPÖ) seems to have diverged from this consensus, publically demanding a more "sincerely neutral" attitude also vis-à-vis Russia in the connection with the 2014 events.

5. For a starting shot for the Austrian discussions see, Heinz Gärtner, 2014. "Neutrality for Ukraine according to the Austria model," *Policy Paper*. Vienna: Austrian Institute for International Affairs. [http://www.oiip.ac.at/fileadmin/Unterlagen/Dateien /Kurzanalysed/UkraineEU_HG1.pdf].

6. Alfred Gusenbauer pointed out in *Format* (March 14, 2014) that in case Ukraine would be pushed too hard to choose between the East and the West, the country in its present shape would split or disintegrate into two. On the other hand, if the country would and the international community would encourage it to choose to be a meeting place for Europe and Russia, tools for the construction of such a role could be offered by the model of Austria. This could mean some type of a self-chosen, voluntary (not imposed) arrangement of "neutrality or non-alignment" based on such agreements that would seem most adequate in today's perspective and be acceptable also to the members of international community. This type of an arrangement would not exclude full EU membership or active partnership with the Nato though it would rule out a full Nato membership. In all cases, the last end decision on the issues of alignment and nonalignment would stay in the hands of the democratically elected political leaders and the people.

7. The attention is restricted here to the spring 2014 debates. Like was the case with the international public attention to the Finland option, also the debate on the Austria model of neutrality for Ukraine calmed down towards the autumn of 2014.

8. The public, at home or abroad, did not always keep pace with the changes in official foreign policy terminologies. Pernille Rieker describes the confusion between the concepts of nonalignment and neutrality in the case of Sweden: "even though nonalignment was the term most frequently used, the neutrality concept was still referred to and Sweden continued to be perceived, both by many Swedes themselves and by foreigners, as a neutral country." She explains this "attachment to neutrality" by noting that neutrality was so widely considered "an important part of Swedish national identity." This applies internationally as well: still in 2000, Jacques Chirac expressed that he knew how important "neutrality" was to the Swedish people. See, Pernille Rieker, 2002. "From territorial defence to comprehensive security. European integration and the changing Norwegian and Swedish security identities," *NUPI Paper* 626. Oslo: Norwegian Institute of International Affairs: 17, 32; also see Walter Carlsnaes, 1993. "Sweden Facing the New Europe: Whither Neutrality?" *European Security* 2(1): 71–89, 83.

9. Neutrality is typically presented a pure necessity of and an instrument for pragmatic national survival in the Cold War. For political science analyses of these narrative patterns and the related identity political implications, see Harle, Vilho, and Sami Moisio, 2000. *Missä on Suomi? Kansallisen identiteettipolitiikan historia ja geopolitiikka.* Vastapaino:Tampere; also Sami Moisio, 2008. "Finlandisation versus Westernisation: Political recognition and Finland's European Union membership debate," *National Identities* 10(1): 77–93; and, especially, Christopher Browning, 2002. "Coming Home or Moving Home? 'Westernising' Narratives in Finnish Foreign Policy and the Re-Interpretation of Past Identities," *Cooperation and Conflict* 37(1): 547–72. There is an interesting similarity between Finland's "Westernising" narrative and the 1980s ideas of Central Europe as "kidnapped, displaced, brainwashed" West as famously presented by Milan Kundera, 1989. "The Tragedy of Central Europe," *The New York Review of Books*, April 26, 1984: 33–38.

10. Chancellor Wolfgang Schüssel (2000–2007, ÖVP) famously equaled Austrian neutrality with the Mozart Kügel and the Lippizzaner horses in the early 2000s. Simultaneously, the "de facto" and "de jure" compatibility of the EU membership and neutrality continued to be frequently debated issues among legal, administrative, and policy experts. However, the popular support of Austria's neutrality remained stable and the political price of the initiation of any reforms continuing to loom too large which discouraged any initiatives. In addition, the social democrats' outspoken lack of support for any amendments regarding neutrality made that for the most part of the 1990s and 2000s the options for gaining the two-thirds majority for changes in parliament were very weak.

11. For an analysis on the deepening cooperation since 2014 see for example, Charly Salonius-Pasternak, 2014. "Deeper Defence Cooperation. Finland and Sweden together again?" *FIIA Briefing Paper* 163. Helsinki: The Finnish Institute for International Affairs. For official Swedish views, see http://www.government.se/government-policy/defence/defence-cooperation-between-finland-and-sweden; For joint statements for example, http://yle.fi/uutiset/finnish_and_swedish_pms_release_joint_statement_serious_threat_to_our_security/8583414. The most recent government report on Finnish foreign and security policy (June 2016) can be found through http://formin.finland.fi/public/default.aspx?contentid=348077&contentlan=2&culture=e and the preceding, government commissioned expert assessment (April 2014) on the possible effects of Finland's Nato membership—suggesting that in case of any moves, such moves such ideally be taken together with Sweden—through http://formin.finland.fi/public/default.aspx?contentid=345685&nodeid=49298&contentlan=2&culture=en-US

12. For neutrality's new meanings and its embedding with Austria's overall security strategy see for example, Bundeskanzleramt, 2013. *Österreichische Sicherheitsstrategie. Sicherheit in einer neuen Dekade—Sicherheit gestalten.* Wien: Bundeskanzleramt. http://www.bka.at/site/3503/default.aspx.

13. For the most recent formulations see http://formin.finland.fi/public/default.aspx?contentid=348077&contentlan=2&culture=e

14. The first article of the treaty obliged Finland "in the eventuality of Finland, or the Soviet Union through Finnish territory, becoming object of an armed attack by

Germany or any state allied with the latter," "true to its obligations as an independent state, [to] fight to repel the attack." Furthermore, the treaty stated that "Finland will in such cases use all its available forces for defending its territorial integrity by land, sea and air, and will do so within the frontiers of Finland in accordance with obligations defined in the present Treaty and, *if necessary*, with the assistance of, or jointly with the Soviet Union." Italics by JRN, the translation is from Greenville, J. A. S. (Ed.). 1974. *The Major International Treaties, 1914–1973.* London: Methuen: 364.

15. The resulting pact between the Soviet Union and Finland differed from the parallel treaties signed with the Eastern European countries. It obligated Finland to take care that its territory would not be used by others to attack the Soviet Union but did not obligate Finland to take part in any military actions anywhere outside Finland's own territory. Further, all possible military cooperation had to be preceded by mutual political consultations whereby the existence of the threat of an attack to the Soviet Union would need to be jointly stated. For more see for example, Jussi Hanhimäki, 1997. *Containing Coexistence. America, Russia, and the "Finnish Solution," 1945–1956.* Kent, OH, London: Kent State University Press: 23–29; Tuomo Polvinen, 1999. *J.K. Paasikivi. Valtiomiehen elämäntyö 4: 1944–1948* [J.K Paasikivi. The lifework of a Statesman]. Porvoo: WSOY: 418–421, 463–517; Max Jakobson, 1968. *Finnish Neutrality: A Study of Finnish Foreign Policy since the Second World War.* London: Hugh Evelym: 38–39.

16. The symbol of this pre-war neutrality was the Copenhagen Declaration of July 1938 in which the so-called Oslo states (Sweden, Norway, Denmark, the Netherlands, Belgium, Luxembourg, and Finland as the core signatories) announced their wish to stay neutral in any upcoming conflict.

17. Finland's wish to stay outside conflicts is formulated in the treaty preamble as "considering Finland's desire to remain outside the conflicting interests of the Great Powers" Greenville 1974: 364.

18. Paasikivi's speech on April 9, 1948, is re-printed in Paasikivi, Juho Kusti (1976) *Paasikiven linja. Puheita vuosilta 1944–1956.* [The Paasikivi Line. Speeches from the Years 1944–1956] Hakalehto, Ilkka ed. Helsinki: Tammi, 114–115.

19. In 1948 the whole issue of neutrality was not of great relevance to the Soviet Union either. Mirroring this relative irrelevance we may also note that Sweden's proposal on a Scandinavian Defense Union (1948) whereby Norway and Denmark would have stayed neutral as well was vehemently resisted by the United States but not particularly actively promoted by the Soviet Union. See for example, Geir Lundestad, 1980. *America, Scandinavia, and the Cold War, 1945–1949.* New York: Columbia University Press; Magne Skovdin, 1990. *Nordic or North Atlantic Alliance? The Postwar Scandinavian Security Debate.* Oslo: Institute for Defense Studies; Poul Villaume, 1989. "Neither Appeasement nor Servility: Denmark and the Atlantic Alliance, 1949–1955," *Scandinavian Journal of History* 14(2): 155–179.

20. Still in September 1953, an internal US position paper had noted that Austria was geostrategically too central to allow a solution "in the model of Finland." Yet it was not seen able to practice "neutrality on the Swiss model" either because of the lack of Austria's political parties' will and capacity to cooperate with another in this

matter. However, in Berlin in April 1954, John Foster Dulles noted that "a neutral status is an honorable status if it is voluntarily chosen by a nation. Switzerland had chosen to be neutral, and as a neutral she has achieved an honorable place in the family of nations. Under the Austrian state treaty as heretofore drafted, Austria would be free to choose for itself to be neutral like Switzerland. Certainly the United States would fully respect its choice in this respect, as it fully respects its choice in the respect of the Swiss nation" (Bischof 1999, 139). When the United States started showing interest in Austria's neutrality, the Soviet Union began to hesitate. In the spring 1955 the process was moving again. The West German integration with the West seeming unavoidable now, the Soviet Union called off the earlier association it had tried to make between the questions of Austria and Germany and, acting in a defensive hurry, pushed for Austria's separate neutrality with the main priority being the clearest possible Anschluss ban. As a guarantee for an enduring existence of Austria (i.e., Anschluss ban), the Austrian diplomatic delegation courtly offered the Swiss model and the Soviet Union approved as the idea of a Swiss type of an internationally guaranteed neutrality. On these events in more detail see, Gerald Stourzh, 2005. "Der österreichische Staatsvertrg in den weltpoliticshen Entscheidungsprozessen des Jahres 1955." In *Der Österreichische Staatsvertarg zwischen internationaler Strateguie und nationaler Identität*. Vienna: Österreichische Akademie der Wissenscahften; Strouzh, G. 1998. *Um Einheit und Freiheit. Staatsvertarg, Neutralität und das Ende der Ost-West-Besatzung Österreichs 1945–1955*. Vienna: Böhlau; also see for example, Vladislav Zubok, 2007. *A Failed Empire: The Soviet Union in the Cold War from Stalin to Gorbachev*. Chapel Hill, NC: University of North Carolina Press: 94–99.

21. The first article of the amendment stated that "for the purpose of the permanent maintenance of its external independence and for the purpose of the inviolability of its territory, Austria, of its own free will, declares herewith its permanent neutrality which it is resolved to maintain and defend with all the means at its disposal" (Verdross 1978, 28).

22. The question of whether there was a need for such consultations was publically raised once by the Soviet Union in 1961. This request led to a personal meeting between President Urho Kekkonen of Finland and Nikita Khrushchev, and as result, the Soviet Union dropped the request.

23. The FCMA treaty that had been renewed in 1983 stayed in force until it was mutually declared invalid by Russia and Finland in early 1992.

24. Regarding Sweden see, for instance, Mikael af Malmborg, 2001. *Neutrality and State-Building in Sweden*. London: Palgrave; also Krister Wahlbäck, 1986. *The Roots of Swedish Neutrality*. Stockholm: The Swedish Institute for International Affairs.

25. The emphasis on the need to avoid any drastic changes—regardless of the simultaneously openness to reconsiderations—is typical to the conclusions of (also) the most recent expert assessment on the effects of Finland's possible nato membership (April 2014) http://formin.finland.fi/public/default.aspx?contentid=345685&nodeid=49298&contentlan=2&culture=en-US

BIBLIOGRAPHY

APA. 2014. "Lunacek: Aktive Neutralitätspolitik statt pro-russischer Pseudo-Neutralität der Freiheitlichen," March 14. http://www.ots.at/presseaussendung/OTS_20140318_OTS0103/lunacek-aktive-neutralitaetspolitik-statt-pro-russischer-pseudo-neutralitaet-der-freiheitlichen

Auffermann, Burkhard. 1992. "Finlandisierung—das abschreckende Beispiel? Zur Problematik eines politischen Kampfbegriffes in der Ära des Kalten Krieges." *zeitgeschichte* 26(6): 347–371.

Bischof, Günter. 1999. *Austria in the First Cold War: The Leverage of the Weak.* Houndmills, Basinstoke, UK: Macmillan Press.

Blomberg Jaakko. 2011. *Vapauden kaipuu. Kylmän sodan loppu ja Suomi.* Helsinki: WSOY.

Browning, Christopher. 2002. "Coming Home or Moving Home? 'Westernising' Narratives in Finnish Foreign Policy and the Re-Interpretation of Past Identities." *Cooperation and Conflict* 37(1): 547–72.

Brzezinski, Zbigniew. 2014. "Russia needs a 'Finland option' for Ukraine." *Financial Times*, Febuary 24.

Bundeskanzleramt. 2013. *Österreichische Sicherheitsstrategie. Sicherheit in einer neuen Dekade—Sicherheit gestalten.* Wien: Bundeskanzleramt. Available through http://www.bka.at/site/3503/default.aspx

Carlsnaes, Walter. 1993. "Sweden Facing the New Europe: Whither Neutrality?" *European Security* 2(1): 71–89.

Cohen, Josh. 2014. "Here's How Ukraine Can take Charge of its Fate: By Declaring Neutrality." *Foreign Affairs*, March 28.

Die Presse (Austria). 2014. *Krim-Krise: Wiener Vier-Punkte-Plan für die Ukraine.* April 2.

Der Tagesspiegel (Germany), "Finnlands Premier Katainen: Wir sind nicht neutral" March 16, 2014.

Final Reports on Deepened Defense Cooperation between Sweden and Finland. Available through http://www.government.se/government-policy/defence/defence-cooperation-between-finland-and-sweden [June 16, 2016].

Gehler, Michael. 2012. "Paving Austria's Way to Brussels: Chancellor Franz Vranitzky (1986–1997). A Banker, Social Democrat, and Pragmatic European Leader." *Journal of European Integration History* 18(2): 159–82.

Greenville, J.A.S. (Ed.). 1974. *The Major International Treaties, 1914–1973.* London: Methuen.

Gruber, Karl. 1953. *Zwischen Befreiung und Freiheit. Der Sonderfall Österreich.* Wien, Berlin: Ullstein

Gruene.at. 2014. Krim-Krise: Grüne Prioritäten. March 7. http://gruene.at.

Gusenbauer, Alfred. 2014 "Die Kampf um die Ukraine." *Format*, March 14.

Gärtner, Heinz. 2014. "Neutrality for Ukraine according to the Austria model" *Policy Paper 1/2014.* Vienna: Austrian Institute for International Affairs. http://www.oiip.ac.at/fileadmin/Unterlagen/Dateien /Kurzanalysed/UkraineEU_HG1.pdf

Hanhimäki, Jussi. 1997. *Containing Coexistence. America, Russia, and the "Finnish Solution," 1945–1956*. Kent, OH, London: Kent State University Press.

Harle, Vilho, and Sami Moisio. 2000. *Missä on Suomi? Kansallisen identiteettipolitiikan historia ja geopolitiikka*. [History of the national identity politics and geopolitics] Vastapaino:Tampere,

Helsingin Sanomat (Finland). 2014. *Ukrainan suurvaltapelissä Suomi on tarjolla vaihtorahaksi* [In the Great Game over Ukraine, Finland is offered as a trade-off"], Febuary 29.

Himanen, Hannu. 2003. "Finland." In *Neutrality and Non-Alignment in Europe Today*, edited by Hanna Ojanen. Helsinki: The Finnish Institute for International Affairs.

Iloniemi, Jaakko. 2014. "The Finnish Experience is very Difficult to Copy" *Financial Times*, March 11.

Jakobson, Max. 1968. *Finnish Neutrality. A Study of Finnish Foreign Policy since the Second World War*. London: Hugh Evelyn.

Kissinger, Henry. 2014. "How the Ukraine Crisis ends" *Washington Post*, March 6, 2014.

Kundera, Milan. 1984. "The Tragedy of Central Europe." *The New York Review of Books*, April 26, 1984: 33–38.

Lipponen, Paavo. 2008. *Järki voittaa. Suomalainen identiteetti globalisaation aikakaudella*. [Finnish Identity in Globalisation's Age] Helsinki: Otava.

Lundestad, Geir. 1980. *America, Scandinavia, and the Cold War, 1945–1949*. New York: Columbia University Press.

Majander, Mikko. 1999. "The Paradoxes of Finladization." In *Northern Dimensions: The Yearbook of the Finnish Institute for International Affairs 1999*. Helsinki: The Finnish Institute for International Affairs.

Malmborg, Mikael af. 2001. *Neutrality and State-Building in Sweden*. London: Palgrave.

Matson, R. 1998. "Finlandization: A Retrospective." In *Charting an Independent Course: Finland's Place in the Cold War and in the US Foreign Policy*, edited by T.M. Ruddy. Camas, WA: Regina Books.

Mearsheimer, John J. 2014. "Getting Ukraine Wrong." *The New York Times*, March 24.

Ministry of Foreign Affairs. 2016. *The Effects of Finland's Possible Nato Membership. An Assessment*. Helsinki: Ministry for Foreign Affairs. http://formin.finland.fi/public/default.aspx?contentid=345685&nodeid=49298&contentlan=2&culture=en-US

Moisio, Sami. 2008. "Finlandisation versus Westernisation: Political recognition and Finland's European Union membership debate" *National Identities* 10(1): 77–93.

Munro, Emily (Ed.). 2005. *Challenges to Neutral and Non-Aligned Countries in Europe and Beyond*. Geneva: Geneva Center for Security Policy.

Nyberg, Réne. 2014. "Finland's History is so Different from Ukraine's." *Financial Times*, Febuary 25.

Paasikivi, Juho Kusti. 1976. *Paasikiven linja. Puheita vuosilta 1944–1956*. [The Paasikivi Line. Speeches from the Years 1944–1956.] Hakalehto, Ilkka ed. Helsinki: Tammi.

Polvinen, Tuomo. 1999. *J.K. Paasikivi. Valtiomiehen elämäntyö 4: 1944–1948* [J.K Paasikivi. The lifework of a Statesman]. Porvoo: WSOY.

Prime Ministers Office. 2016. "Government Report on Finnish Foreign and Security Policy." *Prime Minister's Office Publications*. Helsinki: Prime Minister's Office. http://formin.finland.fi/public/default.aspx?contentid=348060

Railo, Erkka, and Ville Laamanen (Eds.). 2010. *Suomi muuttuvassa maailmassa. Ulkosuhteiden ja kansallisen itseymmärryksen historiaa*. [Finland in a Changing World. History of Foreign Relations and National Self-Perceptions.] Helsinki: Edita.

Rainio-Niemi, Johanna. 2014. *The Ideological Cold War. The Politics of Neutrality in Austria and Finland*. New York and London: Routledge.

Rieker, Pernille. 2002. "From territorial defence to comprehensive security. European integration and the changing Norwegian and Swedish security identities" *NUPI Paper* 626. Oslo: Norwegian Institute of International Affairs.

Salonius-Pasternak, Charly. 2014. "Deeper Defence Cooperation. Finland and Sweden together again?" *FIIA Briefing Paper* 163. Helsinki: The Finnish Institute for International Affairs.

Skovdin, Magne. 1990. *Nordic or North Atlantic Alliance? The Postwar Scandinavian Security Debate*. Oslo: Institute for Defense Studies.

Stourzh, Gerald. 1998. *Um Einheit und Freiheit. Staatsvertarg, Neutralität und das Ende der Ost-West-Besatzung Österreichs 1945–1955*. Vienna: Böhlau.

———. 2005. "Der österreichische Staatsvertrg in den weltpoliticshen Entscheidungsprozessen des Jahres 1955." In *Der Österreichische Staatsvertarg zwischen internationaler Strateguie und nationaler Identität*. Vienna: Österreichische Akademie der Wissenscahften.

Tarkka, Jukka. 2012. *Karhun kainalossa. Suomen Kylmä Sota 1947–1990*. [Finland's Cold War 1947–1990] Helsinki: Otava.

Wahlbäck, Krister. 1986. *The Roots of Swedish Neutrality*. Stockholm: The Swedish Institute for International Affairs.

Wenger, Andreas. 2003. "Swiss Security Policy: From Autonomy to Cooperation." In *Swiss Foreign Policy, 1945–2002*, edited by Gabriel, Jürg Martin and Thomas C. Fischer. Houndmills, Basinstoke, UK: Palgrave Macmillan.

Verdross A. 1978. *The Permanent Neutrality of Austria*. Vienna: Verlag für Geschichte und Politik.

Villaume, Poul. 1989. "Neither Appeasement nor Servility: Denmark and the Atlantic Alliance, 1949–1955." *Scandinavian Journal of History* 14(2): 155–179.

Väyrynen, Raimo. 2003. "Comments on the Finnish Position." In *Neutrality and Non-Alignment in Europe Today*, edited by Hanna Ojanen. Helsinki: The Finnish Institute for International Affairs.

YLE News (Finland). 2014a. *Katainen saksalaisille: Suomi ei ole puolueeton* [Katainen to the Germans: Finland is not neutral], March 16.

———. 2014b. *Kissinger: Suomi toimisi mallina Ukrainalle* [Kissinger Finland could be a model for Ukraine], March 18.

———. 2016. *Finnish and Swedish PMs release a joint statement: "Serious Threat to Our Security,"* January 10.

Zubok, Vladislav. 2007. *A Failed Empire: The Soviet Union in the Cold War from Stalin to Gorbachev*. Chapel Hill, NC: University of North Carolina Press.

Chapter 2

From an Offer for all Cases to a Model Case?

Aspects of the Controversy about the Soviets' Germany, Austria, and Neutrality Policy, 1952–1955, in Current and Recent Research

Michael Gehler

It is one of the most controversial issues of Cold War Historiography if Stalin made a serious offer on March 10, 1952, when proposing a bloc-free (nonaligned and neutral) unified Germany with a national army as a result of all-German free elections. Since the 1980s up to now three generations of historians have been and are involved in an archive-based discussion about that issue. It is interesting that the connection between the Austrian and German Question (1952–1955) often has been ignored in that debate. There was no broad and intensive scholarly discussion if Austria's attempts to sign a state treaty and to reach a status of neutrality (1952–1955) were examples for Germany. When this came up, it was quickly neglected and rejected. This article raises questions of the model case debate in a first chapter. In a second one, it shows how the Austrian Question was in the wake of the Great Powers' Germany Policy (1952–1954). A third chapter demonstrates how the Allied Germany and Austria Policies were interconnected in 1952. The contribution touches also the Soviet Germany and Austrian Policy in 1955 by a fourth chapter. A final conclusion sums up arguments of the validity of the Austrian model case. The state of the art is presented according to new research literature results.

QUESTIONS OF THE MODEL-CASE DEBATE

The signing of the State Treaty, Austria's commitment to neutrality, and the withdrawal of troops from the four occupying powers that followed in 1955 hit like a lightning bolt in the middle of the East-West confrontation. In a historical light, however, it was not such an exceptional operation: Austria was not the first and only place to have Soviet troops withdraw. The Soviet Union also withdrew from Yugoslavia (December 1944), Northern Norway (September 1945), Czechoslovakia (December 1945), Bornholm (April 1946), Manchuria (May 1946), Iran (May 1946), Bulgaria (December 1947), North Korea (December 1948), China (Dairen and Port Arthur, May 1955), Finland (Porkkala-Udd, January 1956), and Romania (July 1958) (Handzik 1993). Old and new questions are raised:

- What were the objectives pursued in Germany and Austria after 1945 by the Soviet leadership?
- Were Stalin's offers in 1952 meant seriously?
- Was it only about the integration of the GDR into the East or, beyond that was the goal of Soviet policy about preventing the Federal Republic of Germany (FRG) becoming bound to a bloc?
- Was the Soviet leadership aiming at Germany in 1955 with the "Austria-example"?
- To what extent could the political structures that had been put in place in Central Europe's after 1945 be revised?

A "so-called theory of a 'model case'" (Stourzh 2005) has been spoken of, but no one has differentiated up to now what was meant by this or how it should be understood. Various questions are connected with the "model":

- Was it primarily about bilateral preliminary talks with the USSR to then be able to sit down in the consultation with the Western powers?
- Did it serve as an amicable quadripartite agreement to solve other questions beyond this?
- Was Austria's neutrality a test case for the relaxation of tensions?
- Was the Austria solution moving to neutrality thus just the result of a failed Soviet policy on Germany or a new and, at the same time, a last attempt at solving the German question?
- Should example effects of the state treaty for a German peace treaty be assumed?
- Was it about neutrality, neutralizing or even a mixture of the two for Germany?
- Or was it about much more than that, namely a neutral, united Germany weakening or even breaking up NATO?

Research has viewed the Soviet position in the spring of 1955 from the "resolute turn" to and "direct contact" with the FRG, "uncertainty" about the

Western Powers and the FRG as well as attempts to influence the Western, especially West German, public (Stourzh 2005, 388–91, 450–85). It did not seem to be more. We will need to come back to these findings.

A comparison of the limits and possibilities of the two countries has already been made (Mueller 2007, 123–54; Gehler 2015, 1115–22). Austria's resurrection was a product of the lost Hitlerite War and the Allied desire for weakening Germany. The FRG and the GDR were themselves artifacts of the Soviet and US empires and their antagonism during the Cold War. The FRG was created by the "London Recommendations" of the Six-Power Conference on June 2, 1948; the year after, the GDR was created at Moscow's behest. In the Second Allied Control Agreement of June 28, 1946, Austria was able to build up a democratic rule of law despite Soviet occupation. The pre-Anschluss borders of 1937 put the four powers until 1949 firmly. State and international law were both German part states as temporary administrative bodies of the occupying powers. Independence for Germany was not promised as it was for Austria in the Moscow Declaration of November 1, 1943. The occupation in the Alpine Republic was provisional; the general government, however, had already been put into operation in 1945. Austria's independence was to be restored and its territorial integrity to remain intact. While the victors took sweeping economic and political measures in the years 1945 to 1949 in their German occupation zones (Krautkrämer 1962, 44–89), Austria was left in political limbo and managed to maintain its economic and monetary unity. The Marshall Plan was for the entire country, which was only the case for the Western zones in Germany.

Despite of these differences the stereotypical argument about the lack of comparability does not rule out knowledge and application possibilities for solving the problem in these two cases. The gradual integration of the nonsovereign FRG in the Western system, the "total integration" (Schwarz 1990, 607) of the "occupied ally" (Rupieper 1991) took place under Western Allied military control and intelligence monitoring. Separately, a contract and military alliance renunciation, however, were the price that Austria had to pay to the USSR for political unity and inner freedom as the State Treaty also imposed restrictions and a constitutional law subsequently imposed neutrality, limiting foreign policy maneuver.

The "rearmament" of the FRG and its accession to the WEU and NATO were the price to gain more "sovereignty," but this was in fact not obtained. The military buildup in the Western zones in Austria under Western Command, however, was not a precondition of mandatory and unilateral Western integration, which would have had the momentous consequence of the partition of the country. The use of its armed forces was left almost entirely to Austria alone, as had been offered in the two Stalin Notes of March 10 and April 9, 1952, for a united Germany (Steininger 1985, 116, 191). From this year onward, the indication was toward separate paths for both countries (Gehler and Böhler 2007): neutrality, unity and Western orientation for Austria on the one hand; NATO, Western integration and division of the country for Germany on the other hand (Gehler and Agstner 2013).

THE AUSTRIA QUESTION IN THE WAKE OF THE GREAT POWERS' GERMAN POLICY, 1952–1954

For the West, the Soviet Germany proposal (German unity and mutual withdrawal of troops for military freedom with a national army) on March 10, 1952, came as a surprise. Immediately, on March 13, Western Allied diplomats presented a substantially abbreviated and far more unfavorable shortened agreement for Austria to the USSR, which also came unexpectedly for Moscow—with a view to the existing draft State Treaty—and they made it into an element of their policy towards Germany (Bischof 1991, 143–83; Gehler 1994a, 243–78; 2015, 140–49). Both proposals offered a basis for negotiations and material for propaganda. Both seemed unacceptable to the other side. While the Western side was forced to respond to the Stalin Note, the Eastern side silently ignored the "abbreviated treaty" that blocked the State Treaty, and thus ruled out the Austrian situation as a model for Germany.

For the relationship between Vienna and Bonn, this did not result in any adverse effects. The Western integration of Germany was well received at the Ballhausplatz. There, the initially propagated short contract promoted the game of the Western powers in the battle of notes with Stalin, while at the same time the place later Austrian demand for separation of the two matters was in Adenauer's interest (Gehler 1994, 243–78).

If the FRG did not want to respond to Stalin's offers, a learning process still resulted for Austria. According to research at this time, Moscow was following neither a policy of neutrality for Austria nor a model case policy for Germany (Ruggenthaler 2013, 490). For the former, however, there is counter-evidence (Mueller 2011, 47). Lack of flexibility and geostrategic intentions to hedge the Eastern Bloc are cited as key reasons for the Soviet attitude (Mueller 2005, 116–18; Ruggenthaler 2011, 198).

However, since 1949/50 the Austrian Communist Party (KPÖ) had propagated a neutrality solution for Austria (Stourzh 2005, 267–68, 321; Ruggenthaler 2013, 483), so one wonders if this could have been carried out unilaterally and without instructions or the approval of Stalin. The fact is, however, that in its policy towards Germany in 1952, the Kremlin gave no hints that could have been helpful to Austria. Therefore, without the USSR making the same or similar proposals regarding Austria, those working at the Ballhausplatz considered whether the Stalin Note was also directed at them and whether it could be used to solve their own problem (Gehler 2015, 132). Foreign Minister Karl Gruber (1945–1953) then formulated his principles of "true neutrality." Vienna took lessons from the Soviet Germany notes and began to adjust to alliancelessness (Gehler 1994b, 379–92, 433).

Bonn was worried—above all with a view to the unfinished Western integration—that there was an analogous situation to Austria in Germany: a four-power agreement with an open end. Alliance freedom that is Neutrality between East and West, as a means of preventing or overcoming the division of Germany was inconceivable for Adenauer. Chancellor Julius Raab could imagine it for Austria, and in 1953, there were Austrian soundings with respect to a policy of alliance freedom, which resulted in a still to be determined neutrality. The uprising on June 17, 1953, in the GDR and the bloody crackdown ruined this initiative for the time being (Gehler 2015, 274–90).

The Berlin Conference of Foreign Ministers in February 1954 did not bring the awaited breakthrough from Vienna (Pfeiffer 2001, 81–98) in the sense of unity and freedom. For the ease and satisfaction of Adenauer, who did not want an Austrian success, however its influence in 1955 was no longer sufficient, to prevent such an undesirable solution (military neutrality and territorial integrity) for the southern neighbor. In Bonn, concern was widespread that Soviet concessions on the Austrian question would cause repercussions in the German population and allow corresponding analogies (Gehler 2015, 360).

In contrast to the "quantité négligeable" Austria, the FRG had central importance for the Western powers. As long as Austria was not only "alliance free" but also remained mentally-culturally and economically westernized, its potential for the West was not lost and removed Soviet influence largely.

The development of the rejection of the European Defense Community (EDC) by the French National Assembly at the end of August 1954 with the emerging NATO entry of West Germany dominated the Paris Agreements and brought movement into the solidified fronts, so that a neutrality solution was now forced upon Austria (Gehler 2015, 413–27).

THE CONTROVERSY ABOUT THE SOVIET'S GERMANY AND AUSTRIA POLICY, 1952

To date, no consensus has been detectable in the historiography: Rolf Steininger (1985), Josef Foschepoth (1990), Melvyn Leffler (1992), Wilfried Loth (1994, 2007), John Lewis Gaddis (1998), and Geoffrey Roberts (2006) argued in terms of Stalin's willingness for German unity, while, oppositely, Hermann Graml (1977, 1981), Hans-Peter Schwarz (1982), Stefan Creuzberger (1997), Gerhard Wettig (1999, 2008, 2015), Jochen Laufer

(2002, 2004), Vladislav Zubok (2007), and Peter Ruggenthaler (2007, 2015) doubted the credibility of Stalin's Germany offers, whereby the most recent studies have had access to Soviet sources.

Most recently, the idea that Stalin intended to have a neutral Germany has been categorically and decidedly rejected (Ruggenthaler 2011, 203; 2015, 227, 349–367, 366). This is argued with the immediate prehistory: In February, 1951—the "Birth year of the Stalin Note" (Ruggenthaler)—the leader of the Socialist Unity Party (SED) Walter Ulbricht had encouraged exploiting the neutralist movement in West Germany in order to prevent Anglo-American rearmament plans for West Germany and "unmask the US warmongers."—Wasn't it serious? The proposal was favored in the Soviet Foreign Ministry by Andrej Wyschinskji and Vyacheslav Molotov (Ruggenthaler 2011, 179–87; 2015, 354, 363). Andrei Gromyko argued for a referendum against the remilitarization of Germany (Ruggenthaler 2011, 182). Even though in 1952, Stalin would decide everything alone—no one would dare do otherwise (Ruggenthaler 2014, 150, 155, 163; 2015, 352)— the idea of mobilizing the West German masses for the neutralization of Germany found support. It was hoped, therefore, that there would be protests against Adenauer (in order to weaken his position or to bring him down?). Next it is argued that Stalin indeed was "lured" to the idea of neutrality for a reunited Germany, but he did not want it (Ruggenthaler 2013, 488; 2015, 197–216).

The last finding is not consistently thought through because what would have happened then had the "temptations" worked? What consequence would that have had considering the presence of the other three Powers in Germany after everything was set in motion, when for Stalin German neutrality was not a real and serious issue? If the fight against "remilitarization" had been successfully concluded, what should and would follow? One argues further that Stalin did not want to sacrifice the GDR but rather only wanted to consolidate it (Ruggenthaler 2013, 487; 2015, 216–227). The "construction of socialism" in the GDR was definitely planned before the offers (Ruggenthaler 2011, 177; 2014, 165, 2015) but this did not rule out another alternative. On the contrary, the old thesis of blaming the West for the German division (Graml 1981) was revived and applied by Ruggenthaler to the West to legitimize the integration of East Germany into the Eastern system, but this greatly reduces the complex offer.

However, this revitalized reading cautiously differs from the traditional position according to which the Stalin Note was pure propaganda and disruptive because it contained concrete aims and pursued several goals, but reportedly should still definitely not be for German neutrality. Concretely, the struggle against West German rearmament and for getting Germans to agitate against the Adenauer government, calling for the "construction of socialism" in the GDR, and its integration into the Eastern Bloc, were real intentions of the notes (Ruggenthaler 2011, 187; 2014, 164; 2015, 227, 364, 366).

However, why had Germany then been offered block and coalition freedom (= neutrality) in the notes? Did Stalin actually want to agree to the division of Germany in 1952 that is reconcile with the transfer of West German potential to the West and give up access to the Ruhr area and therefore renounce reparations from West Germany? The following aspects come up short or are even missing in the error and deception argumentation:

1. The demand for free elections in Germany, the most important concern of the West in its reply (Ruggenthaler 2011, 186), was approved on April 9, 1952, in the second Stalin note. Why did he add this? Critics of its credibility normally neglect this question. The offer of free elections already implied the Austrian model with three practiced free elections in 1945, 1949, and 1953—in the Soviet occupation zone—with the known negative outcome for the Communists, which Moscow had accepted. Stalin could not and would not lay all the cards on the table in the first Note of 10 March. For any negotiations, hc had to have something in hand. The West still had the alternative of raising the Oder-Neisse line in return as a question, which Adenauer had already brought into play at the High Commissioners' meeting in Bonn on March 17, 1952 (Gehler 2015, 695), in case Stalin would offer free elections (what he did on April 9), and Khrushchev proposed again in January 1955 under international control (UN).

2. National Armed Forces are the international legal basis and an integral element of armed neutrality. Without interpreting this aspect, the National Army offer for the whole of Germany in the Stalin Note is only seen as a means to justify the (later) establishment of the National People's Army (NVA) of the GDR (Ruggenthaler 2011, 192), which falls too short.

3. Clearly, the Kremlin could not count on the German Communist Party (KPD) in the FRG (Ruggenthaler 2011, 182). It was too discredited and weak. Nevertheless, the SPD found itself in a far stronger position, really in fundamental opposition to Adenauer's Western course, which could be exploited. The political position of the German Trade Union, the Deutsche Gewerkschaftsbund (DGB), was still not calculable.

4. In the 1952 notes, neither "neutrality" nor the "neutralization" of Germany was spoken of, but "coalition freedom." The seriousness of the offers was not disputed by researchers and in contemporary assessments from the FRG, who simply uncritically accepted them or even saw them as a "preliminary stage of Bolshevism" (Franz-Josef Strauss) (Dittmann 1981, 63): Only one Soviet goal, "neutralization," was equated with "Sovietization" (Adenauer 1966, 263–265), negatively viewed by the whole of Germany, and excessively propagated. The overly stressed question of the

seriousness of the Soviet policy on Germany was used to distract from the stance of the German Chancellor and the Western powers in the context of Soviet notes. In reality Adenauer was convinced of its gravity namely because it would have prevented the Western integration of the FRG.

5. Why the concept of neutrality does not explicitly appear in the notes, can be explained. Soviet international legal doctrine did not actually deal with this idea until later, virtually only after initiating neutrality status for Austria in 1955 and against the backdrop of the nonaligned or neutralist movement among the Afro-Asiatic colonies (Dinkel 2015). The almost simultaneous emergence of the doctrine of "peaceful coexistence" harked back to Soviet foreign policy. A note from the Soviet Foreign Ministry to the Government of the Netherlands on March 7, 1955, bound the USSR to the Hague Conventions of 1899 and 1907. Neutrality was thus conceived as nonalignment as well as a policy in war and in peace, whereby this was understood as permanent neutrality or a policy of neutralism that appeared synonymous in content and concept (Hafner 1969, 215–16, 219, 234; Fiedler 1959; Mueller 2011, 43–47).

Ruggenthaler has discovered a remarkable number of new documents related to the Stalin Note Debate, but it has remained open in his studies what exactly Stalin's concept of neutrality was (if he had one at all—only instrumentalizing neutrality in a negative sense doesn't mean a conception). Not least of all, that would provide information about the seriousness of his Germany policy. If Ruggenthaler is right and Stalin only offered the appearance of neutrality for Germany, then it cannot be seen as a mature concept, only as a negative-abusive instrumentalization (Ruggenthaler 2015, 349).

The Stalin Notes need to be classified not only in a larger historical context but also much more strongly in light of contemporary international relations. For the security context, there was (among other things the French) debate on the EDC (1950 to 1952), to which the FRG was supposed to belong and which was supposed to have been established and the agreement signed in May 1952. Now, immediately after March 10, the French Communists were suddenly in favor of a national army for a united Germany despite of their sharp refusal of any German remilitarization before (Gehler 1988, 75–104), which should mobilize (the left wing) public in France and force the government to negotiate (Loth 2002a, 60). In February 1952 Greece and Turkey had been members of the Transatlantic Alliance as part of a NATO-Far Eastern Command. In the United States, a presidential election campaign was being run under the promising participation of the isolationist Republican Robert A. Taft.

The long-term dimensioning of Soviet foreign policy, based on theories of one of the early pioneers of its interpretation (Meissner 1953, 1970, 16–27), is argued fundamentally with a "three-element theory." This included world revolutionary, meaning universalist, but also nationalist, and totalitarian components. According to Meissner the world revolutionary component had existed at the time of the revolutionary and civil wars, the nationalist since the "revolution from above" by Stalin, and the totalitarian element from the establishment of Stalin's autocracy and dictatorship. All three varieties alternated occasionally from, but persisted partially and were connected to each other. This is understandable in view of the Soviet policy on Germany in 1952. The Stalin note was an offer for all cases (Gehler 2015, 207–17, 212, 214). The following aspects from a long-term historical perspective speak for this:

1. In 1917/18, Berlin and Germany were already seen by Lenin as the main space and a central arena for future revolutionary expectations. The idea was widespread among Bolsheviks and Communists that whoever could achieve his political dreams in the German capital could exert significant influence over Europe. The conquest of Berlin was so important for Stalin that he made great sacrifices for it in 1945.
2. Russian nationalism is a modern phenomenon that seemed to move to the background in the face of communist internationalism under the Bolsheviks, but actually found acceptance under Stalin with "socialism in one country" and had a revival in the context of the "Great Patriotic War" against "Hitler-fascism" and later experienced a mobilization of Soviet patriotism combined with greater Russian and imperialist nationalism. This was combined with some "understanding" for other nations such as Germany, where one felt connected by historical-traditional contracts. Stalin's sentence, "The Hitlers come and go, but the German people, the German state remain" was, on the one hand, propaganda during the war, but on the other hand was not foreign to his thinking.
3. The totalitarian component grew out of the demand to have an ideologically compliant orthodox Marxism-Leninism, while also being committed to continuously pursuing an anti-capitalist and socialist foreign policy, be it in the "homeland" or when facing the revolutionizing of companies and the transformation of power relations over the means of production on a global scale. The totalitarian component allowed Stalin to cooperate with authoritarian systems of government or even totalitarian dictatorships, but they also did not contradict temporary alliances with democracies.
4. Despite all the continuity that was grounded in this programmatic-ideological thinking, there were at the same time mobility and flexibility in the red dictator's foreign and Germany policy, which spoke for keeping options open (1924–1934), and the same pro-Western policy in the League of Nations (1934–1939), then the conclusion of a non-aggression pact with

Hitler (1939–1941)[1] in order to annex Poland and the Baltic countries, and then in sequence through an alliance with the anti-Hitler coalition (1941–1945) brought much of Central and Eastern Europe under his political and military control. Finally, Stalin maneuvered via his policies of seizure of power, repression, and Sovietization in the "socialist countries" and established an ideological-political-economic-military opposition to the Western Powers and thus became a key player in the Cold War (1947–1953).

5. Germany always played an important and varying role for Stalin: an ally (1939–1941), a main opponent in the war (1941–1945), an area of partial influence and control (1945–1949), and a partial-state ally and partial-state opponent (from 1949). How far the categories of the three-element theory (Meissner) played a role here, still remains an area for future research.

Studies of Soviet policy toward Germany after 1945 have elaborated three different components: First, the orientation of a "socialist" united and later East Germany; second, the concept of a "hard peace"; and third, a "moderate version" that a bourgeois democratic German State preferred, obeying Soviet foreign policy, seeing reason and the solution of border and reparations issues analogous to ideas that the Kremlin accepted. These strategy patterns ("socialist" whole or partial Germany, "hard peace," and a "bourgeois-democratic German state") competed with each other. The other variations played a certain role as tactical means. The "hard peace" came from the time of the inter-Allied discussions during the war and socialism as an all-German variant was not even seriously pursued as propaganda. These options served the purpose of "preventive or lasting effects to the real or perceived uncooperative steps of the West in postwar Germany in order to resist and bring about cooperative solutions." The "use of inadequate policies as supposedly suitable tactics was theoretically highly questionable." They led in practice "First to loss of confidence among the Allies" and "then to heavy defeats for Soviet policy in Germany" (Filitov 1999, 51–52, 54).

The discussion about the intentions of Germany policy of the USSR has found a result in the research literature on Soviet military administration (SMAD) in the GDR insofar as both the unity of Germany and the Sovietization of the Stalin's Soviet occupation zone were both simultaneously kept open as options, which in practical terms meant the policies of the SMAD should gradually result in a Sovietization (Naimark 1995; Creuzberger 1996; Foitzik 1999). What, however, spoke for Stalin in 1952 to suggest military nonalignment and the reunification of Germany?

1. The thinking of Soviet policy after the war and, above all, after the Potsdam Conference (July 17–August 2, 1945) viewed Germany as a total complex. The establishment of an East German state was initially neither

intended nor planned for the long term, even if the research believes that Stalin had consistent thoughts of dividing Germany (Laufer 2009, 298, 304, 604–605). However, that did not rule out another and opposite policy after 1945 and even after 1949.

2. The reaction to the founding of West Germany in May was the founding of GDR in October 1949, which was a byproduct of the failed Berlin blockade of 1948/49, the first and most serious defeat for the Soviet Union in the Cold War (Falin 1993), the result of a failed Soviet policy on Germany. In the following Soviet offers, Germany as a whole is repeatedly mentioned—A peace treaty for the GDR neither existed nor was an option for Moscow, at least until the Khrushchev Ultimatum in 1958/59 and also afterwards.

3. The formal "recognition" or "sovereignty" of the GDR did not come immediately after its establishment, and it was only after Stalin's death that it was "granted" by the Kremlin. The GDR never had true or full sovereignty. The same was true for the FRG.

4. The "rearmament" of West Germany in combination with US military potential and the projection of US nuclear technology was more than an alarm signal for Stalin; it was a horror scenario, especially since there were even several German Wehrmacht officers with "Russian experience" waiting to be employed, and the Soviet victory in the "Great Patriotic War" would have been unthinkable without the support of the United States.

5. A West Germany firmly integrated in the ECSC, EDC, and NATO context, compared to a nonaligned and controllable undivided Germany, was the worst of all solutions for Stalin in the German question. This would be made possible by "accelerating the conclusion of a peace treaty" with Germany (Loth 2002a, 59).

Preliminary Conclusion: Stalin's proposal for a nonaligned Germany was an offer for all cases: it contained, on the one hand, publicly available propaganda and on the other hand, serious diplomacy and policy negotiation elements for a peace treaty with Germany outside of the Western bloc. The Notes showed defensive and offensive elements. They raised hopes and expectations, but also included threats, dangers and risks both for Germany and for the West. With this multidimensional policy, Stalin kept all possible options open: incitement, mobilization and uncertainty towards the Adenauer government in the West German public, division and confusion in the Western camp, blaming the FRG and the West for the division of Germany, facilitating the Eastern integration of the GDR, preventing the Western integration of the FRG and its removal from the transatlantic-European alliance, fomenting anti-Western neutralist moods, the creation of a single bloc-free, nonaligned, neutral, or neutralized Germany to reverse the rotation of the arms race and weaken NATO. Stalin simultaneously pursued minimum and maximum targets via this multidimensional strategy. In principle, delaying or preventing the Western integration of the FRG. For that reason alone, his offer was meant seriously and credibly. Overall, the Stalin Notes of March and April 1952 were serious compared to the propaganda of the following two Notes. They were dynamic, flexible, open and ambiguous offers, which had also enabled their various interpretations (Gehler 2015, 207–17, 212, 214).

Singling out only each isolated individual aspect of the Notes and stiffening them, as has been done in the research literature sometimes falls short. The one direction spoke of a "trap" and "feint" of "temptations" and "siren song," a "disruptive" or even an "attempt to deceive," the other of "seriousness," "substance" and a "lost opportunity." Interpretations that exclude the abovementioned issues miss the variety of the offers and the reality behind their intentions and strategies.

For decades in the various archives, most recently in Moscow, researchers have looked for definitive evidence and collected documents, on which one or the other thesis has been based. Previously the definitive proof of "Stalin's Bluff" (Ruggenthaler) or the exclusive seriousness of his Germany Notes could not be provided despite contrary announcements and book titles. It was a composite of true partial aspects that did not contradict itself, but could not be combined with each other. Thus, also the succinct theses from "disruptive maneuvers" (Graml 1977; 1981) and the "lost opportunity" (Steininger 1985), among other things with a view to Adenauer.

However, relativism does not mean devaluation because the German Chancellor played a key role in the context of the defense against the Stalin Note and the spread of Western treaty policy in 1952. Although he was not an addressee of Stalin's proposals, a lot depended on his judgment. Had he pushed for an exploration of the offers, it would have been possible to check them, but he was not interested in this. This would undoubtedly have contributed to relieving and legitimizing his policy. Seen in this way, Adenauer had in reality missed a chance: If the argument is correct that the Stalin Notes were made only on the assumption that the West would in any case not act on the Soviet neutralization offers it received (Ruggenthaler 2007, 14–19), it was a unique opportunity for Adenauer and the Western Powers that was lost in order to uncover and expose the supposed "insincerity" of Stalin. Thus, a chance was missed to confirm and demythologize the "legend of the lost opportunity" (Graml 1981; Schwarz 1982). If this was the case, it is more than doubtful but wrong that "Chancellor Adenauer rightly recognized that it was a pure propaganda move and did not act on it" (Ruggenthaler 2007, 37). If it was true, then one wonders why then the opportunity was missed. Unmasking Stalin to the German public and his "maneuvers" as propaganda to the eyes of the world? Truly, Adenauer feared the seriousness of the offer as well as the associated risks and therefore spared the risk of entering into it—especially since he had to understand logically it as a serious attempt to stop the Western integration of Germany, which was one of the main motives of the "Red Czar." Adenauer's policy puts his refusal to investigate possibilities in 1952 and casts a shadow on his Germany policy even today.

If in the research the question has been asked whether the Soviet Union had really shown willingness for unity in freedom in Germany in the first decade after the war (Wettig 1999, 295–327; 2015, 162–85) and this has been strongly doubted, so one wonders why the Western powers and Adenauer did not openly say this and get rid of any doubt as to the seriousness of their own policy on Germany? So, had they not, as British foreign secretary Anthony Eden said, won "the battle of the notes," but even—at least morally—lost it? If Stalin had only gone about blaming the West for the German division, one would have to agree. Meanwhile, it is also argued that the central battle was not an attempt to overcome the Cold War, but an expression of the status quo assurance. That would have served the West and the East. Moreover, the consolidation of the German division had only leveled the road to Austria's neutrality (Ruggenthaler 2013, 483, 490) and, therefore, it was only a byproduct of the deepening of the division of Germany. By contrast, one could however argue that denial helped to create a neutral solution in accordance with the model case. Austria then definitely not only consolidated but also extended the German division?

Would Stalin have been willing to give up the GDR? He was consistently willing to sacrifice others repeatedly—even against his own followers and party members. In 1939 after completion of the non-aggression pact with the "Third Reich," he surrendered the German Communists in exile in Moscow to Nazi Germany, and he probably would have sacrificed SED politicians for a bloc-free, neutralized, and united Germany in 1952. This dictator was capable of doing almost anything to consolidate and expand his power. To move the Americans, British, and French to withdraw from Germany would have been another big success for the USSR after the "Great Patriotic War." Stalin, however, was not able to reach this maximum goal.

For all the brilliance of the Soviet Germany note of March 1952, they led to no positive result for Moscow, so it meant a "lost victory" for Stalin, similar to Hitler a decade earlier. Above all, Stalin had lost time, which is irretrievable. In 1950/51, still more could have been achieved on the German question, but even in 1952 not everything was lost.

If for 1952 one talks about a "lost opportunity" (Steininger 1985), one should also not ignore that the Soviet Union, both before and during this time, left no discernible mark on Austria, a country that forced itself into a comparison with Germany and offered a demonstration of the credibility of the opportunity for the policy on Germany. This fact is all the more important because the costs of such a policy for Moscow—compared to Germany—would not have been that great. If Stalin's offers did not have only propagandistic intentions, then a chance was also lost in terms of the Austrian "test case" by the Soviet side (Gehler 1994, 243–78; Ruggenthaler 2007, 121–23). Stalin's notes accordingly fell victim to their Germany-fixation and their ignorance about Austria.

CONTROVERSIES ABOUT THE SOVIET GERMANY AND AUSTRIA POLICY, 1955

Soviet foreign policy after Stalin's death, particularly in 1954, was designed and conducted primarily by Molotov. The leadership was supposedly split into three groups (Georgi Malenkov—Nikita S. Khrushchev—Vyacheslav Molotov) (Brzezinski 1962, 188). Following the dismissal of Malenkov as prime minister, different actors (Bulganin, Khrushchev, Molotov) were used differently and active. With the elimination of the "anti-party group" in 1957 at latest, it was first assumed that Khrushchev alone determined Soviet foreign policy (Meissner 1999, 60–61). The changing internal power constellations from 1953 to 1955 explain the sway of Soviet policy.

In considering Soviet Germany and Austria Policy in 1955, one needs to differentiate between the first and second half of the year, otherwise one loses sight of differences between the—alternating—imminent and existing—"two-state theory" and two-state *rhetoric* as a result of a Western policy of accomplished facts and the intransigence of Adenauer's emerging two-state *policy* and two-state *practice*. The latter options were not yet established definitively until the middle of 1955. The status quo was consolidated in Central Europe until the autumn of 1955 (Thoß 1993, 171–88), which led to unsatisfactory results in terms of the maximum objective of the Soviet policy on Germany, the "split against its will" (Loth 1996, 283–97).

In the research, it has been argued for 1952 as well as for 1955 that the Soviet Union was not pursuing a model plan for Germany with Austria (Ruggenthaler 2011, 198). That conclusion is opposed by another argument: "The Austria Question was also always part of the German Question for Soviet foreign policy" (Ruggenthaler 2013, 483; Ruggenthaler 2015). As apparently in the Kremlin there was clarity about the fact that Soviet concessions to the Western powers in Austria affected the expectations of Germans: "Above all, the population in the Soviet Zone of Occupation/GDR looked at what the USSR did in Austria" (Ruggenthaler 2013, 484).

So what were the intentions of the Soviet Union with respect to Germany and Austria in 1955? As long as the GDR had no peace treaty, it was still up for grabs and you sometimes had in the Kremlin the vision of a united from East to West, open, Soviet-friendly Germany à la the Weimar Republic. Austria's ambassador in Moscow, Norbert Bischoff in January 1955, saw the first and overriding goal of Russian policy in the shift or even prevention of the ratification of the Paris Agreements. According to him, the Soviets would consider the situation in Europe as "very serious" and "still hold their old basic notions of the desirable solution to the German question," a "united, peace-loving Germany (i.e., not intent on territorial gain in the East), non-militaristic, and of course, not in a military alliance with America," in Molotov's own words, an "improved Weimar Republic." In such a Germany, the German Communist Party (KPD) would "only play a rather modest role." Nevertheless, this solution of a division of Germany would be decidedly preferable.[2] Bischoff recapitulated the Soviet policy on Germany of the previous years and recalled the Notes from 1952 to bring about a peace treaty for Germany and for the prevention of the EDC Treaty to "pathetic calls from the German people" by Malenkov on the eve of the general elections in 1953, the proposal by Molotov at the Berlin Conference in 1954 to drop the EDC and enter into a pan-European security pact on the basis of the unity of Germany, the Soviet Note of January 15, 1955, the offer of free elections under international control this same year, and Molotov's speech to the Supreme Soviet from February 8, at which this proposal was repeated. Bischoff recognized the key position of Adenauer in rejecting these proposals, saying, "That the integration of West Germany into the Atlantic world is more important to him than the restoration of a united Germany."[3]

After a talk with the Germany expert in the Soviet Foreign Ministry, Vladimir B. Semenov, Bischoff held the Soviet main objectives, namely increasing resistance to ratification of the Paris agreement in West Germany, delaying its ratification, and perhaps even preventing it. Semenov was so clear that no doubts existed about the Soviet intentions (Gehler and Agstner 2007, 245–247).[4]

Bischoff had spoken, according to the words of Semenov, of Soviet diplomacy, which was distinct from Soviet propaganda and Soviet policy. The Soviet positions in the Germany question moved in this multidimensional, partially independent three-level system: The Kremlin *policy* held a concrete and realistic political solution for Austria in April and May 1955 in the German question debate, thus creating a lasting sting in the flesh of the FRG, although after the Geneva summit in July the definitive Eastern integration of the GDR should have gotten higher priority. Until then, it was still expected in the West with serious offensives terms "neutralization" of Soviet policy, especially since the Soviet diplomacy suggested ways of dropping the Socialist Unity Party (SED) regime. The central model case function of Austria in 1955 for both Soviet policy as well as for its diplomacy was still the prevention of West German NATO integration but also using the State Treaty negotiation procedure as a model for a German Peace Treaty. Moscow was still open to the Geneva Summit to provide the Pankow puppet system a Western Allied troop withdrawal from Germany within the framework of free elections. Below the politics and diplomacy of the USSR were the actions of the occupation authorities in both countries, deploying and pursuing propaganda activities and the aspirations of Sovietization, which could be mitigated as required or disavowed and stopped when the policy (as in East Germany in the spring or in Austria from the summer of 1953). Still, in the first half of the 1950s Sovietization was relatively ineffective in practice as could be seen on June 17, 1953. Neither the companies and economic structures of Austria nor those of Germany were as communist as the comrades would have liked. The help of the Soviet Union and the support of the CPSU for the KPÖ and the SED remained ambivalent, calculating, and halfhearted, however the parties varied in significance On June 17, 1953, Moscow was in the case of the GDR ready to replace the SED leadership. In May 1955, the Austrian Communist Party in the Kremlin perceived as a negligible size, meaning they were seen as marginal, close to Soviet occupation policy on the respective Austria and Germany policy, and virtually back to only one dimension of the complex and multi-Soviet attitudes, postures, and positions.

Soviet *diplomacy* aimed deliberately at Western, especially French diplomacy. The Soviet (foreign) *policy* was guided by pragmatic considerations and realizable objectives, but varied due to inconsistency and indecision. It was flexible after Stalin's death and open, although inconsistent due to uncertain leadership constellations, while Soviet *propaganda* remained ideologically dogmatically fixed as an instrument of the Cold War, and the Western, especially the West German public aimed at delegitimizing and disempowering its ideological enemies, which would not succeed. Anticommunism was a dominant and manifest element of continuity of both political cultures in Germany and Austria.

The SED, which brought Moscow into play as a seemingly independent actor, according to research always followed detailed instructions (Wettig 1999, 185–234; 2015, 131–61). If this finding is true, the dedicated recommendation of the Austria model for the solution of the German question by Walter Ulbricht in April and May 1955 can be understood as a desire and a vision from the Soviet side for the future (Gehler 2015, 732–37).

The model case function of the (Austrian-Soviet) treaty preparations, the inter-allied and Austrian negotiations of the treaty, and the Austrian implementation of the agreements in the period before and after May 15, 1955, attracted a broad and long-lasting debate at all levels of Western demoscopy, diplomacy, politics and journalism. The "Austria-example" of the German question (bilateral preliminary investigations in Moscow, quadripartite negotiations on troop withdrawal for alliance freedom) was taken to be quite conceivable internally and semi-public, a viable and reliable way to solve the German question, and even after ratification of the Paris agreements taken into consideration and further debated (Gehler 2015).

Given the reference to missing Soviet files, Notes on prevention of West German rearmament, and striking a balance between the advantages and disadvantages of a neutral Germany in Moscow (Ruggenthaler 2011, 186), one wonders if this necessity existed, even if it was internally all too clear and obvious.

Obviously, this was being weighed in the State Department. There, it was believed at the intelligence level, a neutralized, Western-oriented Germany was quite possible and feasible without jeopardizing their own positions after the FRG had joined NATO in July 1955 (Gehler 2015, 912–31).[5]

Had Adenauer given a hint to the largely German-controlled press in Bonn (Gehler 2015, 1027–31) that, according to the Allensbach Demoscopic Institute, the impressionable and wavering mood in Germany would, possibly be rapidly changed (Gehler 2015, 550–52). The "Austria solution" was much less about "uncertainty" in the West for the Soviet leadership (Stourzh 2005, 478–80) with the national governments and populations the same as in 1952, but rather a policy with strong elements of confidence-building. The "model case" did not have to have to mean automatically and necessarily the "neutralization" of Germany, as hysterical contemporaries in defensive positions in Germany or later historians stuck in their views argued.

In the academic debates on the "model case" up to now, there has been no distinction between the approach and the solution itself. In the spring of 1955, the Soviet Union still sought a four-power conference on Germany in order to conclude a German Peace Treaty. The result was open. For the Soviets, it was neither a conference on the FRG nor a conference about the GDR. First, and then until the spring of 1955, the USSR still wanted to negotiate the Austria Question at such a conference, together with the whole of Germany (Thoß 1993, 113–116). For this, Adenauer's Western integration policy was highly dangerous and for Austria stressful until the end, and yes the Ballhausplatz succeeded in maneuvering itself out with a fateful package deal.

The central problem of the security needs of the Soviet Union lay not in relation to Austria, Finland, and Yugoslavia, but in the far more tangential German question. By way of four-power control, this initially seemed solvable. To even think of an arrangement, let alone reach one as was confidence-building and—closely connected—a minimum level bilateral contact as a precursor for quadripartite control. Austrian diplomacy had grasped that in the spring of 1955. The Soviets demonstrated this symbolic and psychologically important scenario with satisfaction to the FRG and the Western world.

It was about the credibility of the policy in the specific example, as a bloc in Europe can be overcome by granting neutrality.

The Kremlin showed itself to still be quite open-minded about the idea of a reunified, neutralized Germany, above all at the Geneva Summit (18 and 23 July 1955) (Loth 1994, 220–21; Wettig 2011, 46–48; Gehler 2015, 950–87) but significantly less so at the Foreign Ministers' Conference (October 27 to November 16, 1955) (Wettig 2011, 48–49), (despite all mental reservations and resistance), (Gehler 2015, 950–87, 1052–74; Steininger 1993, 205).

On July 19, 1955, at the Geneva Summit, British prime minister Anthony Eden had a "frank and intimate talk" with his Soviet counterpart Nikolai A. Bulganin outside the conference, which was "in a long experience of talks with Russians [. . .] one of the most important and certainly the frankest conversations that I have known":

> Bulganin plunged into the problem of Germany. He explained in familiar terms how real the Soviet fears of a German recovery were. Almost every family in Soviet Russia, including his own, had suffered some personal loss. Eden replied that they in Britain also had no reason to feel tenderly toward the Germans after the experience of two wars. Nevertheless, one had to look to the future, and whatever the fear of Germany had been, he could not believe that in the nuclear age Germany could really be a formidable danger to Russia. Bulganin however, would not altogether accept this. He admitted that the Germans might not be able to make hydrogen bombs, but later all they could be given to them. Then Bulganin said that he wanted to say something to Eden 'which he had said to nobody else': ["] It was not possible for his Government to return to Moscow from this Conference having agreed to the immediate unification of Germany. They were a united Government and reasonably solidly based in the country but this was something that Russia would not accept and if they were to agree to it, neither the Army nor the people would understand it and this was not come to weaken the Government . . . In further discussion with him, and later with Khrushchev it emerged that while they could not agree to the unification of Germany now, they might be prepared to consider terms of reference for the Foreign Secretaries, which would contemplate such unification together with other compensating conditions.["] (Steininger 1990, 117–18).

Bulganin and Khrushchev were therefore willing to give Molotov orders for the Geneva Conference of Foreign Ministers: You should discuss the issue of "reunification" and request matching services that will achieve a European security agreement with the USSR (Steininger 2002, 330–31). This could also hold true for the Stalin successors: No NATO integration, but only a loose alliance (= neutrality). A unified Germany with appropriate security guarantees for the Four Powers.

If you read the conversation Bulganin-Eden exactly, it can hardly be doubted that the thinking of the Soviet political leadership, the fear of the Germans was still deeply rooted ten years after the war ended. The fear of the German threat had not vanished—on the contrary, the threat was objective and remained subjectively, considering that since the end of the war when the "German threat" threatened not to increase, an alliance of the Western powers and the United States with the Germans was a threat scenario for Moscow. The fact that facing such a situation for the Soviet Union, an "Austria-solution" appeared desirable for Germany can hardly be disputed. The recognition of the security interests of the former allies of the anti-Hitler coalition was an essential concern of the Kremlin, but this was ignored by Adenauer and the West.

Khrushchev was the most politically decisive man in the Kremlin after 1955. He preferred according to the French Foreign Minister Christian Pineau, who reproduced his words precisely, "[having] 20 million Germans who were with him, over 70 million Germans who were against him, even if they were neutralized." This did not mean, according to Pineau that Khrushchev "was against a neutral Germany, but only against a reunified Germany, which was opposed to [sic] being neutralized." It is much more important, however, "at a reunification that the social achievements of East Germany [should] not be lost." The Soviet Union could be "currently a reunification of Germany just imagine if the united Germany were communist or if it somehow would consist of two parts, of which the other would be free and communist." Austrian ambassador Alois Vollgruber drew the conclusion, "that the Russians would be most willing to withdraw from East Germany and maybe sooner or later also from the satellite state, but that communism must remain," he added. "We wanted neither the Russians nor communism in Central Europe." Pineau replied to the hopelessness of the situation that one must continue to speak with "the Russians," and referred to "such tremendous changes" in the interior of Russia that would cause "significant changes in terms of foreign policy."[6] This should not be the case in the coming years, although albeit somewhat late in 1989/90.

To obtain "Unity and Freedom" (Stourzh 2005) in the 1950s as well as in 1989–1990, there was no way around a quadripartite arrangement, as the Soviet Union would show clearly and convincingly in the case of Austria. The scenario should also take place right in front of Bonn. The fundamental insight into a quadripartite solution was not ruled out by Austria's government leaders. They succeeded. The FRG leadership was above all in favor of partial-state freedom, not entire state unity, which marked the difference between Bonn's and Vienna's policies. That negotiations had to take place with all four powers—assuming one was interested in an integral solution—was the main realization of Austria solution of 1955.

Premature disclosure of the GDR without an agreement on the withdrawal of Western troops from Germany was not to be expected from the Kremlin leadership in the 1950s, as it might have been conceivable even under Lavrenti Beria by redeeming the policy of "building socialism" in the GDR in the spring of 1953 and appeared possible (Wettig 1994, 195). Anything else would be a considerable loss of prestige two years later, if not a capitulation of the USSR before its ideological enemies, the West equaled, as was determined internally in the CPSU Presidium Malenkov in January 1955. This was also in line with the GDR leadership (Stourzh 2005, 476–78). This had to be not a contradiction to the "model case" thesis: "Double or multiple strategies with different timeframes were part of the armamentarium of Soviet policy, and ideological justifications always came for each step in any direction" (Stourzh 2005, 587).

Germany was and remained a central element of Soviet policy in Europe. Therefore, it was still seen as a whole in 1955. Therefore, Moscow at first had no forced interest in establishing diplomatic relations with West Germany before the summer of 1955, especially since the issue of international recognition of the GDR would have been raised. This step was taken after the Geneva Summit. The special emphasis of the two-state theory by Khrushchev only happened afterwards (Meissner 1999, 63). Consistently and logically, the formal establishment of diplomatic relations with the GDR by the Soviet Union continued after the Adenauer visit in Moscow from 8 to 14 September 1955 and the establishment of diplomatic relations with the FRG.

When, since the end of 1954 start-up planning for the Warsaw Pact, in the case against the Austria-example was brought to bear, it must be pointed out that the existence of the envisaged pact system had been made dependent from the Soviet side on the continuation of NATO. Only and only in the case of involvement of Germany in the Atlantic Alliance was the solution to the question of German unity to be addressed by Moscow (Thoß 1993, 67–68).

In a remarkable speech in Warsaw on May 11, 1955—a few days before the establishment of the Eastern security pact—Bulganin had stated that the establishment of a united, free and democratic Germany was not only necessary, but also to be implemented readily with good will. He pointed to the case of Germany as the necessary waiver to a remilitarization and criticized the good will of the Western powers for making acceptable proposals.[7] This position was and remained a touchstone of Soviet policy on Germany from 1952 to 1955.

Before the Paris Agreements entered into force, there were still not only opportunities to discuss Germany as a whole but also for negotiation. With this, the USSR was not interested in the West. The inclusion of the GDR in the Warsaw Pact system remained analogue to the integration of the FRG into NATO. The Warsaw Pact establishment and launching of the GDR were not actions but reactions with offensive elements and "countermeasures" (Wettig 1999, 279, 281, 282–86; 2015, 101–14) of the Soviet Union after NATO's founding and the scheduled entry of the FRG into the Atlantic alliance. The GDR remained "in military terms, spared for the time being." It had no place in the United High Command of the Warsaw Pact, its position there has been reserved as a subsequent regulation. In terms of assistance agreements between member states, it was not suspected wrongly that there was also a discrimination of the Eastern part of the country. It was only in January 1956 that the Soviet Union and its "brother states" decided the integration of the armed forces of the GDR into the common military alliance (Wettig 1999, 283–284, 286).

The USSR was already on the defensive in 1955 with regard to the economic, trade and nuclear technological level (The embargo policy in the context of the COCOM lists within the framework of the OEEC started in the early 1950s. It was breaking as they hit the economy of the Soviet Union and its allies). It responded to the German question in the first half of the 1950s far more often and acted on neutrality policy offensively (Mueller 2014). The "model case" could remain reserved as a future scenario in view of the irrefutable realities established in the course of 1955. Realpolitik thus could no longer be made from the summer of 1955 onward.

The classic State Treaty historiography has denied the model question for Germany traditionally as well as tendentiously (Stourzh 2005) and has thereby been modeled on a German military historical interpretation that sees "not the function of a model case for Germany but a test case for relaxation of tensions" (Thoß 1988, 136; 1993, 119–120). This neither was a contradiction, nor unlike Germany policy a maximal target of Soviet Austria Policy. The contentious issue in any event has been left open for lack of compelling evidence. Behind the corresponding chapter in the mentioned book, there is also a question mark: "Soviet Austria Policy in the Spring of 1955 and its Motivations: The NATO-Defense, 'Model Case' for Germany or More?" (Stourzh 2005, 450–85).

The question of whether the Soviet leadership actually considered the Austrian solution a model for Germany, despite the results achieved there, cannot be categorically denied. On the contrary: With certainty, Soviet political intentions for Germany in their Austria Policy cannot be ruled out during the first half of 1955 (Gehler 2015, 491–92).

It turns out that in the more recent studies on the history of the treaty, the newly raised question of whether the Soviet Union with its Austria policy (beyond Germany?) possibly (still?) wanted more. This approach was therefore based on earnest intentions by the Soviet Union, ruled out disruption and deception maneuvers, as was evident in the examples of Finland, Yugoslavia, or Austria. Already in individual contributions, this "controversial issue" has been referred to base on files from the French Foreign Ministry that have not thus far been systematically used by the researchers. That Soviet Austria Policy 1955 was mainly about Germany is based on a paper from the Quai d'Orsay and the estimates derived from there (Gehler 1995, 259–97).

After further reading, it appears that the Soviets possibly wanted far more than just a chance at Germany using Austria (Stourzh 2005, 480–85). They also wanted a concession recognizing the seriousness of their policy, which also practically amounts to an admission, suggesting that for the USSR it was not primarily about the Alpine Republic but about following a policy with regard to Austria and pursuing other, even more important global concerns (Stourzh 2005b, 965–95).

Thus, it appears that for the Anglo-Americans in 1955, the risky and disruptive State Treaty was not urgent in view of the Western integration of the FRG coupled with "freely" chosen and self-proclaimed neutrality. From the Soviet point of view, it appeared primarily as a means of achieving various other purposes—a "model case" for entirely different reasons.

The following results are certain for the German-policy dimension of the Austria policy of the Great Powers in 1955:

1. Relevant circles of French diplomacy saw in the Soviet Austria Policy a target direction that was "only aimed at Germany" (Gehler 1995, 263–64; Stourzh 2005, 467).
2. In the Anglo-American camp, the view predominated that the USSR meant Austria to be a model case for Germany, which was a "dangerous solution"—also for the Soviet Union itself (Gehler 1995, 270–72; Stourzh 2005, 467–68). Western assessments of the Stalin notes from the spring of 1952 were similar (Steininger 1985).
3. Adenauer himself saw Moscow's Austria policy as opposed to the Western integration of the FRG. He saw it as a great danger. The "model case" and its effects were taken seriously by him. In a negative way, the German Chancellor saw, as did the European Western powers, the "model case" as a threatening alternative to his Western integration course, meaning a prejudice for the Allied policy towards Germany. The four should not be discussing and negotiating about Germany over his head. That was the underlying cause of his anger over Austria, which had indeed already been negotiating with the four powers since 1954 on a ministerial level.
4. The model of the "Austria" solution consisted among other things in the sudden appearance of bilateral agreements in Moscow (April 11 to 15) and the rapidly conducted quadripartite negotiations in Vienna (May 2 to 13) at ambassadorial and finally at foreign-minister level. The Soviets wanted to negotiate even more in March 1955, namely at ministerial level and taking into account the German question and a peace treaty for Germany.

5. The publicly expressed approval for a belt of neutral states in Europe by US President Eisenhower and his expressed sympathy for armed neutrality according to the Swiss model (e.g., at the Berlin Conference of Foreign Ministers in February 1954) as well as related fears of a redeployment of US troops from Europe were the real reasons for Adenauer's frustration and the core of his anger. The unfavorable treatment of West Germany in the question of German assets in the State Treaty only added to his hostile and contemptuous attitude towards Austria (Gehler 2015, 1145, 1153, 1217–18).

6. With the Austria solution, Moscow attempted to provide evidence of its goodwill and a confidence-building measure to contribute to the relaxation of tensions rather than merely contributing to uncertainty, which meant reducing confrontation and conflict potential.

7. In this regard, it was only logical that the possibility of the central question of Soviet security policy in Europe, the German question was included and should be part of such a solution. The factor of Yugoslavia in the new and flexible Soviet policy of 1955 has been recognized and mentioned in the research for quite some time (Gehler 1995, 265–268).

8. In April and May 1955, the idea of a neutral zone of countries for Europe was launched, which the USSR played via Western media—open and contentious in this case was whether Germany was part of this "belt of neutral states" (Gehler 2015, 879–901). This was indeed doubted (Stourzh 2005), but could neither be falsified nor refuted, according to which the Soviet Union "ostensibly said Austria, but really meant Germany" (Thoß 1993, 116), especially since the German question for Moscow in 1955 was still a key problem for economic, political and military developments at the center of Europe. It was also still essential to the security interests of the Soviet Union after the founding of the Warsaw Pact in May 1955, especially after the situation had worsened with the FRG expressing its intention to join NATO.

9. Moscow wanted to stimulate German opposition to Adenauer's Western course in the first half of 1955 and thereby indirectly delay the "rearmament" of Germany, which already in 1952 played a role. Seen as part of the intended "model case" effect on the one hand as well as a cheeky "attempt to interfere" against the Western Block involvement of FRG can be understood on the other hand also as a constructive contribution to an amicable settlement of the question of Germany between East and West in order to contribute to creating a European security system. This, however, would be created only twenty years later after Austria's State Treaty and neutrality: The Helsinki Final Act (1975) and the CSCE follow-up process represented a comprehensive political-military strategy change in the West during the Cold War (Peter 2015, 1–19, 533–43). Involuntarily,

one wonders what would have happened if this change of strategy had started earlier. Was not the Austrian model in 1955 a small example with State Treaty and neutrality what was called later on the Final Act by Hans-Dietrich Genscher the first diplomatic-historical example of the reversal of Soviet interests (unity and freedom with a democratic Western model and a function of destabilization in the East)? One year after Austria's State Treaty and neutrality the Hungarian uprising broke out—thirty-three years before the "fall of the wall."

SUMMARY

It seems to be clear that Austria's example in Soviet foreign policy from 1952 to 1954 was not a model for Germany (Ruggenthaler 2013, 490). However, the Western proposal of the abbreviated treaty made every even theoretically conceivable Soviet Austria model case impossible as a policy for Germany (1952–1953). In most cases, the relationship between Germany and the Austria question were not included in long-lasting and extensive research on the Soviet Germany policy. Thus torn from this context and only as a sporadically occurring hint, it is not surprising in the context of the preparations for the presentation of the 1951 Russian Note from March 10, 1952, that in all advisory bodies in Moscow participants agreed that "for Germany, the Austria model—democracy internally and neutrality to the outside—could not be used" (Wettig 1999, 206). Austria so designated and serving as the pattern was at this time, however, not even neutral, but took over this status only by constitutional law on October 26, 1955.

The real intentions of the foreign, European, and Germany policies of the late Stalin era (1952–1953) and the first years after his death (1953–1955) have until recently remained in semi-darkness, since the balance of power in the Soviet Union was muddled at this time and the opinion-forming and decision-making processes in the Kremlin were mixed. Consequently, they were and are not unique for making historical reconstructions. What the red dictator and his successors, Beria, Malenkov, Bulganin and Khrushchev (1953–1955), planned in detail, in theory, and in practical fact wanted, is not yet continuously and unequivocally certain on the basis of sources.

We still do not know, despite many Stalin biographies, enough about his policy towards Germany and what exactly his "concept" of neutrality—except only functional, instrumental, and negative *thoughts* but not a real concept—was, even though it is repeatedly argued to draw all too exclusive, valid, and far-reaching conclusions. This impression is confirmed after reading the recent and contemporary literature with differing and fluctuating judgments (Filitov 2005, 121–43; Loth 2010, 229–45; Ruggenthaler 2015, 183–290, 349–67).

It is still far from everything clear. Much is still interpretation despite the newly revealed sources and some remains speculation. The partial opening of Soviet archives and their use, for example, by German and Austrian historians of the past 20 years (Loth, Laufer, Mueller, Wettig, Ruggenthaler) has provided insightful secondary and sometimes, temporarily relevant individual results, but not the "definitive proof" of the sincerity or insincerity of Soviet policy on Germany in the first half of the 1950s. The "definitive evidence" practically does not exist. There is virtually none—despite such decidedly dramatic book titles like "Stalin's Big Bluff" (Ruggenthaler 2007) or previous and forthcoming judgments regarding the "legend of the missed opportunity" (Graml, Schwarz, and Loth 2002, 653–64).

Unlike historians who have assumed the alternatives of Western integration policy and represented this hypothesis incessantly, it can be argued that in German and European policy development until the year 1955, the opportunity and scope still existed for an Austrian solution to the German Question in East and West (bilateral preliminary investigations, quadripartite negotiations with troop withdrawal for alliance freedom), options that could have shaken the foundations of Adenauer's policy more heavily than they already had anyway.

It was far less the lack of enforceability of an alternative policy of neutrality by the Western Allies—there were still points of contact with the strongest power of the Western Three, the United States, to take a turn—but rather the lack of will of the German Federal Chancellor himself.

The development up to the Geneva Conference of Foreign Ministers was still open, and the situation was not irreversible. The twelve divisions of the Western German army had not yet been established, and the NVA neither justified nor was part of the Warsaw Pact. For the Soviet leadership in Germany, the question of the possibility of a reversal existed in 1955 had Adenauer and the West showed signs of giving in. The "model case" was publicly cast as a "trap," "allurement" or "propaganda maneuver," and on the other hand rated internally as a conceivable, possible and legitimate option, but perceived as a "dangerous" and "risky" solution. However, which policy operates without danger and risk, especially when it is about a divided nation during the Cold War and determines the fates of millions of people behind the "Iron Curtain"? Such a risk-free policy could neither be had nor made. The policy of Western integration was dangerous and risky for Adenauer too. It took not only the maintenance of the established confrontation and military potential in Western and Eastern Europe and thus a nuclear war into consideration, but also the continuation of the division of Germany for an indefinite period—In the end, this would take forty years.

Austria's government and top diplomats were in favor of "unity and liberty" (Stourzh 2005)—with some exceptions and opponents in their own country as well as a few representatives from the parties—and took the risk of a possible negotiated settlement with the Soviet Union—despite concerns, worries, and warnings from London, Paris, and Washington, and the prophecies of doom in Western journalism. Vienna would win. Bonn did not even want this and thus saved its own status as a Western state. The West was relieved that Adenauer unswervingly stuck to his course, which in itself was clearly evident in advance, but above all, it proved Soviet policy was not working intensively beyond Austria, although Soviet diplomacy endeavored to achieve this, still at the first Geneva but then afterwards the signs were to let the matter drop.

Dutch foreign minister Joseph Luns was convinced that if Moscow's Austria initiative had come three months earlier—that is, parallel to the Soviet Government statement of January 15, 1955, on the recent approval of free elections for the whole of Germany under international control, meaning also under UN supervision—the conclusion of the Paris Agreements could thus have been disrupted (Gehler 2015, 681). The Kremlin leadership was late with the proposals for the settlement of the German question in 1952 as in 1955, even to reach maximum targets that were in its interest. That was the result of differing and inconsistent interpretations together with a lack of determination in the Kremlin itself. Although after 1955 the Soviet Union tried to make the DDR acceptable at the international level, one can hardly ignore that a nonaligned and unified Germany would have been the better solution for Moscow than a NATO-integrated FRG with the European Western powers and a nuclear-armed United States in the background. There can be no doubt about this maximum goal of Soviet leaders but there can be doubt about their faith that they could turn the German question to their advantage.

Until the Geneva Summit and Foreign Ministers' Conference in July and the autumn of 1955, the Soviet interest was still to negotiate on Germany as a whole and that, of course, under the conditions repeatedly mentioned by the USSR on the German question, just as they had also clearly acted on the Austrian precedent. Their goal was to lead by example and decide quickly and credibly in the first half of 1955: military alliance or alignment/neutrality, national armed forces, and having free elections at the national level in Austria (1945, 1949 and 1953), which took place without problems. If it was in the Soviet interest to inaugurate a policy of relaxation ("peaceful coexistence"), the Kremlin needed its central focus on the conflict in Central Europe in terms of defusing and neutralizing the German threat.[8] That was the "big" solution (Hillgruber 1987, 25; Gehler 2005, 105–31) in the sense of an intermediate zone-aligned state from the North through central Europe to the Balkans. Should not reaching for Germany begin in the neighborhood and in peripheral zones: Austria, Yugoslavia, and Finland could be added logically in such a concept that did not make Germany essential. That only a "small" solution was possible for the Soviet Union in the second half of 1955 with

Austria's permanent neutrality, did not primarily relate to an unwillingness to negotiate about Germany in Moscow's policy, as described by contemporary witnesses and as a result by historical research as well, but primarily because of the West continuously rejecting Soviet proposals for freedom of alliance for Germany since 1952. In terms of the integration of the GDR in the Eastern alliance and economic system and placing blame for the division of Germany on the West, Stalin was probably successful (Ruggenthaler 2015). Then the Austria solution was as merely a little "Stalin Note from the year 1955" (Gehler, 1996; 2009, 580) and only a small victory in the great Soviet political defeat of Germany with regard to the maximum performance of the Kremlin.

Although Moscow could not reach the initial maximum objective of preventing the West Germany's entry into NATO with the achieved Austria solution, it demonstrated a permanent "good example" by agreeing to Austria's neutrality, indeed this became a model for its "peaceful coexistence policy" for the time from end of the 1950s and 1960s. Austria was not only praised and recommended by Moscow, but also repeatedly prompted and encouraged to bring its good offices to bear to solving the German question and the Berlin Crisis (Mueller, 2011, 275–86, 286; 2014, 279–95), which was what Austria also tried to do many times under Julius Raab and Bruno Kreisky as well between Bischoff and his German ambassador colleague Hans Kroll (Gehler 2015, 1187–1201, 1212–21). Reversing the West's Germany policy decisions from the time before 1955 became increasingly difficult: The founding of the GDR was not only a result of the founding of the FRG by the Western Allies (1948–1949), but also the GDR's continued existence was a result of the refusal of Adenauer to negotiate about a neutral Germany (1952–1955), especially since he did not pursue reunification as a priority. Adenauer was the key figure in the question of rejecting of the Austria model. Decades later in 1978, Kreisky recalled his memories of confidential discussions with Adenauer when the British prime minister James Callaghan had asked him what the Western attitude should be, "if the two Germanys revive the issue of reunification." The Austrian chancellor replied:

> As a Catholic, Adenauer had never favored reunification since he knew that a Catholic majority would be unobtainable in a united Germany. For years, everybody had talked about unification but very few really believed in it. If it became a real issue, the German people might rally to it; but it was unlikely to figure as an issue at, for example, the next General Election in the FRG. The FRG was now richer and more influential than ever before and had no reason to wish for change.[9]

Adenauer also had a party political and electioneering motif based on the historical, religious and cultural differences with the Protestant East of

Germany: Many of the root areas for SPD voters were in the GDR. With the "Soviet Zone," Germany as a whole would have become, if not social democratic, still more protestant than the FRG. That argument could not be waved away, which French foreign minister Robert Schuman already knew in 1952 (Steininger 1985, 46).

Even though because of the solidifying division of Germany, it was becoming increasingly unlikely that either the idea of the Austria model or the neutralization of Germany would occur after 1955, these ideas were not entirely dead. They could always be revived by the Soviets as a possible solution (Gehler 2015, 1212–15). Even in the 1980s and in 1989/90, this was the case (Gehler 2007, 512; 2015, 1228–1230; 2015b, 451).[10] The rejection took place immediately from Bonn and the West. This reflects the decisions of the early years of the East-West German postwar history: The division of Germany by the Soviets, provoked through their actions in their zone (1945–1946), and the Berlin Blockade (1948–1949) and then was decided by the West (1948–1949) and pushed through together with Adenauer (1952–1955). There were alternative options and solutions like alliancelessness, neutrality and neutralization, but they were ignored or refused. The price was the division of Germany and Europe.

NOTES

1. The German Field Marshal Erich von Manstein in his published 1955 memoir "Lost Victory" described the positions of the Soviet army in eastern Poland in May and June 1941—that is, before the German attack on the USSR—as a "deployment for all cases" and highlighted these findings. Erich von Manstein, *Lost Victories*, Bonn 1955, pp. 179–180—Stalin's Germany policy "for all cases" in principle had not changed by March and April 1952.

2. Report No. 6/P "Zur jüngsten Deutschland-Erklärung der Sowjetregierung" ("About the recent Germany-Declaration of the Soviet Government," Austrian Embassy Moscow, Norbert Bischoff to Leopold Figl, January 18, 1955. Austrian State Archives, Archiv der Republik, BKA/AA, II-pol, Zl. 319.725-pol/55 (GZl. 319.014-pol/55).

3. Report No. 38-Pol/56 "Die Sowjetunion und der 'Status quo' in Deutschland" ("The Soviet Union and the 'Status Quo' in Germany"), Austrian Embassy Moscow, Norbert Bischoff to Leopold Figl, June 7, 1956. ÖStA, AdR, BKA/AA, II-pol.

4. Austrian Embassy Moscow, Norbert Bischoff to Leopold Figl, February 21, 1955. ÖStA, AdR, Nachlass Norbert Bischoff, E/1770: 157.

5. "Problems and Policies of a reunified and neutralized Germany," July 1955. National Archives Record Administration (NARA), Washington, RG 59, Lot File 58 D 776, Box 12.

6. Strictly confidential report from the Austrian Embassy Paris "Conversation with the Foreign Minister," Alois Vollgruber to Figl, June 7, 1956. ÖStA, AdR, II-pol, Zl. 40-pol/56.

7. "Warschau ohne Säbelrasseln" (Warsaw without Saber Rattling), *Salzburger Nachrichten*, May 12, 1955.

8. In the British Foreign Ministry, it was clear, "the approaching power balance in Europe is for the Russians disquieting, and the only obvious means of lightening the western scale is to reduce the 'menace' of Germany," Confidential Report of the British Embassy Vienna, "Austro-Soviet talks: Information from Figl and Dr. Kreisky," June 7, 1955 to Southern Department, Foreign Office. S.W. 1. United Kingdom National Archives (UKNA), FO 371/117803/1071/495.

9. Confidential Record of the prime minister's discussion with the Chancellor Kreisky of Austria, in plenary sesssion at 10 Downing Street on July 4, 1978, AT 1725. UKNA, Visit of Dr. Kreisky, Chancellor of Austria, to UK, July 1978, FCO 33/3367.

10. Interview with Hans Modrow, November 21, 2014, the last non-free elected Ministerpresident of the GDR, who presented a three-stage plan for Germany in January 1990 (contractual community—confederation with monetary union—neutrality).

BIBLIOGRAPHY

Adenauer, Konrad. 1966. *Erinnerungen 1953–1955*. Stuttgart: Deutsche Verlagsanstalt.

Besson, Waldemar. 1970. *Die Außenpolitik der Bundesrepublik. Erfahrungen— Maßstäbe*. München: Piper.

Bischof, Günter. 1991. "Karl Gruber und die Anfänge des 'Neuen Kurses' in der österreichischen Außenpolitik 1952/53." In *Für Österreichs Freiheit. Karl Gruber—Landeshauptmann und Außenminister 1945–1953 (Innsbrucker Forschungen zur Zeitgeschichte 7)*, edited by Lothar Höbelt and Othmar Huber, 143–183. Innsbruck: Haymon.

Bjørnstad, Stein. 1996. *Soviet Policy and the Stalin Note of 10 March 1952*. University of Oslo: Hovedoppgrave.

Bott, Sandra, Jussi M. Hanhimaki, Janick Schaufelbuehl, and Marco Wyss (Eds.). 2015. *Neutrality and Neutralism in the Global Cold War: Between or within the blocs?* London: Routledge.

Bonwetsch, Bernd. 2008. "Die Stalin-Note 1952—kein Ende der Debatte." *Jahrbuch für Historische Kommunismusforschung*, 106–113.

Brzezinski, Zbigniew K. 1962. *Der Sowjetblock. Einheit und Konflikt.* Köln, Berlin: Kiepenheuer & Witsch.

Creuzberger, Stefan. 1996. "Die sowjetische Besatzungsmacht und das politische System der SBZ." *Schriften des Hannah-Arendt-Instituts für Totalitarismusforschung* 3. Weimar, Köln, Wien: Böhlau-Verlag.

———. 1997. "Abschirmungspolitik gegenüber dem westlichen Deutschland im Jahre 1952." In *Die sowjetische Deutschland-Politik in der Ära Adenauer* (Rhöndorfer Gespräche 16), edited by Gerhard Wettig, 12–36. Bonn: Bouvier.

Dinkel, Jürgen. 2015. "Die Bewegung bündnisfreier Staaten. Genese, Organisation und Politik (1927–1992)." *Studien zur Internationalen Geschichte 37*. Berlin, München, Boston: de Gryuter.

Dittmann, Knud. 1981. *Adenauer und die deutsche Wiedervereinigung. Die politische Diskussion des Jahres 1952*. Düsseldorf: Droste.

Falin, Valentin. 1993. *Politische Erinnerungen*. München: Droemer Knaur.

Fiedler, Heinz. 1959. *Der sowjetische Neutralitätsbegriff in Theorie und Praxis: Ein Beitrag zum Problem des Disengagement*. Köln: Verlag für Politik und Wirtschaft.

Filitow, Alexej. 1999. "Stalins Deutschlandplanung und -politik während und nach dem Zweiten Weltkrieg." In *50 Jahre sowjetische und russische Deutschlandpolitik sowie ihre Auswirkungen auf das gegenwärtige Verhältnis (Studien zur Deutschlandfrage 14)*, edited by Göttinger Arbeitskreis, Boris Meissner, and Alfred Eisfeld, 43–54. Berlin: Duncker & Humblot.

―――. 2005. "The Post-Stalin Succession Struggle and the Austrian State Treaty." In *Der österreichische Staatsvertrag 1955. Internationale Strategie, rechtliche Relevanz, nationale Identität/The Austrian State Treaty 1955. International Strategy, Legal Relevance, National Identity (Österreichische Akademie der Wissenschaften, Philosophisch-Historische Klasse, Historische Kommission/Archiv für österreichische Geschichte Band 140)*, edited by Arnold Suppan, Gerald Stourzh, and Wolfgang Mueller, 121–143. Wien: Verlag der Österreichischen Akademie der Wissenschaften.

Foitzik, Jan. 1999. "Sowjetische Militäradministration in Deutschland (SMAD) 1945–1949. Struktur und Funktion." *Quellen und Darstellungen zur Zeitgeschichte 44*. Berlin: Akademie Verlag.

Foschepoth, Josef (Ed.). 1990. *Adenauer und die Deutsche Frage*. Göttingen: Vandenhoeck & Ruprecht. 2nd edition.

Gaddis, John Lewis. 1998. *We Know Now: Rethinking Cold War History*. Oxford: Clarendon Press.

Gehler, Michael. 1988. "Ein wiedervereinigtes und blockfreies Deutschland mit Nationalarmee und die französischen Kommunisten im Jahre 1952." *Militärgeschichtliche Mitteilungen* 44: 75–104.

―――. 1994a. "Kurzvertrag für Österreich? Die Stalin-Noten und die Staatsvertragsdiplomatie 1952." *Vierteljahreshefte für Zeitgeschichte* 4: 243–278.

――― (Ed.). 1994b. *Karl Gruber. Reden und Dokumente 1945–1953. Eine Auswahl (Institut für Zeitgeschichte der Universität Innsbruck, Arbeitskreis Europäische Integration, Historische Forschungen, Veröffentlichungen 2)*. Wien, Köln, Weimar: Böhlau.

―――. 1995. "L'unique objectif des Soviétiques est de viser l'Allemagne. Staatsvertrag und Neutralität 1955 als 'Modell' für Deutschland?" In *Österreich in den Fünfzigern* (Innsbrucker Forschungen zur Zeitgeschichte 11), edited by Thomas Albrich, Klaus Eisterer, Michael Gehler, and Rolf Steininger, 259–297. Innsbruck, Wien: Studienverlag.

―――. 1996. "Österreich, die Bundesrepublik und die deutsche Frage 1945/49–1955. Zur Geschichte der gegenseitigen Wahrnehmungen zwischen Abhängigkeit und gemeinsamen Interessen." In *Ungleiche Partner? Österreich und Deutschland in ihrer gegenseitigen Wahrnehmung. Historische Analysen und Vergleiche aus dem 19. und 20. Jahrhundert (Beiheft 15 der Historischen Mitteilungen der Leopold von Ranke-Gesellschaft)*, edited by Michael Gehler, Rainer F. Schmidt, Harm-Hinrich Brandt, and Rolf Steininger, 535–580. Stuttgart: Steiner. Reprint: Innsbruck, Wien, Bozen: Studienverlag, 2009.

———. 2005. "Neutralität und Neutralisierungspläne für Mitteleuropa? Österreich, Ungarn, Tschechoslowakei und Polen." In *Neutralität—Chance oder Chimäre? Konzepte des Dritten Weges für Deutschland und die Welt 1945–1990*, edited by Udo Wengst, and Dominik Geppert, 105–131. München: Oldenbourg.

———. 2005. "Neutralität und Neutralisierung in der bipolaren Welt: Zusammenfassung und weiterführende Thesen." In *Neutralität—Chance oder Chimäre? Konzepte des Dritten Weges für Deutschland und die Welt 1945–1990*, edited by Udo Wengst, and Dominik Geppert, 203–206. München: Oldenbourg.

———. 2007. "Eine Außenpolitik der Anpassung an veränderte Verhältnisse: Österreich und die Vereinigung Bundesrepublik Deutschland-DDR 1989/90." In *Verschiedene europäische Wege im Vergleich. Österreich und die Bundesrepublik Deutschland 1945/49 bis zur Gegenwart*, edited by Ingrid Böhler, and Michael Gehler, 493–530. Innsbruck, Wien, Bozen: Studienverlag.

———. 2015. *Modellfall für Deutschland? Die Österreichlösung mit Staatsvertrag und Neutralität 1945–1955.* Innsbruck, Wien, Bozen: Studienverlag.

———. 2015b. "Austria, the Revolutions and the Unification of Germany." In *The Revolutions of 1989. A Handbook (Österreichische Akademie der Wissenschaften/ Philosophische Historische Klasse/Institut für Neuzeit- und Zeitgeschichtsforschung/ Internationale Geschichte/International History 2)*, edited by Wolfgang Mueller, Michael Gehler, and Arnold Suppan, 437–466. Wien: Österreichische Akademie der Wissenschaften.

Gehler, Michael and Rudolf Agstner (Eds.). 2013. *Einheit und Teilung. Österreich und die Deutschlandfrage 1945–1960. Eine Edition ausgewählter Akten. Festschrift für Rolf Steininger zum 70. Geburtstag.* Innsbruck, Wien, Bozen: Studienverlag.

Gehler, Michael and Ingrid Böhler (Eds.). 2007. *Verschiedene europäische Wege im Vergleich. Österreich und die Bundesrepublik Deutschland 1945/49 bis zur Gegenwart. Festschrift für Rolf Steininger zum 65. Geburtstag.* Innsbruck, Wien, Bozen: Studienverlag.

Graml, Hermann. 1977. "Nationalstaat oder westlicher Teilstaat. Die sowjetischen Noten vom Jahre 1952 und die öffentliche Meinung der Bundesrepublik Deutschland." *Vierteljahrshefte für Zeitgeschichte* 24: 838–842.

———. 1981. "Die Legende von der verpaßten Gelegenheit. Zur sowjetischen Notenkampagne des Jahres 1952." *Vierteljahrshefte für Zeitgeschichte* 29: 307–341.

Hafner, Gerhard. 1969. "Die permanente Neutralität in der sowjetischen Völkerrechtslehre—Eine Analyse." *Österreichische Zeitschrift für öffentliches Recht* 19: 215–258.

Handzik, Helmut. 1993. "Politische Bedingungen sowjetischer Truppenabzüge 1925–1958." *Internationale Politik und Sicherheit* 34. Baden-Baden: Nomos.

Hilger, Andreas, Mike Schmeitzner, and Clemens Vollnhals (Eds.). 2006. "Sowjetisierung oder Neutralität? Optionen sowjetischer Besatzungspolitik in Deutschland und Österreich 1945–1955." *Schriften des Hannah-Arendt-Instituts für Totalitaris-musforschung* 32. Göttingen: Vandenhoeck & Ruprecht.

Hillgruber, Andreas. 1987. *Alliierte Pläne für eine "Neutralisierung" Deutsch-lands 1945–1955 (Rheinisch-Westfälische Akademie der Wissenschaften Vorträge G286).* Opladen: Westdeutscher Verlag: 5–31.

Krautkrämer, Elmar. 1962. *Deutsche Geschichte nach dem zweiten Weltkrieg. Eine Darstellung der Entwicklung von 1945 bis 1949 mit Dokumenten.* Hildesheim: Lax Verlag.

Laufer, Jochen. 2002. "Stalins Friedensziele und die Kontinuität der sowjetischen Deutschlandpolitik 1941–1953." In *Stalin und die Deutschen. Neue Beiträge zur Forschung,* edited by Jürgen Zarusky, 131–158. München: Oldenbourg.

———. 2004. "Die Stalin-Note vom 10. März 1952 im Lichte neuer Quellen." *Vier-teljahrshefte für Zeitgeschichte* 1: 99–118.

———. 2009. "Pax Sovietica. Stalin, die Westmächte und die deutsche Frage 1941–1945." *Zeithistorische Studien* 46. Köln, Weimar, Wien: Böhlau.

Leffler, Melvyn. 1992. *A Preponderance of Power: National Security, the Truman Administration and the Cold War.* Stanford: Stanford University Press.

Loth, Wilfried. 1992. "Die Historiker und die Deutsche Frage. Ein Rückblick nach dem Ende des Kalten Krieges." *Historisches Jahrbuch* 112(2): 366–382.

———. 1994. *Stalins ungeliebtes Kind. Warum Moskau die DDR nicht wollte.* Ber-lin: Rowohlt.

———. 1996. "Spaltung wider Willen. Die sowjetische Deutschlandpolitik 1945–1955." *Tel Aviver Jahrbuch für deutsche Geschichte* 24: 283–297.

———. 2000. *Die Teilung der Welt. Geschichte des Kalten Kriegs 1941–1955.* München: dtv. Extended new version.

———. 2002a. "Die Entstehung der 'Stalin-Note.' Dokumente aus Moskauer Archiven." In *Die Stalin-Note vom 10. März 1952. Neue Quellen und Analysen. Mit Beiträgen von Wilfried Loth, Hermann Graml und Gerhard Wettig,* edited by Jürgen Zarusky, 19–115. München: Oldenbourg.

———. 2002b. "Das Ende der Legende. Hermann Graml und die Stalin-Note. Eine Entgegnung." *Vierteljahrshefte für Zeitgeschichte* 50: 653–664.

———. 2007. *Die Sowjetunion und die deutsche Frage. Studien zur sowjetischen Deutschlandpolitik.* Göttingen: Vandenhoeck & Ruprecht.

———. 2010. "The Crucial Issues of the Early Cold War. The German question from Stalin to Khrushchev: The meaning of new documents." *Cold War History* 10(2): 229–245.

Maelstaf, Geneviève. 1998. *Que faire de l'Allemagne? Les responsables français, le statut international de l'Allemagne et le problème de l'unité allemande (1945–1955). Direction des Archives Ministère des Affaires Étrangères.* Paris: Ministère des Affaires Étrangères.

Meissner, Boris. 1953. "Russland, die Westmächte und Deutschland. Die sowje-tische Deutschlandpolitik 1943–1953." *Abhandlungen der Forschungsstelle für Völkerrecht und ausländisches Recht der Universität Hamburg* 5, Hamburg: H. H. Nölke.

————. 1970. "Triebkräfte und Faktoren der sowjetischen Außenpolitik." In *Grund-fragen sowjetischer Außenpolitik*, edited by Boris Meissner and Gotthold Rhode, 9–40. Stuttgart, Berlin, Köln, Mainz: Kohlhammer.

————. 1999. "Die sowjetische Deutschlandpolitik unter Chruschtschow." In *50 Jahre sowjetische und russische Deutschlandpolitik sowie ihre Auswirkungen auf das gegenseitige Verhältnis. Studien zur Deutschlandfrage 14*, edited by Boris Meissner, and Alfred Eisfeld, 55–74. Berlin: Duncker & Humblot.

Meissner, Boris and Gotthold Rhode. 1970. *Grundfragen der sowjetischen Außenpolitik*. Stuttgart, Berlin, Köln, Mainz: Kohlhammer.

Mueller, Wolfgang. 2007. "Sowjetische Deutschland- und Österreichpolitik 1941 bis 1955 im Vergleich: Die Fragen der staatlichen Einheit und des Friedensvertrages." In *Verschiedene europäische Wege im Vergleich. Österreich und die Bundesrepublik Deutschland 1945/49 bis zur Gegenwart. Festschrift für Rolf Steininger zum 65. Geburtstag*, edited by Michael Gehler and Ingrid Böhler, 123–154. Innsbruck, Wien, Bozen: Studienverlag.

————. 2005. "Gab es eine „verpasste Chance"? Die sowjetische Haltung zum Staatsvertrag 1946–1952." In *Der österreichische Staatsvertrag 1955. Internationale Strategie, rechtliche Relevanz, nationale Identität/The Austrian State Treaty 1955. International Strategy, Legal Relevance, National Identity. Österreichische Akademie der Wissenschaften, Philosophisch-Historische Klasse, Historische Kommission/Archiv für österreichische Geschichte 140*, edited by Arnold Suppan, Gerald Stourzh, and Wolfgang Mueller, 89–120. Wien: Verlag der Österreichischen Akademie der Wissenschaften.

————. 2011. *A Good Example of Peaceful Coexistence? The Soviet Union, Austria, and Neutrality, 1955–1991*. Wien: Verlag der Österreichischen Akademie der Wissenschaften.

————. 2014. "A Special Relationship with Neutrals? Khrushchev's Coexistence, Austria, and Switzerland, 1955–1960." *Zeitgeschichte* 41(5): 279–295.

Mueller, Wolfgang, Arnold Suppan, Norman M. Naimark, and Gennadij Bordjugov (Eds.). 2005. *Sowjetische Politik in Österreich. Dokumente aus russischen Archiven: Sovetskaia politika v Avstrii: Dokumenty iz Rossiiskikh arkhivov 1945–1955*. Wien: Verlag der Österreichischen Akademie der Wissenschaften.

Naimark, Norman. 1995. *The Russians in Germany. The History of the Soviet Zone of Occupation, 1945–1949*. Cambridge, MA: Harvard University Press.

————. 1997. *Die Russen in Deutschland. Die Sowjetische Besatzungszone 1945 bis 1949*. Berlin: Ullstein.

Peter, Matthias. 2015. *Die Bundesrepublik im KSZE-Prozess 1975–1983. Die Umkehrung der Diplomatie*. Berlin, München, Boston, Oldenbourg: De Gruyter.

Pfeiffer, Rolf. 2001. "Kein guter Beginn. Das konfliktreiche deutsch-österreichische Verhältnis im Jahr 1954." In *Geschichte ist Vielfalt. Natur—Gesellschaft—Wissenschaft. Festgabe für Peter Krüger anlässlich seines 65. Geburtstages*, edited by Katja Wüstenbecker, 81–88. Münster: LIT-Verlag.

Roberts, Geoffrey. 2006. *Stalin's Wars: From World War to Cold War 1939–1953*. New Haven CT: Yale University Press.

Ruggenthaler, Peter (Ed.). 2007. "Stalins großer Bluff. Die Geschichte der Stalin-Note in Dokumenten der sowjetischen Führung." *Schriftenreihe der Vierteljahrshefte für Zeitgeschichte 95.* München: Oldenbourg.

———. 2011. "The 1952 Stalin Note on German Reunification. The ongoing Debate." *Journal of Cold War Studies* 13(4): 172–212.

———. 2013. "Zur Rolle der sowjetischen Besatzung Österreichs in der Außenpolitik Stalins." In *Licencer to detect. Festschrift für Siegfried Beer zum 65. Geburtstag. Schriftenreihe des Instituts für Geschichte 19,* edited by Alfred Ableitinger and Martin Moll, 474–492. Graz: Leykam Verlag.

———. 2014. "Neutrality for Germany or Stabilization of the Eastern Bloc? New Evidence on the Decision-Making Process of the Stalin Note." In *Imposing, Maintaining, and Tearing Open the Iron Curtain,* edited by Mark Kramer, and Vit Smetana, 149–170. Lanham, Boulder, New York, Toronto, Plymouth UK: Lexington Books.

———. 2015. *The Concept of Neutrality in Stalin's Foreign Policy, 1945–1953.* Lanham, Boulder, New York, London: Lexington Books.

———. 2015. "Die Sowjetunion und die österreichische Neutralität im Kalten Krieg." In *Die österreichische Neutralität. Chimäre oder Wirklichkeit?* edited by Gerald Schöpfer, 137–153. Graz: Leykam Verlag.

Rupieper, Hermann-Josef. 1991. *Der besetzte Verbündete. Die amerikanische Deutschlandpolitik 1949–1955.* Opladen: Leske & Budrich.

Schwarz, Hans-Peter. 1982. *Die Legende von der verpaßten Gelegenheit. Die Stalin-Note vom 10. März 1952.* Stuttgart, Zürich: Belser.

———. 1990. "Die Eingliederung der Bundesrepublik in die westliche Welt." In *Vom Marshallplan zur EWG. Die Eingliederung der Bundesrepublik in die westliche Welt. Quellen und Darstellungen zur Zeitgeschichte 30,* edited by Ludolf Herbst, Werner Bührer, and Hanno Sowade, 593–612. München: Oldenbourg.

Steininger, Rolf. 1985. "Eine Chance zur Wiedervereinigung? Die Stalin-Note vom 10. März 1952. Darstellung und Dokumentation auf der Grundlage unveröffentlichter britischer und amerikanischer Akten." *Archiv für Sozialgeschichte Beiheft* 12. Bonn: Verlag Neue Gesellschaft, 1986. 2nd edition.

———. 1990. *The German Question. The Stalin Note of 1952 and the Problem of Reunification.* New York: Columbia University Press.

———. 1993. "Zwischen Pariser Verträgen und Genfer Gipfelkonferenz: Großbritannien und die Deutsche Frage 1955." In *Die doppelte Eindämmung. Europäische Sicherheit und deutsche Frage in den Fünfzigern. Tutzinger Schriften zur Politik 2,* edited by Rolf Steininger, Jürgen Weber, Günter Bischof, Thomas Albrich, and Klaus Eisterer, 177–211. München: von Hase und Koehler.

———. 2002. *Deutsche Geschichte. Darstellung und Dokumente in vier Bänden. Bd. 2: 1948–1955.* Frankfurt/Main: S. Fischer Verlag.

———. 2005a. *Der Staatsvertrag. Österreich im Schatten von deutscher Frage und Kaltem Krieg 1938–1955.* Innsbruck, Wien, Bozen: Studienverlag.

Stourzh, Gerald. 2005. "Um Einheit und Freiheit. Staatsvertrag, Neutralität und das Ende der Ost-West-Besetzung Österreichs 1945–1955." *Studien zu Politik und Verwaltung* 62. Wien: Böhlau. 5th revised version with a biographical commentary.

————. 2005b. "Der österreichische Staatsvertrag in den weltpolitischen Entscheidungsprozessen des Jahres 1955." In *Der österreichische Staatsvertrag 1955. Internationale Strategie, rechtliche Relevanz, nationale Identität/The Austrian State Treaty 1955. International Strategy, Legal Relevance, National Identity*, edited by Arnold Suppan/Gerald Stourzh/Wolfgang Mueller, 965–995. Wien: Verlag der Österreichischen Akademie der Wissenschaften.

Thoß, Bruno. 1993. "Der Beitritt der Bundesrepublik Deutschland zur WEU und NATO im Spannungsfeld von Blockbildung und Entspannung (1954–1956)." In *Die NATO-Option. Anfänge westdeutscher Sicherheitspolitik 1945–1956* 3, edited by Militärgeschichtliches Forschungsamt, 3–234. München: Oldenbourg.

————. 1988. "Modellfall Österreich? Der österreichische Staatsvertrag und die deutsche Frage 1954/55." In *Zwischen Kaltem Krieg und Entspannung. Sicherheits- und Deutschlandpolitik der Bundesrepublik im Mächtesystem der Jahre 1953–1956*, edited by Bruno Thoß and Hans-Erich Volkmann, 93–136. Boppard/Rhein: H. Boldt.

Wettig, Gerhard. 1982. "Die sowjetische Deutschland-Note vom 10. März 1952. Wiedervereinigungsangebot oder Propagandaaktion?" *Deutschland Archiv* 2: 130–148.

————. 1994. "Zum Stand der Forschung über Berijas Deutschlandpolitik im Frühjahr 1953." In *Die Deutschlandfrage von der staatlichen Teilung Deutschlands bis zum Tode Stalins*, edited by Göttinger Arbeitskreis, 183–200. Berlin: Duncker & Humblot.

————. 1999. *Bereitschaft zu Einheit in Freiheit? Die sowjetische Deutschland-Politik 1945–1955*. München: Olzog.

————. 2008. *Stalin and the Cold War in Europe: The Emergence and Development of East-West-Conflict, 1939–1953*. Lanham: Rowman & Littlefield.

————. 2011. "Sowjetische Deutschland-Politik 1953 bis 1958. Korrekturen an Stalins Erbe, Chruschtschows Aufstieg und der Weg zum Berlin-Ultimatum." *Quellen und Darstellungen zur Zeitgeschichte* 82. München: Oldenbourg.

————. 2015. *Die Stalin-Note. Historische Kontroversen im Spiegel der Quellen.* Berlin: be.bra verlag.

Zarusky, Jürgen (Ed.). 2002. *Die Stalin-Note vom 10. März 1952. Neue Quellen und Analysen*. München: Oldenbourg.

Zubok, Vladislav. 2007. *A Failed Empire. The Soviet Union from Stalin to Gorbachev.* Chapel Hill: University of North Carolina Press.

Chapter 3

The Persistence of Neutrality in Post–Cold War Europe

Liliane Stadler

For over twenty years after the end of the Cold War, most of Europe's neutral states have remained ambiguously neutral. Where the discourse is concerned, Switzerland still proclaims itself to be neutral, as do Austria and Ireland (Goetschel 2011, 312). Finland and Sweden now prefer the term "non-allied" (Goetschel 2011, 312). Furthermore, according to Kostas Ifantis and Sotiris Serbos, where the practice is concerned "neutrality survives only insofar as military non-alignment persists" (Ifantis and Sotiris 2013, 219).[1]

Bearing this in mind, Ireland was the first neutral state to join the European Communities (EC) in 1973. Austria, Finland and Sweden followed suit, joining the European Union (EU) in 1995. Today, each of these states is an active participant in the EU's Common Foreign and Security Policy (CFSP) and of its Common Security and Defence Policy (CSDP). Furthermore, all five states—including Switzerland—have signed Partnership for Peace (PfP) agreements with the North Atlantic Treaty Organization (NATO) over the course of the 1990s. Consequently, most of them have enhanced the interoperability of their own armed forces and command structures with those of NATO, participated in joint military exercises with NATO members or contributed directly to NATO operations (Cottey 2013, 448). Strictly speaking, it would seem that these developments are incompatible with the concept of neutrality, whose purpose it is to avoid military entanglements.

Nevertheless, to date, none of the Cold War neutrals have completely abandoned both neutrality and non-alliance. In other words, what is puzzling about this pattern is that for some reason neutral states find it difficult to make a complete transition from neutrality to non-neutrality. This raises the following question: Why have neutral European states remained neutral after the end of the Cold War?

In order to answer this question, I will apply process tracing to three diverse case studies, namely Switzerland, Sweden and Austria. In doing so, I will test two competing theoretical explanations for the ambiguous persistence of neutrality and will suggest amendments to these existing theoretical frameworks. The first is path dependence, which accounts for the persistence of neutrality by conceptualizing it as an institution, from which it would be costly to diverge. The second explanation is ontological security. This is a relatively novel theory in International Relations, developed primarily by Jennifer Mitzen of the University of Chicago during the mid-2000s. It conceptualizes neutrality as a defining aspect of state identity, which permits neutral states to routinize their interactions with others and to thereby monitor their threat environment more accurately than otherwise. My main argument is that ontological security theory is better able to explain the persistence of neutrality in post-Cold War Europe, yet that it requires refinement concerning the manner in which states accommodate their routines. This is because while the states explored here have chosen only reversible and no irreversible foreign policy options to date where their neutrality is concerned. Before discussing both theoretical frameworks in detail and applying them to my case studies, however, I will briefly dwell on my understanding of neutrality and on my methodological framework.

THE CONCEPT OF NEUTRALITY

The word neutrality is derived from the Latin word neuter, meaning neither (Boczek 1989, 3). I here understand it in accordance with the definition advanced by Harto Hakovirta, who argues that, "in an international conflict, a policy is the more neutral the less it interferes in said conflict, the more equally it benefits or harms the parties concerned and the less it affects the outcome of the conflict" (Hakovirta 1988). Note here that understood in this way, neutrality applies to conflict situations rather than peace.

In order to be neutral, a state should adhere to three principles: impartiality, non-belligerence and self-defence. The first implies that a neutral must treat all parties to a conflict equally in the military and in the nonmilitary sector, such that it does not favor any given party (Boczek 1989, 3). The second implies that it may not initiate or participate in hostilities (Fischer, Köck and Verdross 1980, 314; Radovan 1989, 29). The last principle implies that a state must be able to defend its own territory against attack or against the misuse of a belligerent for military purposes (Neuhold 1988, 16, 99). In other words, for neutrality to be respected, it must be defended forcefully and this is the only permissible use of force for a neutral state. What this means in practice is that neutral states may not commit their military capabilities to the pursuit of other states' objectives, that they may not join alliances, and that they must be able to rely on their own resources to secure their defence (Boczek 1989, 1). The goal of a neutral state is maximum independence from foreign interference (Von Däniken 2016, 45).

However, beyond what is sometimes referred to as this "common denominator," the manifestations of neutrality are diverse (Boczek 1989, 2). Neutrality can be temporal or permanent. It can be applied to all or only to a few states and it can result from a multilateral treaty, a unilateral declaration or forced neutralization. These may be combined to differing degrees, which gives rise to the highly idiosyncratic nature of neutrality in practice (Schaub 1995, 6). The cases selected here are intended to reflect this diversity among the notably small population of neutral states to date.

One last distinction to bear in mind at this stage is the one between *neutrality law* and *neutrality policy* (Lezzi 2016). Neutrality law, which here mainly refers to the three principles of neutrality, has evolved through the writings of legal scholars, as well as international custom over centuries and has been codified in the Conventions of The Hague of 1907. Yet strictly speaking, neutrality law only applies to neutrality in war time. Hence, it does not extend to the unilateral formulation of neutrality policy during peacetime. The latter refers to measures that a neutral state takes, which exceed and reinforce its obligations under neutrality law. The primary purpose of neutrality policy is to enhance the credibility and the predictability of neutral foreign and security policy internationally (EDA 2015). At first sight, it also appears as though there exists a correlation between neutrality law and irreversible foreign policy choices, as well as between neutrality policy and reversible foreign policy choices. While neutrality law entails a firm and often formal commitment, neutrality policy does not. Over the course of this chapter, I intend to explore whether this is in fact the case.

METHODOLOGY: PROCESS TRACING

As to my methodological framework, in order to tell, whether path dependence or ontological security applies, I will use process tracing. Process tracing is here understood as the examination of evidence within an individual case to test alternative explanations for the outcome of said case (Bennett 2008, 704). As such, it will involve testing for the presence or absence of causal process observations (CPO), the steps in the causal chain that each of the two competing explanations argue ought to be present to produce the observed outcome.

I will use two tests for this purpose, namely *hoop tests* and *smoking gun tests*. Hoop tests determine whether an argument demonstrates certitude, whereas smoking gun tests determine whether it demonstrates uniqueness (Waldner 2015, 127). In other words, passing a hoop test does not confirm an argument, but failing it eliminates it. This also means that the presence of a CPO is a necessary condition for an argument to be valid (Goertz and Mahoney 2012, 93). A smoking gun test, on the other hand lends decisive support in favor of a very particular argument, yet failing it does not eliminate it (Goertz and Mahoney 2012, 94). In this context, the presence of a CPO is a sufficient condition for the validity of the argument (Goertz and Mahoney 2012, 95). Please note that neither of these tests may provide absolute certainty. Tests that both confirm an explanation and eliminate competing explanations are called "doubly decisive tests" (Bennett 2008, 706). Evidence for such tests is exceptionally rare in the social sciences and that is why they will not be attempted here.

COMPETING EXPLANATIONS AND THEIR PROCESS TRACING

Path Dependence

As to the first theory I will test, path dependence explains the persistence of institutions (Gerard 2001, 235; Crouch and Farrell 2004, 6). In accordance with the definition provided by Oran Young, an institution is here understood as the conjunction of convergent expectations and patterns of behavior or practice (Young 1979, 16). This means that actors who adhere to an institution become accustomed to responding to repeating situations in a consistent manner. In the case of permanently neutral states, this may mean that in the event of an armed conflict and even beyond, they remain non-belligerent, impartial, and they strive to prevent the violation of their territorial integrity.

In order to explain the persistence of neutrality beyond the end of the Cold War in terms of path dependence, there needs to be compelling evidence that an institution has become "locked in" and that it becomes resistant to critical junctures as a result of this. This means that change and innovation become difficult as a result of recurrent practice (Crouch and Farrell 2004, 30).

"Lock-in" phenomena have been studied in the context of economics, in order to challenge the assumption of decreasing returns. The idea of decreasing returns encourages rational economic actors to converge towards an efficiency-maximizing equilibrium (Crouch and Farrell 2004, 8). This process is also known as negative feedback. Increasing returns—or positive feedback—on the other hand, imply that once adopted, a process may also deliver increasing benefits (Mahoney 2000, 508). Cumulative investments in a profitable venture are an example of this. Having invested large sums of

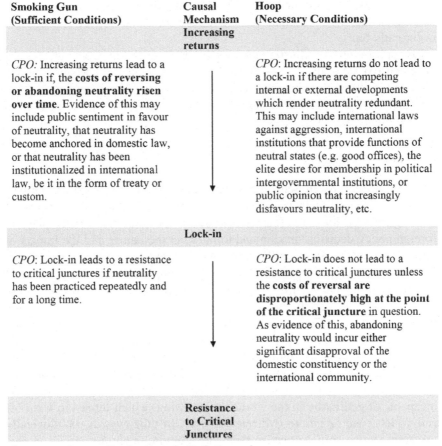

Smoking Gun (Sufficient Conditions)	Causal Mechanism	Hoop (Necessary Conditions)
	Increasing returns	
CPO: Increasing returns lead to a lock-in if, the **costs of reversing or abandoning neutrality risen over time**. Evidence of this may include public sentiment in favour of neutrality, that neutrality has become anchored in domestic law, or that neutrality has been institutionalized in international law, be it in the form of treaty or custom.		*CPO*: Increasing returns do not lead to a lock-in if there are competing internal or external developments which render neutrality redundant. This may include international laws against aggression, international institutions that provide functions of neutral states (e.g. good offices), the elite desire for membership in political intergovernmental institutions, or public opinion that increasingly disfavours neutrality, etc.
	Lock-in	
CPO: Lock-in leads to a resistance to critical junctures if neutrality has been practiced repeatedly and for a long time.		*CPO*: Lock-in does not lead to a resistance to critical junctures unless the **costs of reversal are disproportionately high at the point of the critical juncture** in question. As evidence of this, abandoning neutrality would incur either significant disapproval of the domestic constituency or the international community.
	Resistance to Critical Junctures	

Figure 3.1   Process Tracing Tests for Path Dependence.

money, reversing or changing the process becomes highly costly. The process has become locked in and the result of this is the stable reproduction of a particular outcome (Mahoney and Schensul 2006).

Three factors are characteristic of these processes: Firstly, they are particularly sensitive to initial conditions. These conditions are contingent, meaning that they cannot be readily explained on the basis of prior events and they often take states by surprise. Mahoney argues that another way of understanding this is that an explanation of an event appears to fall outside of existing theoretical frameworks (Mahoney 2000, 514). Such events are referred to as critical junctures. Secondly, once such contingent events or critical junctures have taken place, path dependent sequences are relatively deterministic and marked by considerable inertia (Mahoney 2000, 510–511). Lastly, this inflexibility increases farther down any given process, which accounts for the notion of a lock-in (Arthur 1994, 112–113). In other words, critical junctures that occur later on in a sequence do not have the same impact as those that occur early on.

Overall, Figure 3.1 illustrates how path dependence may account for the persistence of neutrality in post-Cold War Europe. Note that the smoking gun tests and the hoop tests below refer to the arrows, which connect each stage. The hoop test and the smoking gun test that I will carry out are marked in bold in Figure 3.1.

Ontological Security

Ontological security presents a new and alternative explanation for the per-sistence of neutrality in post-Cold War Europe. The aim of the theory of ontological security is twofold. It is to assess the role that identity plays in foreign policy decision-making and to interpret the nature and the impact of threats to identity (Steele 2005, 520). Whereas most mainstream theories in International Relations presume that security implies survival and physical security, ontological security refers to the security of identity (Mitzen 2006, 129). Security of identity means that a social actor can act rationally on the basis of ordered preferences, because these are based on a consistent and strong sense of self. It is analogous to certainty and self-confidence.

In order to make this argument, ontological security extrapolates from the level of the individual. When an individual feels insecure, for example, she does not necessarily fear for her survival (Steele 2005, 525). Instead, she feels incapable of getting by in the world, not knowing, which threats to ward off and which ones to ignore (Mitzen 2004, 3). In other words, ontologically insecure people cannot organize their threat environment as a result of per-vasive uncertainty (Mitzen 2004, 3–4). Uncertainty is here understood as the inability to assess the relations between decisions and outcomes.

According to Jennifer Mitzen, understanding why states fear uncertainty requires the integration of insights from both constructivism and rationalism. Rational agency rests on the ability to make choices that lead to preferred ends (Mitzen 2004, 19). This assumes that actors know their preferences, the available courses of action and the consequences of each. In reality, however, according to Mitzen, states may not always possess this knowledge. This results in uncertainty (Mitzen 2004, 20). And when a state does not know how to relate means and ends to each other, agency becomes problematic.

Ontological security-seeking, therefore, is the drive to minimize uncer-tainty by imposing cognitive order on one's environment (Mitzen 2006, 346). In this way, it enables both rational action and choice (Mitzen 2006, 344). According to Mitzen, what follows from this is that ontological security is "the condition that obtains when an individual has confident expectations, even if they are probabilistic, about the means-ends relationships that govern social life" (Mitzen 2006, 345).

The mechanism through which identity and ontological security are maintained is routinization. A routine is a set of responses to stimuli that become relatively automatic or habitual (Mitzen 2004, 4). In other words, when X happens, an actor responds with Y. Routines reduce uncertainty, because they facilitate rather than inhibit action. They do this by regularizing social life and by thus generating conditions under which an actor feels it has reliable knowledge about means-ends relations (Mitzen 2004, 4). Here, the difference between institutions and routines is that the former are intended to maximize utility and minimize costs, while the latter are intended to enhance agency and reduce uncertainty.

Crucially, however, cognitive disorder may arise when routinization fails (Bayley 2015, 821). Such tends to be the case in a so-called "critical situation." Once again, this term is very similar to the term "critical juncture" used and applied to path dependence. For the purpose of this chapter, I will treat critical situations and critical junctures as the same phenomena and will refer to them as critical moments. In ontological security terms this kind of situation renders an actor unable to continue to function as its "old self," because its identity is no longer compatible with the external conditions of the international environment (Cupać 2012, 27). The most obvious example of this is the Russian Federation after the dissolution of the Soviet Union in 1991.

In order to overcome uncertainty and anxiety, an agent must reform its behavior to accommodate any changes to its environment (Steele 2005, 526). This is the chief difference between path dependence and ontological security. Furthermore, there is a subdivision within ontological security theory. Jennifer Mitzen here distinguishes between two types of routines: healthy and maladaptive ones (Mitzen 2004, 19). Maladaptive routines are routines in which an agent incessantly follows a habit or routine, rather like path dependence. The difference between maladaptive routines and path dependence is that in the case of the former, a routine is maintained due to pervasive uncertainty and hesitation. In the case of the latter, an institution is maintained more obviously as a result of a rational cost-benefit analysis.

Healthy routines, on the other hand, can tolerate a certain degree of uncertainty, which may be overcome through slight adaptations in light of external developments (Browning and Joenniemi 2013, 496). The difference between path dependence and healthy routines is that path dependence argues that it is more rational to maintain an institution as it is, while a healthy routine presupposes that at times it is more rational to make slight changes to a routine. Therefore, the way in which I can dismiss either path dependence or ontological security is by identifying whether a neutral state has maintained all of its neutrality practices from before the critical moment in its aftermath. If yes, path dependence applies. Yet if I detect alterations in a neutral's practices

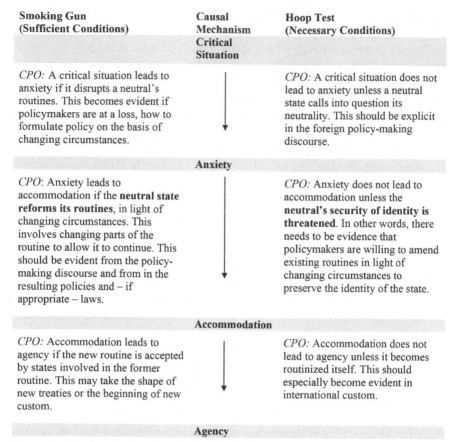

Smoking Gun (Sufficient Conditions)	Causal Mechanism Critical Situation	Hoop Test (Necessary Conditions)
CPO: A critical situation leads to anxiety if it disrupts a neutral's routines. This becomes evident if policymakers are at a loss, how to formulate policy on the basis of changing circumstances.	↓	*CPO:* A critical situation does not lead to anxiety unless a neutral state calls into question its neutrality. This should be explicit in the foreign policy-making discourse.
	Anxiety	
CPO: Anxiety leads to accommodation if the **neutral state reforms its routines**, in light of changing circumstances. This involves changing parts of the routine to allow it to continue. This should be evident from the policy-making discourse and from in the resulting policies and – if appropriate – laws.	↓	*CPO:* Anxiety does not lead to accommodation unless the **neutral's security of identity is threatened**. In other words, there needs to be evidence that policymakers are willing to amend existing routines in light of changing circumstances to preserve the identity of the state.
	Accommodation	
CPO: Accommodation leads to agency if the new routine is accepted by states involved in the former routine. This may take the shape of new treaties or the beginning of new custom.	↓	*CPO:* Accommodation does not lead to agency unless it becomes routinized itself. This should especially become evident in international custom.
	Agency	

Figure 3.2   Process Tracing Tests for Ontological Security.

without abandoning neutrality, ontological security applies. Bearing this in mind, just like in Figure 3.1, Figure 3.2 accounts for the persistence of neutrality from the perspective of ontological security and highlights the tests I will carry out in bold.

CASE STUDY: SWITZERLAND

Bearing in mind the previous, I will now apply my process tracing tests to the first case study: Switzerland. In 1993, the Bundesrat under the presidency of Adolf Ogi introduced the "Report on Swiss Foreign Policy for the Nineties" (hereafter Report of 1993). As previous foreign policy reports had done, it again expressed support for Switzerland's permanent and armed neutrality. However, unlike before, it also argued that, "Neutrality should remain an instrument of foreign and security policy only as long as it is better able to implement Swiss national interests than other concepts" (EDA 1993, 6). It further stated that neutrality was, "neither unchangeable in content nor unchangeable in duration" (EDA 1993, 6). On the basis of these considerations, the report reminded its readers that Swiss foreign policy was also driven by solidarity and that Switzerland would become increasingly committed to, "Sharing responsibility for the greatest problems of our time and to take an active part in international efforts to resolve them" (EDA 1993, 12). What this meant in practice was that firstly, in light of the precedent set by the First Gulf War, Switzerland would take part in nonmilitary sanctions imposed on any state by the UN and secondly, that neutrality would no longer pose an obstacle to EU membership (EDA 1993, 28). In 1993, this was unprecedented, raising the question why Switzerland retained the three core duties of neutrality, while loosening its foreign policy restrictions to include measures it had traditionally considered to contradict neutrality.

Process Tracing Test for Path Dependence

In order for path dependence to explain why Switzerland has retained elements of neutrality to date, the costs of abandoning neutrality must have been demonstrably too high in the aftermath of the Cold War. This test passes, because, giving up neutrality would have incurred tremendous resistance at the domestic level (Gehler 2001, 97).

Already in 1946, Federal Councillor Max Petitpierre had argued that, "Giving up our neutrality is like asking the United Kingdom to give up its monarchy or the United States to give up the republic" (Trachsler 2011, 111). In fact, yearly national opinion polls conducted by the Centre for Security Studies (CSS) at the Swiss Federal Institute of Technology (ETH) in Zurich show that the overwhelming majority of the Swiss population has consistently supported neutrality over time (Tresch et al. 2015).

Figure 3.3 displays the development of Swiss public opinion on neutrality between 1989 and 2015. On average, 1,111 people were interviewed each year. Each person was asked the question, "In your opinion, how can Switzerland best maintain its interests while contributing to world security at the same time?" Respondents were subsequently asked to rate their approval of three possible responses in percentage points. These responses were:

A. Switzerland should maintain its neutrality.
B. In case of a political conflict abroad, Switzerland should take sides. In case of an armed conflict, it should remain neutral.
C. Switzerland should also take sides in case of an armed conflict (de facto abandonment of neutrality).

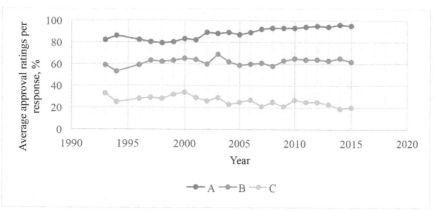

Figure 3.3   Popular Attitudes Towards Neutrality.

The average percentage of approval that each response received over time is displayed in Figure 3.3.

What Figure 3.3 reveals is that Swiss voters would have disapproved of any government which would have attempted to give up neutrality between 1989 and 2015. Given the nature of Swiss direct democracy, a likely consequence of such an attempt may very well have led to a popular referendum to reverse it. Swiss policymakers in turn were very aware of the popularity of neutrality and acted accordingly (Thalmann 2016). This is why there appears to be convincing evidence in support of the claim that the costs of abandoning neutrality were too high in 1993. Path dependence passes this hoop test and it is possible that Switzerland remained neutral after the end of the Cold War as a result of a cost-benefit calculation.

However, in order to exclude ontological security as an explanation, the costs of abandoning neutrality must also have increased prior to the critical moment. This is because ontological security theory argues in the opposite direction, namely that a critical moment renders it more feasible that a routine will be adapted to accommodate changing circumstances. This being said, it appears to me that path dependence does not pass this smoking gun test, because after the end of the Cold War, some costs of maintaining neutrality actually increased.

Although the Swiss public has remained emotionally attached to the idea of neutrality, the proliferation of international regimes to address transnational security threats has rendered non-participation counterproductive and has confronted Swiss policymakers with a dilemma. Contemporary security threats appeared to require collaborative responses. Neutrality, however, was an ill-suited concept to combat intra-state conflict, terrorism, organized crime or the proliferation of weapons of mass destruction. Even the core of neutrality, as it was codified in The Hague in 1907, only guides foreign policy in the event of an interstate conflict (Trachseler 2011, 109).

At this point it is useful to recall the changes to Swiss neutrality policy introduced by the Report of 1993 and discussed in the introduction to this case study. The aforementioned dilemma is why this report retained a commitment to the law of neutrality, more specifically to its three core principles, but abandoned all of the additional elements of neutrality policy prevalent during the Cold War. These in turn had resulted from the so-called Bindschedler Doctrine of 1954. Said doctrine obliged Switzerland to refrain from joining collective security organizations, taking part in economic sanctions or participating in international conferences and organizations. Bearing in mind the proliferation of international regimes to address transnational security threats, the costs of maintaining the Bindschedler Doctrine have actually increased up until 1993. Finally, Report 1993 came at the cost of only the Bindschedler Doctrine, not of Swiss national identity or of the predictability and credibility of its foreign policy. Hence, the explanation of path dependence does not pass this smoking gun test and it does not disconfirm ontological security, to which I will now turn.

Process Tracing Tests for Ontological Security

According to ontological security theory, in order to regain a stable self-understanding and a capacity for rational, goal-oriented action, a state needs to accommodate its routines in the wake of a critical moment. This was evidently the case for Swiss neutrality during the post-Cold War period. As discussed, the obligations contained in the Bindschedler Doctrine of 1954, were gradually abandoned during the early 1990s (Lezzi 2016; Von Däniken 2016). The Report of 1993 elaborated on this new mode of thinking by remarking that the expedience of neutrality should be re-examined from time to time, depending on the geopolitical climate (EDA 1993, 6).

It is important to bear in mind, however, that these changes only affected neutrality policy and not neutrality law, which is why they were never put neither to a popular referendum nor to a parliamentary vote. The aforementioned reports served the purpose of informing parliament and public on the foreign and security strategy of the Bundesrat (Goetschel 2016).

As a result, by 1996 Switzerland enhanced its commitment to international cooperation on security (EDA 2000, 3; Thalmann 2016; Schmid 2016). It actively participated actively in the Geneva Disarmament Conference, the Organization for Security and Cooperation in Europe (OSCE) and it entered into a PfP agreement with NATO. Lastly, but perhaps most importantly, Switzerland joined the UN in 2002. Hence, Switzerland has neither joined NATO nor the EU to date. While the Bundesrat under the presidency of René

Felber did apply for membership of the European Economic Area (EEA), Swiss voters terminated the Council's aspirations in a national referendum on the December 6, 1992 (Gehler 2001, 50). Nevertheless, what this goes to show is that Switzerland did reform its routines and that ontological security passes this test.

What remains to be tested is whether all of the previous was done in service of Switzerland's security of identity. I believe that Switzerland passes this last test for two reasons. Firstly, the end of the Cold War posed a threat to Switzerland's security of identity and secondly, the changes that Switzerland subsequently made to its neutrality policy were such that they permitted Switzerland to retain neutrality despite challenges from its external environment. In fact, there appears to be a clear distinction between two types of foreign policy options resulting from this dilemma: Reversible ones and irreversible ones. Reversible foreign policy options are options that entail a lesser level of risk and commitment. In practice, they refer to changes in Swiss neutrality policy. Irreversible ones refer to sincere and often multilateral commitments. In practice, these here entail changes in Swiss neutrality law. What is interesting about Switzerland is that the former were extensively invoked, while the latter were not invoked at all. Furthermore, I believe this distinction to have been made on the basis of Swiss policymakers' recognition of both the external threats to Switzerland's security of identity and of the unwavering and overwhelming domestic support for neutrality.

Switzerland's response, was to participate in selective collective security ventures, as long as these required no treaty commitments while remaining neutral both under international treaty law and international custom. It participated in economic sanctions by the UN Security Council and the EU and the eventually became a UN member in 2002. Furthermore, it contributed to the aforementioned PfP with NATO in the form of peacekeeping missions and training centers. Interestingly, none of these or of the other aforementioned cooperative ventures included treaty obligations in violation of Swiss neutrality. As such, they pre-empted any form of a breach of its previous commitments to neutrality under international law, an un-winnable binding referendum or any uncertain responses by other states who had become accustomed to Swiss neutrality (Bundestaat 1999a, 7690). What is more, in case of further alterations to Switzerland's security environment, these reversible foreign policy commitments could be withdrawn. After all, this is precisely how ontological security theory stipulates that security of identity is maintained.

I would therefore suggest that ontological security include this slight nuance in its theoretical framework in order to distinguish between reversible and irreversible changes to a routine. There exists a similarity between path dependent institutions and irreversible policy options, namely that they deter change. Their difference, however, is that path dependence deters it with a view to the past, more specifically, in light of increasing returns and increasing costs of change in the past. As has been demonstrated here, this logic does not hold in the case of Switzerland.

Irreversible foreign policy options, on the other hand, deter change with a view to the future. These options do not broaden, but constrain a state's freedom of action in the future and may hence lead to maladaptive routines. Switzerland does not fall under this category either. Instead, it has opted for a series of reversible foreign policy changes to accommodate its needs for both ontological and physical security. This had the dual benefit of protecting Swiss neutrality, which remains highly popular among Swiss citizens, and preventing the country from entering into any maladaptive routines in the future.

CASE STUDY: SWEDEN

Sweden is very different from Switzerland. In 2002, Swedish Prime Minister Göran Persson declared in a speech in Jyväskylä, Finland, that Sweden would militarily assist any EU member state in the event of an armed attack (Sanomat 2002). Hence, since 2002, Sweden can no longer be considered neutral (Bring 2016). Yet it continues to be non-allied, sometimes also referring to itself as "militarily non-aligned" (Hjelm-Wallén 2016; Bring 2016; Sanomat 2002). According to Ove Bring, professor emeritus of international law and former legal adviser at the Swedish Ministry of Foreign Affairs from 1976 to 1993, the difference between neutrality and non-alliance is that strictly speaking neutrality only applies to the event of an armed conflict. Non-alliance, on the other hand, can also be a peacetime policy. Furthermore, non-alliance does not entail non-belligerence in the event of war.

In fact, Sweden has never been a permanently neutral state (Bring 2016). Rather, it pursued a foreign policy that was very similar to permanent neutrality. It has remained non-allied and has routinely declared neutrality in the event of most armed conflicts for approximately two hundred years. This has produced similar expectations among other states as permanent neutrality would have. However, Swedish neutrality, unlike Swiss neutrality, has never been based on an international treaty obligation and is not mentioned in the Swedish constitution (Logue 1989, 36). Swedish neutrality has always been a unilaterally chosen and routinely implemented policy, rather than the product of neutrality law (Åström 1989, 16). In other words, until 2002, it has always been a reversible foreign policy option for Sweden, the utility of which depended on the prevailing circumstances (Vaahtoranta and Forsberg 2000, 21). This is also why, unlike Switzerland, Sweden became a member of the UN in 1946, and a member of the EU in 1995. In fact, in the case of Sweden, the accession to the EU was a critical moment. This is because it rendered both the rationale and the practice of its neutrality policy increasingly ambiguous between 1990 and the present.

It began with a radical reversal of Swedish neutrality policy in 1990. In May of that year, Socialist Prime Minister Ingvar Carlsson declared that the political union considered by the EC as a result of the Single European Act of 1986, represented the "definitive borderline" for Swedish neutrality and that because of this, Sweden would not join the EC (Goldman 1991, 13). Five months later, however, during the opening ceremony of the Swedish Riksdag[2] on the October 2, 1990, the same Ingvar Carlsson argued that, as a result of the positive developments on the continent, "Swedish membership in the EC is in the national interest, provided that her policy of neutrality is retained" (Carlsnaes 1993, 82).[3] The Swedish government subsequently announced on the October 26, 1990, that it would prepare to submit an application for membership, while, in an article in *The Economist* from the November 8, 1990, Carlsson explained that Sweden's rapid change of course was principally due to economic difficulties, including high inflation, large budget deficits and low growth rates (Rieker 2002, 14). The Swedish Riksdag concurred with Carlsson in December of the same year, when it formally approved the decision to seek EC membership with 90 percent of delegates supporting the motion, as long as Swedish neutrality would be retained (Miles 1997, 97). The formal application was presented to the EC on the July 1, 1991.

Bearing in mind the previous, the case study on Sweden asks a question similar to that of the preceding case study on Switzerland, namely: Why has Sweden subsequently abandoned neutrality and retained non-alliance after the end of the Cold War? I will keep the same hoop tests and smoking gun tests applied to path dependence and ontological security in the case study on Switzerland before. As in the previous case study, I will argue that path dependence does not pass all of its process tracing tests, while ontological security does. It also appears to me that all of Sweden's reforms to its routine were reversible rather than irreversible.

Process Tracing Tests for Path Dependence

This first hoop test fails. While the costs of abandoning non-alliance may have been too high for Sweden during the period of 1990 to 2009, the costs of abandoning neutrality were not. The most illustrative example of this argument is the complete reversal of opinion, which the Parliamentary Standing Committee on Foreign Affairs underwent in little over a year between 1988 and 1989. While in early 1988, the Standing Committee decided that Swedish neutrality was not compatible with EC membership, it argued that it was possible in late 1989 (Carlsnaes 1993, 82). The arguments they advanced in support of this sudden change clash directly with path dependent reasoning. The first was that unlike other neutrals, Sweden was not bound either by international law or constitutional considerations in its neutrality policy and that it could hence adapt to changing international conditions as it saw fit (Carlsnaes 1993, 82). The second argument was that since the end of the Cold War, a functioning all European security and cooperative structure had become feasible and that hence, a substantive change in policy would be justified for the first time (Carlsnaes 1993, 83). If neutrality had been a path dependent institution for Sweden, it would have been able to resist this critical moment.

These arguments do not apply to non-alliance, however. In fact, the Swedish public has consistently declined to join NATO in national opinion polls (Vaahtoranta and Forsberg 2000, 36; Novus 2014; Reuters 2014). It was only in October 2014 that a survey conducted by the polling firm Novus revealed that an extremely narrow margin of 1 percent of Swedish citizens polled were in favor of joining NATO. As shown in Figure 3.4, 37 percent of Swedes were in favor of joining NATO in October 2014, while 36 percent were against (Novus 2014). This represents a substantial increase from only 31 percent in April of 2014, but only a slight increase from 35 percent polled in April of 2013.

Prime Minister Stefan Lofven was nevertheless swift to rule out NATO membership and it is likely that he did so on account of three reasons (Reuters 2014; Bring 2016). The first is that joining NATO would in all likelihood have entailed a national consultative referendum (Bring 2016). This would have been very risky. The margin between the supporters and the opponents of NATO membership was only one percent, which in all likelihood fell within the margin of error that the polling firm Novus did not actually report. In addition, there was a substantial number of undecided voters. Secondly, according to Ove Bring, Sweden would only consider joining NATO if Finland did the same (Bring 2016). Lastly, because of this, if both Sweden and

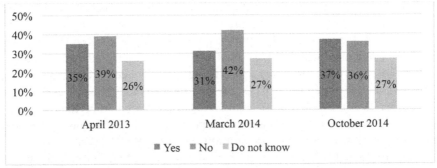

Figure 3.4   Public Opinion Poll on Swedish NATO Membership of October 2014.

Finland were to join NATO, this would have drastically altered the security constellation in the Baltic region and the effects of this on relations with the Russian Federation might have been adverse (Vaahtoranta and Forsberg 2000, 68). Therefore, this hoop test fails, seeing as the costs for abandoning neutrality were low in the aftermath of Sweden's accession to the Cold War, while costs of abandoning non-alliance remained high.

Recall that the nature of a smoking gun test is such that an explanation is only sufficient, if this test holds. This is not so for path dependence in the case of Sweden, because the costs of abandoning neutrality declined for Sweden at the end of the Cold War. The same cannot be said for non-alliance even though the costs of abandoning non-alliance arguably declined as well.

Those in favor of path dependence have argued that neutrality has become a central tenet of Swedish national identity over time (Dahl 1997). However, seeing as neutrality has never formed part of Swedish law or of the Swedish constitution, only of Swedish foreign policy, it is neither formally institutionalized nor is the public directly involved in the process of its formulation. Furthermore, after the end of the Cold War, public discussion increasingly turned on neutrality. Especially in light of Sweden's EU membership, it appeared to many journalists, commentators, politicians and academics, like Sweden ought to abandon neutrality and to contribute to the Western security community (Malmborg 2001, 170). According to Mikael Af Malmborg, "It was a matter of bringing Swedish official foreign policy and self-understanding in harmony with long-since clear economic, political and partly military affiliation with the West" (Malmborg 2001, 170). Further, according to Lee Miles, "In essence, rationales for Swedish neutrality had declined as Europe and its bloc arrangement was revised" (Miles 1997, 96). It was on the basis of these considerations, that it was possible to drastically reformulate neutrality policy in 1992 and to abolish it in 2002.

The effect of these policy changes were to decouple neutrality and non-alliance from each other, abandoning the former, while retaining the latter. Yet despite the costs associated with NATO membership in terms of public opinion discussed before, this is strange because the physical costs of joining NATO had actually declined by the end of the Cold War and especially in light of its PfP agreement of 1994. Despite refusing to join NATO in 1949, Sweden cooperated with NATO covertly throughout the Cold War, installing secret lines of communication, permitting NATO overflights and preparing Swedish air bases for NATO aircraft, for instance (Nilsson 2009, 287; Tunander 1999). Sweden's PfP with NATO of 1994 could be interpreted as the logical continuation of long-term cooperation and it subsequently became one of the closest forms of cooperation of any PfP state (Dahl 2011, 10). As an article in *The Economist* pointed out in 2014, Sweden participates in NATO exercises, commits troops to the NATO rapid reaction force and takes part in out-of-area peacekeeping operations (*The Economist* 2014). Further, in 1997, Sweden established a PfP training center and joined the Euro-Atlantic Partnership Council (Vaahtoranta and Forsberg 2000, 16). In fact, as the *The Economist* has also pointed out, Sweden actually incurs a cost by not joining NATO, namely that of not being able to participate in its decision-making structure (*The Economist* 2014).

It hence appears to me that the costs of abandoning neutrality appeared to have declined especially after the end of the Cold War and in light of the fact that neutrality has never become formally institutionalized in Sweden. Yet the costs of abandoning non-alliance, although in my opinion, on the decline especially after the end of the Cold War, have remained too high for Sweden to date. This has led to a split between the two, which I believe is uncharacteristic of path dependence. I will therefore proceed to apply my process tracing tests for the theory of ontological security.

Process Tracing Test for Ontological Security

In my opinion, abandoning neutrality in favor of non-alliance indicates that Sweden strongly passes this hoop test. I believe that it did so in order to accommodate itself to the EU. Yet it also influenced the EU to accommodate its non-alliance.

The main causal process observations for this hoop test are three reformulations of Swedish neutrality policy in 1992, 2002 and 2009. The first reformed Swedish neutrality to "non-participation in alliances during peacetime, aiming at neutrality in the event of war." The second reformed the first into "non-participation in military alliances with the aim of making it possible for [Sweden] to remain neutral in the event of war in our vicinity" (Riksdag 2001). Lastly, the so-called Solidarity Declaration of 2009 may by some be interpreted as the complete abandonment of neutrality, because it reassured its Nordic neighbors and fellow EU members that Sweden would not remain passive in the event of an act of aggression (Möller and Bjerfeld 2010, 365; Winnerstig 2014, 41).

However, bearing in mind this reconfiguration of Swedish foreign and defence policy, it is important to bear in mind that Sweden did not merely abandon its neutrality in order to appeal to the EU. In fact, Sweden has considerably influenced the EU such as to make its rules and regulations compatible with non-alliance as well, and therein lies a significant aspect of Sweden's accommodation process with the EU. Once in the EU, both Sweden and Finland were able to influence the CFSP. The most prominent CPO in this context were the Petersberg Tasks of 1992 and the Amsterdam Treaty of 1997. The initial aim of the Amsterdam Treaty had been to incorporate the WEU into the EU and hence to expand the collective defence capabilities of the EU (Malmborg 2001, 184). However, as a result of Swedish and Finnish lobbying, these ambitions were limited to crisis management, humanitarian, and rescue operations, as well as peacekeeping, contained in the Petersberg Tasks (Malmborg 2001, 184; Vaahtoranta and Forsberg 2000, 14). As such, both Sweden and Finland could remain non-allied within the context of the EU and outside of NATO and this is in itself indicative of a reformed Swedish policy on neutrality and non-alliance.

At this stage, recall the Swedish and the Finnish Solidarity Declarations of 2009, which stipulate that neither state would remain passive if another EU state or a Nordic neighbor were to experience an act of aggression or a natural disaster. In addition, they expected solidarity to be reciprocal (Dahl 2011, 10). It is important to note that although they may resemble NATO's Article 5, these declarations were purely unilateral and included no precise political or military commitments. In other words, they were therefore reversible.

According to Nils Andrén, "Whatever its formal justification, the status of neutrality is basically an adjustment to the international environment" (Andrén 1989, 175). I disagree with this statement, because Sweden has so far been willing to accept almost everything in the field of security cooperation since the end of the Cold War except collective defence (Vaahtoranta and Forsberg 2000, 6). While Sweden agreed to actively and constructively participate in the EU, it excluded military guarantees and it was only ever an observer to the WEU. Furthermore, as mentioned previously, both Sweden and Finland actively promoted the so-called Petersberg Tasks of 1992, which effectively reduced the military mandate of the WEU to that of crisis management, humanitarian, and peacekeeping tasks both prior to and after their incorporation into the Treaty of the EU during the Summit of Amsterdam of 1997. Further, where the Treaty of Lisbon is concerned, Sweden remains protected from its collective security obligations under Article 42.7 by the so-called Irish clause within that same article, which stipulates that obligations of aid and assistance "shall not prejudice the specific character of the security and defence policy of certain Member States" (EU 2007).

Lastly, the reason why non-alliance is irreversible whereas neutrality has been reversible for Sweden is not very enigmatic at all. Firstly, entering an alliance entails a treaty obligation and secondly, as mentioned before, it would entail a consultative referendum. These hurdles did not exist for Swedish neutrality, because Swedish neutrality has only ever been a policy and never a legal commitment. As such, it has been continuously adjusted over the past two decades. However, this has been an elite-led process and according to Ove Bring, this means most Swedish citizens still perceive Sweden to be neutral (Bring 2016). This, in conjunction with the skepticism that remains prevalent among the Swedish public with regards to NATO, is an almost certain guarantee that any consultative referendum on NATO membership would fail. In other words, although Sweden has adjusted its neutrality to the prevailing spirit of solidarity in post-Cold War Europe, it has taken only reversible steps in this direction and like Switzerland, it has not chosen any foreign policy options that would be irreversible and maladaptive, the paradoxical reason for this being the continued attachment of the Swedish public to neutrality as a source of national identity. In conclusion, therefore, I argue that ontological security theory can explain why Sweden abandoned neutrality and retained non-alliance after the end of the Cold War, while path dependence cannot.

CASE STUDY: AUSTRIA

This leaves Austria as the final case study. Austria is a case, which I believe underwent two critical moments: Austria's accession to the EU in 1995, yet prior to it, the Single European Act of 1986. The latter formulated the goal of the EC to establish a single European market by December 31, 1992 and to pursue a coordinated foreign and security policy under the framework of European Political Cooperation, the forerunner of the CFSP (EU 2010; Lantis and Queen 1998, 155). This presented Austria with a problem. On one hand, Austria desired inclusion into the European market and it appeared as though Austria would be left at a major economic disadvantage if it were to be left outside of it (Bundeskanzleramt 2001; Gehler and Kaiser 1997, 95). On the other hand, according to the Austrian Constitutional Federal Statute of 1955, its neutrality served "the purpose of the permanent maintenance of its external independence" (Bundeskanzleramt 1955).

The Austrian government under Franz Vranitzky attempted to circumnavigate this issue in its report to the Austrian legislature entitled "On the Future Arrangement of Austrian Relations to the European Communities" of the 17th of April 1989. The report stated that, with its application, Austria expresses its desire to participate fully in European integration and that it is therefore prepared to adopt the rights and responsibilities of an EC member state, while retaining its status of permanent neutrality (CVCE 2012).

However, following an overwhelmingly positive referendum in 1994, in which 66.6 percent of voters consented to EC membership with a voter turnout of 81 percent, Austria entered the EU on January 1, 1995 without any significant reservations concerning its neutrality (Bundesministerium für Inneres 1994; Bundeskanzleramt 2001). A number of developments ensued from this, which were unfavorable for Austrian neutrality. Following the Maastricht Treaty of 1992, the Treaty of Amsterdam of 1997 further refined and enhanced the CSDP. First of all, it fused the decision-making

and the operational aspects of the WEU and the CSDP. Secondly, it incorpo-
rated a collective defence obligation into the Treaty of the European Union
(Gustenau 2000, 1). These developments stood in contradiction to Austrian
neutrality and arguably represented the very reason why Austria refrained
from joining the EC for most of the Cold War. What is puzzling about this is
that to date, the Constitutional Federal Statute of 1955 remains in place. Especially the Social Democratic Party, Sozialdemokratische Partei Österreichs
(SPÖ), and the Green Party have prevented any changes to this article of the
constitution to date (Gehler 2014, 567). Hence, this once again raises the
question, why has Austria remained neutral during the post-Cold War period?

Process Tracing Tests for Path Dependence

As mentioned before, Austria's permanent neutrality remains enshrined in its
constitution to date. In fact, no amendments have been attempted to remove
permanent neutrality from the Austrian constitution (Schilchegger 2011, 16).
This is indicative of the fact that neutrality is not something that Austria could
easily give up, even in light of its accession to the EU in 1995. It is further
indicative of path dependence, because if anything is a mark of institutionalization, forming part of a state's constitution is it. This is because changing
the constitution, in the parlance of path dependence, is costly.

Bearing this in mind, however, while removing Austria's permanent
neutrality has not been attempted to date, joining the EU clearly has been
attempted successfully, despite the fact that throughout the Cold War, the
two were regarded as mutually exclusive. This is puzzling. In fact, in terms
of legal hurdles, joining the EU was roughly equally costly as abandoning
neutrality. According to the Austrian constitution, both required a two-thirds
majority support in parliament in addition to approval by the Federal Council
and a binding popular referendum (Lantis and Queen 1998, 155). Furthermore, both required the consent of the four former occupying powers, who
had agreed to Austrian neutrality on April 5, 1955 and, in the case of EU
accession, it required the consent of the EU itself (Ionescu 1968, 413).

These costs were evidently not insurmountable when Austria applied for
EU membership. Some political parties even considered EU membership
a logical extension of previous trade agreements with the EC. Predictably,
both government parties at the time, the SPÖ and the moderately conservative Österreichische Volkspartei (ÖVP), campaigned strongly in support of
EU membership, arguing mainly that it would secure economic growth and
competitiveness, as well as employment (Luther 1995, 128). The only party
that opposed the planned membership was the right-wing Freiheitliche Partei
Österreichs (FPÖ). Strikingly, all major interest groups were also in support
of membership, including environmental organizations, corporate lobby

groups, unions and the majority of the media (Gehler and Kaiser 1997, 96). This preordained both the required two-third majority in parliament and the approval by parliament. Lastly, as mentioned previously, the popular referendum of the 12th of June 1994 produced an overwhelming majority of 66.6 percent in favor with a voter turnout of 81 percent.

Hence, while path dependence fulfils the first necessary condition, that giving up neutrality remains too costly for Austria, joining the EU despite permanent neutrality has not been. In other words, the interpretation of the compatibility between neutrality and EC membership has changed. This in turn is important, because it could also be indicative of the fact that Austria may simply be reforming the routines of its neutrality in the manner that ontological security theory suggests. In other words, this hoop test confirms path dependence, because it attests to the persistence of neutrality, but it does not exclude ontological security.

In order for path dependence to serve as a sufficient explanation, there also needs to be evidence that the costs of abandoning neutrality have also increased over the course of its history as a result of its institutionalization. I will argue here that this was in fact not the case.

I believe that in fact, a number of developments took place within the EU which actually made neutrality costlier to maintain. This is because it was arguably in contradiction with Austria's obligations under the Treaty of Maastricht of 1992, the Treaty of Amsterdam of 1997 and the Treaty of Lisbon of 2007. These treaties obliged Austria to participate in the EU's CFSP, which essentially contradicts the Constitutional Federal Statute of 1955. The latter states that the purpose of Austrian neutrality is that of independence (Bundeskanzleramt 1955, Art. 1).

Instead of voicing concerns, however, Austria amended its constitution. Article 23(f) henceforth stipulated that Austria would participate in the CFSP on the basis of the Treaty of Amsterdam of 1997 (Bundeskanzleramt 1998, Art. 23f (1)). It was updated regularly and replaced by Article 23(j) and to refer to the Treaty of Lisbon after 2007. According to this article, decisions by the European Council concerning the defence of the EU and the integration of the WEU into the EU would require the adoption of a corresponding resolution by both chambers of the Austrian legislature (Bundeskanzleramt 1998, Art. 23f (1)). In its Neutrality Doctrine of 2001, however, the government of Wolfgang Schüssel even interpreted Article 23(f) to mean that Austria's participation in the CSDP would no longer be impaired by neutrality (Bundeskanzleramt 2001). Even more explicitly, the doctrine stipulated that as a result of its unconditional participation in the CFSP, Austria's "status of permanent neutrality had changed enduringly" and furthermore that, "In international comparison, Austria's status under international law no longer corresponds to neutrality but to non-alliance" (Bundeskanzleramt 2001).

Hence, the conclusion to draw from this is that while neutrality may have been resistant to the critical moment of 1986, it was not thoroughly resistant to the critical moment of 1995 and subsequently underwent significant changes. Because this test was a smoking gun test, however, only passing it can render path dependence a sufficiently convincing explanation of the persistence of Austrian neutrality during the post-Cold War period.

Process Tracing Tests for Ontological Security

In light of the previous, I believe it is appropriate to say that Austria reformed its routines where both neutrality and the EU are concerned. However, it also altered its respective relationships with the UN and NATO. Where the UN was concerned, Austria gave precedence to UN Security Council resolutions over neutrality law as a result of the First Gulf War of 1990. In this respect, it was very similar to Switzerland (Bundeskanzleramt 2001; Gustenau 2000, 5). Its relations with NATO were also similar to those of both Switzerland and Sweden after joining the PfP in 1995. Austria was the third-largest contributor to the Kosovo Force (KFOR) and the largest contributor to the Stabilization Force in Bosnia (SFOR). In addition to this, it provided logistic support, communication units and liaison officers on a regular basis (Gärtner 2016, 4). However, it remained outside of the NATO alliance. The SPÖ-ÖVP government of Viktor Klima did propose the so-called Options Report of 1998, which initiated a discussion on Austria's potential membership of NATO. The report failed to gather sufficient support among Austria's political parties, however (Gehler 2014, 566).

Overall, Austria remains neutral under constitutional law to date, while adhering to Security Council decisions and participating in NATO's PfP. Where the EU is concerned, it is important to bear in mind that both Articles 23(f) and 23(j) did not derogate neutrality. Strictly speaking, they were additions and not amendments to the constitution. The Constitutional Federal Statute of the 26th of October 1955 has never been changed (Schilchegger 2011, 16, 20). Furthermore, Art. 42(7) allows Austria to exempt itself from any collective security obligations within the CFSP. Hence, ontological security passes this test. Austria has accommodated its neutrality to the demands for solidarity from the UN, NATO and the EU, yet without making irreversible legal commitments. The core principles of Austrian neutrality remain intact and Austria may not join a military alliance, participate in a war or station foreign troops on its territory (Feichtinger 2016).

Just as in the cases of Switzerland and Sweden, I would argue that successive Austrian governments since those of Chancellor Franz Vranitzky have implicitly made a distinction between reversible and irreversible foreign policy options where their impact on Austrian neutrality is concerned.

The following foreign policy changes are reversible in my opinion: The policy that UN Security Council resolutions trump Austrian neutrality commitments and Austria's commitment to participate in peacekeeping operations that carry a UN Security Council mandate. These provisions are contained in Article 23(j) of the Austrian constitution, as is its commitment to the CFSP, which I also think is reversible. Some argue Article 23(j) derogates and even suspends neutrality vis-à-vis the EU. The reason why I disagree and why I refer to the obligations contained within this article as reversible is because since the publication of Article 23(f) in 2012, this article has been amended successively. Furthermore, it now refers to Austria's commitment to the CFSP as it is formulated in the Treaty of Lisbon of 2007. Yet as of the Treaty of Lisbon, Austrian neutrality is protected by the so-called Irish Clause contained in Article 42(7), because it "shall not prejudice the specific character of the security and defence policy of certain Member States" (EU 2007). In other words, it is true that Austria has pursued a number of foreign policy options which were not compatible with neutrality in theory.

Yet in practice, the Constitutional Federal Statute of the 26th of October 1955 persists (Feichtinge 2016; Winkler 2016; Gärtner 2016). I would further argue that it has persisted because firstly, abandoning it would have been an irreversible decision and secondly, it would have undermined the sole remaining function of neutrality: Its identity function (Feichtinger 2016). Reconciling Austrian neutrality with its security needs and its security needs with those of the EU have effectively side-lined the contribution that neutrality has made to Austrian physical security over the course of the Cold War, namely its ability to credibly withdraw from great power politics. As shown just before, however, the steps that have been taken towards this end during the Cold War period are reversible without exception. The one irreversible step, that of joining an alliance, has been decisively rejected. Recall the Options Report of 1998, which introduced the possibility of Austria's NATO membership. It failed decisively as no other political party besides the ÖVP was willing to support it. Since then, there has emerged a solid consensus on this matter among both Austria's political elite and its citizens. For this reason, and bearing in mind the distinction between reversible and irreversible reforms, ontological security passes this test.

CONCLUSION

To conclude, therefore, the process tracing tests that I have applied to each case study have revealed that the theory of ontological security appears to render a more nuanced explanation for the ambiguous persistence of

Table 3.1   Process Tracing Test Results

	Path Dependence		Ontological Security	
	Hoop Test	Smoking Gun Test	Hoop Test	Smoking Gun Test
Switzerland	Pass	Fail	Pass	Pass
Sweden	Fail	Fail	Pass	Pass
Austria	Pass	Fail	Pass	Pass

neutrality in post-Cold War Europe than does path dependence. This conclusion can be deduced from Table 3.1.

Table 3.1 shows that in the cases of Switzerland and Austria, path dependence passed its hoop tests, namely that the costs of abandoning neutrality at the time of the critical moment were too high. This means that path dependence meets the necessary conditions in order to be able to explain the persistence of neutrality for each of these cases. It does not meet the necessary conditions in the case of Sweden. Furthermore, path dependence fails its smoking gun test for all three cases. This is because there was no sufficiently compelling evidence that the costs of maintaining neutrality increased over time, which is the hallmark of path dependence. If path dependence were to apply, there ought to be evidence that reversal of the path becomes costlier, the further one has taken the path. However, what this test has revealed in most cases is that in fact, the circumstances for making changes to neutrality policy actually became beneficial during the post-Cold War period.

Hence, as may also be deduced from Table 3.1, the theory of ontological security passes all of its tests for all of its cases. This is also why at first glance ontological security may be accepted as a sufficiently convincing explanation for the persistence of neutrality in post-Cold War Europe. However, I have also tried to show that the relatively new theory of ontological security is in need of refinement. The principal reason for this is that it extrapolates from the level of the individual to the level of the state without distinguishing between the sentiments of its political elites and its citizens. In each of the cases covered in this study, the two are interdependent and the intricacies of this interdependence matter.

Over the course of conducting my process tracing tests, I have come to find that political elites have been more prone to adapt neutrality to the external circumstances prevailing in the aftermath of a critical moment, while citizens of each state considered here have been much more reluctant to do so. This, in addition to binding international treaty commitments in the cases of Switzerland and Austria, has hindered policymakers in these two states to encroach upon neutrality. In the case of Sweden, which has no international treaty obligations to be neutral, neutrality was actually phased out to the point of rendering Sweden a non-allied state. However, changes to its routine have gone no further than this.

Reversible and Irreversible Foreign Policy in Ontological Security Theory

The question is why? The answer is this: Going any further, in the case of each of these three states, would have entailed an irreversible divergence from neutrality or non-alliance. This is different from path dependence, which argues not that the divergence from an institution is irreversible, but that the institution itself is irreversible. This difference is important and it is the principal reason why path dependence is not sufficiently compelling. What needs to be explained is the reluctance of neutrals to diverge irreversibly from neutrality and non-alliance.

Ontological security theory could account for this. In accommodating their routines, each state discussed here has embarked on a number of foreign policy options, which were reversible and which did not entail either international legal commitments or domestic referenda to change the role of neutrality in the constitution. In order to better account not only for the persistence of neutrality, but perhaps other phenomena in International Relations as well, the theory of ontological security needs to differentiate between reversible and irreversible foreign policy options to accommodate existing routines to critical moments. While reversible policy changes may protect a state's ontological security, irreversible or maladaptive foreign policy changes may threaten it further. Neutrality is a clear instance of a healthy routine rather than a maladaptive one. As such it requires flexibility and reversibility.

NOTES

1. Note that the term military nonalignment is here understood to be synonymous with non-alliance, not with the Cold War nonaligned movement.

2. The Riksdag is the unicameral Swedish legislature.

3. Also see Pernille Rieker, 2002. *From Territorial Defense to Comprehensive Security? European Integration and the Changing Norwegian and Swedish Security Identities*. Oslo: Norsk Utenrikspolitisk Institutt. Available at: http://webcache.google-usercontent.com/search?q=cache:DmtGfw3lFQIJ:mercury.ethz.ch/serviceengine/Files/ISN/27374/ipublicationdocument_singledocument/90eefbe1–6079–487d-8976–443b2cc71e9a/en/626.pdf+&cd=1&hl=en&ct=clnk&gl=ch&client=safari [Accessed November 18, 2015]; Lee Miles, 1997. "Sweden and Security." In *The 1995 Enlargement of the European Union*, edited by John Redmond, 97. Aldershot: Ashgate.

BIBLIOGRAPHY

Af Malmborg, Mikael. 2001. *Neutrality and State-Building in Sweden*. Basingstoke: Palgrave.

Andrén, Nils. 1989. "Swedish defence: Traditions, perceptions and policies." In *Between the Blocs: Problems and Prospects for Europe's Neutral and Non-Aligned States,* edited by Joseph Kruzel and Michael H. Haltzel, 175–199. New York: Woodrow Wilson International Center for Scholars.

Arthur, W. Brian. 1994. *Increasing Returns and Path Dependence in the Economy.* Ann Arbor: University of Michigan Press.

Åström, Sverker. 1989. "Swedish Neutrality: Credibility Through Commitment and Consistency." In *The Committed Neutral: Sweden's Foreign Policy,* edited by Bengt Sundelius, 15–33. Boulder: Westview Press.

Bayley, Martin J. 2015. "Imperial ontological (in)security: 'Buffer states', IR and the case of Anglo-Afghan relations, 1808–1878." *European Journal of International Relations* 21(4): 816–840.

Bennett, Andrew. 2008. "Process Tracing: A Bayesian Perspective." In *The Oxford Handbook of Political Methodology,* edited by Janet M. Box-Steffensmeier, Henry Brady, and David Collier, 703–721. Oxford: Oxford University Press.

Boczek, Boleslaw A. 1989. "Introduction: The Conceptual and Legal Framework of Neutrality and Nonalignment in Europe." In *Europe's Neutral and Non-Aligned States: Between NATO and the Warsaw Pact,* edited by S. Victor Papacosma and Mark R. Rubin, 1–42. Wilmington: Scholarly Resources.

Bring, Ove. 2016. *Interview on Swedish Neutrality.* Interviewed by Liliane Stadler [telephone interview] March 13, 2016, 9:00.

Browning, Christopher and Pertti Joenniemi. 2013. "From Fratricide to Security Community: Re-theorising Difference in the Constitution of Nordic Peace." *Journal of International Relations and Development* 16: 483–513.

Bundeskanzleramt. 1955. *Bundesverfassungsgesetz vom 26. Oktober 1955 über die Neutralität Österreichs.* https://www.ris.bka.gv.at/GeltendeFassung.wxe?Abfrage =Bundesnormen&Gesetzesnummer=10000267.

———. 1998. *83. Bundesverfassungsgesetz: Änderung des Bundes-Verfassungsgesetzes (NR: GP XX IA 791/A AB 1255 S. 130. BR: AB 5691 S. 642.)* https://www. ris.bka.gv.at/Dokumente/BgblPdf/1998_83_1/1998_83_1.pdf.

Bundeskanzleramt. 2001. *Sicherheits- und Verteidigungsdoktrin.* http://www.bka. gv.at/2004/4/4/doktrin_d.pdf.

Bundesministerium für Inneres. 1994. *Ergebnisse bisheriger Volksabstimmungen.* http://www.bmi.gv.at/cms/BMI_wahlen/volksabstimmung/Ergebnisse.aspx.

Bundesrat. 1999. *Sicherheit durch Kooperation: Bericht des Bundesrates an die Bundesversammlung über die Sicherheitspolitik der Schweiz (SIPOL 2000).* Bern: EDA.

Carlsnaes, Walter. 1993. "Sweden Facing the New Europe: Whither Neutrality?" *European Security* 2(1): 71–89.

Centre Virtuel de la Connaissance sur l'Europe (CVCE). 2012. *Bericht der Bundesregierung über die Beziehungen Österreichs zu den Europäischen Gemeinschaften: Auszug über den Binnenmarkt und über die Neutralität (1989).* Wien: Bundesregierung. http://www.cvce.eu/content/publication/2006/7/17/ bac95640–902b-414a-b8f6-b9f3cf26ccdc/publishable_de.pdf.

Cottey, Andrew. 2013. "The European Neutrals and NATO: Ambiguous Partnership." *Contemporary Security Policy* 34(3): 446–472.

Crouch, Colin and Farrell Henry. 2004. "Breaking the Path of Institutional Development? Alternatives to the New Determinism." *Rationality and Society* 16(1): 5–43.

Cupać, Jelena. 2012. "Ontological Security of International Organizations: NATO's Post-Cold War Identity Crisis and 'Out-of-Area' Interventions." *СИНТЕЗИС* 4(1): 19–43.

Dahl, Ann-Sofie. 1997. "Not If But How: Sweden's Future Relations with NATO." *NATO Review* [e-journal] 45(3): 19–22. http://www.nato.int/docu/review/1997/9703–5.htm.

———. 2011. "Sweden, Finland and NATO: Security Partners and Security Producers." In *Nordic-Baltic Security in the 21st Century: The Regional Agenda and the Global Role*, edited by Robert Nurick and Magnus Nordenman, 6–11.Washington DC: The Atlantic Council.

Eidgenössisches Departement für auswertige Angelegenheiten (EDA). 1993. *Bericht zur Neutralität*. Bern: EDA.

———. 2000. *Swiss Neutrality in Practice—Current Aspects*. Bern: EDA.

———. 2015. *Das Wichtigste zur Schweizer Neutralität*. https://www.eda.admin.ch/content/dam/eda/de/documents/aussenpolitik/voelkerrecht/PDF_Haupttext_Neutralitaet_de_06_.pdf

European Union (EU). 2007. *Treaty of Lisbon Amending the Treaty of the European Union and the Treaty Establishing the European Community*. European Union. Available at: http://eur-lex.europa.eu/legal-content/EN/TXT/?uri=celex%3A12007L%2FTXT.

———. 2010. *Single European Act*. European Union. http://www.consilium.europa.eu/uedocs/cmsUpload/SingleEuropeanAct_Crest.pdf.

Feichtinger, Walter. 2016. *Interview on Austrian Neutrality*. Interviewed by Liliane Stadler [telephone interview] 29th of March 2016, 16:00.

Fischer, Peter, Heribert Franz Köck and Alfred Verdross. 1980. *Völkerrecht und Rechtsphilosophie*. Berlin: Duncker & Humblot.

Gärtner, Heinz. 2016. *Interview on Austrian Neutrality*. Interviewed by Liliane Stadler [telephone interview] March 30, 2016, 13:00.

———. (in press). "Austria: Engaged Neutrality." In *The European Neutrals and NATO*, edited by Andrew Cottey, 1–14. Basingstoke: Palgrave.

Gehler, Michael. 2001. *Finis Neutralität? Historische und Politische Aspekte im Europäischen Vergleich: Irland, Finnland, Schweden, Schweiz und Österreich*. Bonn: Zentrum für Europäische Integrationsforschung.

———. 2014. "Vom Friedensvertrag von Saint-Germain bis zum EU-Vertrag von Lissabon: Österreichs Weg in die Europäische Union mit seiner langen Vorgeschichte (1919–2009)." In *Österreich und die Europäische Integration seit 1945: Aspekte einer wechselvollen Entwicklung*, edited by Michael Gehler and Rolf Steininger, 531–580. Wien: Böhlau Verlag.

Gehler, Michael and Wolfram Kaiser. 1997. "A Study in Ambivalence: Austria and European Integration 1945–95." *Contemporary European History* 6(1): 75–99.

Gerard, Alexander. 2001. "Institutions, Path Dependence and Democratic Consolidation." *Journal of Theoretical Politics* 13(3): 249–70.

Goertz, Gary and James Mahoney. 2012. *A Tale of Two Cultures: Qualitative and Quantitative Research in the Social Sciences.* Princeton: Princeton University Press.

Goetschel, Laurent. 2011. "Neutrals as brokers of peacebuilding ideas?" *Cooperation and Conflict* 46(3): 312–333.

———. 2016. *Interview on Swiss Neutrality.* Interviewed by Liliane Stadler [interview in person] February 22, 2016, 17:00.

Goldman, Kjell. 1991. "The Swedish Model of Security Policy." *West European Politics* 14(3): 122–143.

Gustenau, Gustav E. 2000. "Die Europäische Gemeinsame Außen- und Sicherheitspolitik—eine Herausforderung für die 'Post-Neutralen'?" *Sicherheitspolitischer Dialog Österreich—Slowenien* 2: 1–12.

Hakovirta, Harto. 1988. *East-West Conflict and European Neutrality.* Oxford: Clarendon Press.

Helsingin Sanomat. 2002. Prime Minister insists Sweden will not join NATO. http://www2.hs.fi/english/archive/news.asp?id=20021111IE2.

Hjelm-Wallén, Lena. 2016. *Interview on Swedish Neutrality.* Interviewed by Liliane Stadler [telephone interview] February 23, 2016, 10:00.

Ifantis, Kostas and Sotiris Serbos. 2013. "OSCE: A Natural Home for Europe's Neutrals?" *International Journal of Humanities and Social Science* 3(11): 212–222.

Ionescu, Ghita 1968. "The Austrian State Treaty and Neutrality in Eastern Europe." *International Journal* 23(3): 408–420.

Lantis, Jeffrey and Matthew F. Queen. 1998. "Negotiating Neutrality: The Double-Edged Diplomacy of Austrian Accession to the European Union." *Cooperation and Conflict* 33(2): 152–182.

Lezzi, Bruno. 2016. *Interview on Swiss Neutrality.* Interviewed by Liliane Stadler [personal interview] January 14, 2016, 15:00.

Logue, John. 1989. "The Legacy of Swedish Neutrality." In *The Committed Neutral: Sweden's Foreign Policy,* edited by Bengt Sundelius, 35–66. Boulder: Westview Press.

Luther, Kurt Richard. 1995. "An End to the Politics of Isolation? Austria in Light of the 1994 Elections." *German Politics* 4(1): 122–140.

Mahoney, James. 2000. "Path Dependence in Historical Sociology." *Theory and Society* 29(4): 507–548.

Mahoney, James and Daniel Schensul. 2006. "Hisotrical Context and Path Dependence." In *The Oxford Handbook of Contextual Political Analysis,* edited by Robert E. Goodin and Charles Tilly, 454–471. Oxford, Oxford University Press.

Miles, Lee. 1997. "Sweden and Security." In *The 1995 Enlargement of the European Union,* edited by John Redmond, 86–124. Aldershot: Ashgate.

Mitzen, Jennifer. 2004. "Ontological Security in World Politics and Implications for the Study of European Security." *CIDEL Workshop—From Civilian to Military Power: The European Union at a Crossroads.* Oslo, Norway, 22–23 October 2004. Columbus: The Ohio State University.

————. 2006. "Ontological Security in World Politics: State Identity and the Security Dilemma." *European Journal of International Relations* 12(3): 341–370.

Möller, Ulrika and Ulf Bjerfeld. 2010. "From Nordic Neutrals to Post-Neutral Europeans: Differences in Finnish and Swedish Policy Transformation." *Cooperation and Conflict* 45(4): 363–386.

Neuhold, Hanspeter. 1982. "Permanent Neutrality on Contemporary International Relations: A Comparative Perspective." *Irish Studies in International Affairs* 1(3): 13–26.

————. 1988. "The Neutral States of Europe: Similarities and Differences." In *Neutrality: Changing Concepts and Practices,* edited by Alan T. Leonhard and Nicholas Mercuro, 97–144. New York.

Nilsson, Mikael. 2009. "Amber Nine: NATO's Secret Use of a Flight Path over Sweden and the Incorporation of Sweden in NATO's Infrastructure." *Journal of Contemporary History* 44(2): 287–307.

Novus. 2014. *TV4 Novus om Nato och beredskap.* http://novus.se/nyhet/tv4-novus-om-nato-och-beredskap/.

Reuters. 2014. *Poll Shows More Swedes in Favour of NATO for First Time.* http://www.reuters.com/article/us-sweden-nato-idUSKBN0II1XN20141029.

Rieker, Pernille. 2002. *From Territorial Defense to Comprehensive Security? European Integration and the Changing Norwegian and Swedish Security Identities.* Oslo: Norsk Utenrikspolitisk Institutt. http://webcache.googleusercontent.com/search?q=cache:DmtGfw3lFQIJ:mercury.ethz.ch/serviceengine/Files/ISN/27374/ipublicationdocument_singledocument/90eefbe1–6079–487d-8976–443b2c-c71e9a/en/626.pdf+&cd=1&hl=en&ct=clnk&gl=ch&client=safari.

————. 2004. "Europeanization of Nordic Security: The European Union and the Changing Security Identities of the Nordic States." *Cooperation and Conflict: Journal of the Nordic International Studies Association* 39(4): 369–392.

Riksdag. 2001. *Riksdagens snabbprotokoll 2000/01:62 Onsdagen den 7 februari.* http://www.riksdagen.se/sv/Dokument-Lagar/Kammaren/Protokoll/Riksdagens-snabbprotokoll-2000_GO0962/?html=true.

Schaub, Adrian R. 1995. *Neutralität und Kollektive Sicherheit: Gegenüberstellung zweier unvereinbarer Verhaltenskonzepte in bewaffneten Konflikten und These zu einem zeit- und völkerrechtsgemässem modus vivendi.* Basel: Lichtenhahn.

Schilchegger, Michael. 2011. "Die österreichische Neutralität nach Lissabon." *ZÖR* 66(5): 5–24.

Schmid, Samuel. 2016. *Interview on Swiss Neutrality.* Interviewed by Liliane Stadler [interview in person] February 22, 2016, 11:00.

Steele, Brendt. 2005. "Ontological Security and the Power of Self-Identity: British Neutrality and the American Civil War." *Review of International Studies* 31(3): 519–540.

Thalmann, Anton. 2016. *Interview on Swiss Neutrality.* Interviewed by Liliane Stadler [telephone interview] January 27, 2016, 9:30.

The Economist. 2014. What Price Neutrality? http://www.economist.com/news/europe/21604586-russia-stokes-fresh-debate-among-nordics-about-nato-member-ship-what-price-neutrality.

Trachsler, Daniel. 2011. "Von Petitpierre bis Calmy-Rey: Wiederkehrende Debatten um die Schweizer Aussenpolitik." *Bulletin zur Schweizerischen Sicherheitspolitik*: 107–136.

Tresch, et al. 2015. *Sicherheit 1015. Aussen-, Sicherheits- und Verteidigungspolitische Meinungsbildung im Trend.* Zurich: Center for Security Studies, ETH Zürich and Militärakademie an der ETH Zürich. http://www.css.ethz.ch/content/dam/ethz/special-interest/gess/cis/center-for-securities-studies/pdfs/Sicherheit-2015.pdf

Tunander, Ola. 1999. "The Uneasy Imbrication of Nation-State and NATO: The Case of Sweden." *Conflict and Cooperation* 34(2): 169–203.

Vaahtoranta, Tapani and Tuomas Forsberg. 2000. *Post-Neutral or Pre-Allied? Finnish and Swedish Policies on the EU and NATO as Security Organizations.* Helsinki: The Finnish Institute of International Affiars.

Von Däniken, Franz. 2016. *Interview on Swiss Neutrality.* Interviewed by Liliane Stadler [interview in person] February 23, 2016, 9:45.

Vukadinović, Radovan. 1989. "Various Conceptions of European Neutrality." In *Between the Blocs: Problems and Prospects for Europe's Neutral and Non-Aligned States,* edited by Joseph Kruzel and Michael H. Haltzel, 29–48. New York: Woodrow Wilson International Center for Scholars.

Waldner, David. 2015. "What makes process tracing good? Causal mechanisms, causal inference and the completeness standard in comparative politics." In *Process Tracing: From Metaphor to Analytical Tool,* edited by A. Bennett and J. T. Checkel, 126–152. Cambridge: Cambridge University Press.

Waltz, Kenneth. 1979. *Theory of International Politics.* New York: McGraw Hill.

Winkler, Hans. 2016. *Interview on Austrian Neutrality.* Interviewed by Liliane Stadler [telephone interview] March 30, 2016, 11:00.

Winnerstig, Mike. 2014. "From Neutrality to Solidarity? Sweden's Ongoing Geopolitical Reorientation." In *Advancing U.S.-Nordic-Baltic Security Cooperation,* edited by Daniel S. Hamilton, András Simonyi, and Debra Cagan, 35–47. Washington DC: Center for Transatlantic Relations (CTR).

Young, Oran. 1979. *Compliance and Public Authority: A Theory with International Applications.* Baltimore: Johns Hopkins Press.

Chapter 4

Are Neutral States Middle Powers?

Laurent Goetschel

The history of neutrality has intimately been linked to the structure of the international system: The concept emerged at a time when wars regularly threatened the existence of small states. Some of these states saw abstention from military warfare as a survival strategy. At the same time, in order not to be seen as "soulless" or uncommitted to international affairs, neutral states developed compensatory activities in the fields of humanitarian and peace policies. These two dimensions, of which the first one may be called realist and the second one idealist, have marked neutrality since its inception, though the relative weight of both dimensions has significantly varied over time and from state to state. Over the last decades, the development of international politics and technology have reduced the significance of states' size as security criteria. Neutral states who also tended to be smaller states became structurally less weak. In parallel, parts of their idealist dimension of neutrality became more relevant in international politics. So one could assume neutral states achieved a double gain in power making them "middle powers." The article provides a nuanced answer to this assumption: it adopts a differentiated view on the idealist dimension of neutrality looking into the evolution of the foreign policy role concepts of European neutral states compared to the political environment. Having become more normal or pragmatic in their peace policies, neutral states may also have lost some of their impact on international politics. The article is structured the following way: It introduces its understanding of neutrality and looks into specific power dimensions of small states before turning to a comparative analysis of the evolution of European neutral states' foreign policy role concepts and finally to some concluding remarks.[1]

THE ESSENCE OF NEUTRALITY

Neutrality emerged as a survival strategy: small states were in permanent danger of being overrun by larger ones. They were not usually primary targets, but conquering them was a way to prevent these states from either falling to one side or freely siding with the other. The consequences of being large or small were not always just relative. The categorization of states according to their territorial extension or the size of their population used to be of crucial importance. What today is called strategic depth and military manpower were essential factors which decided on the survival of states. Small states were not just smaller than others; the consequences of this relative quality could be absolute. Thus, neutrality's original purpose was to help states defend their interests in an international environment marked by interstate conflicts (Goetschel 2011a).

In a realistic perspective, this legitimate right of a neutral state not to wage war aimed at increasing its chances of maintaining its independence and territorial integrity. Neutrals also had to make some concessions, that is, to offer other states some direct interests. Well-known in this respect was neutrality's international equilibrium function: for example, Switzerland acted as the guardian of Alpine passes in monarchical Europe, served together with Austria as the "neutral separator" in Cold War Europe, and Sweden was the centerpiece of the "Nordic Balance" in the same period (Gehler 2001; Riklin 1992; Thomas 1996). However, besides these so-called realistic functions, neutrality also showed an idealistic component based on its core commitment to avert war and promote non-violent means of conflict resolution. This originated from these states' renunciation of projecting their own military power and from their commitment to restrict and regulate use of force in international relations (Joenniemi 1993). At the end of the day, neutrality was and remains far more than a tradition of standing apart and refusing to take sides in violent conflicts between third parties. Neutrality also contained ideas and norms of behavior that neutral states tried to export. For example, neutral states acted as arbitrators and mediators as well as provided their so-called "good offices" (Probst 1989).

These attributes of neutrality and its contribution to a nation's political identity build on neutrality's political core and not on its legal dimension. Neutrality was at the origin of both realistic and idealistic role conceptions. The first one emanated from neutral states' military absenteeism, the second one from the basic commitment of neutral states to regulate and limit use of force. The relative importance of both categories depends on the international structure in which neutral states operate. In a state system characterized by a clear reduction of interstate military conflicts, the idealistic role conception has gained significance compared to the realistic one. As will be shown thereafter, neutrality's role as a foreign-policy identity provider has become its most important function since the end of the Cold War. It is based on what used to be neutrality's secondary function, that is, its idealism or missionary belief. Neutral states used to be experts in compensating for their lack of military force and engagement with other power and activity dimensions. Neutrality may keep this function as long as neutral states actively contribute to promotion of peaceful international relations. Neutrality should not be seen as encouraging passive contemplation of injustice, violence, and oppression. Nor was neutrality defined as a neutral attitude towards attempts to prevent military conflicts (Goetschel 2011a).

POWER DIMENSIONS OF SMALL STATES

Historically, quantitative criteria for the qualification of a state as small or large—such as geographic extent, size of population, GNP or the number of diplomatic representations—were believed to indicate the degree to which a given state would seek to influence affairs beyond its immediate environment and, more critically, the degree to which its leaders would be prepared to assume risks in the pursuit of extra-regional ends (Vital 1971; Small and Singer 1973). It was the capacity of the state to withstand stress, on one hand, and its ability to pursue a policy of its own devising, on the other, which were traditionally seen as the key criteria of smallness (Vital 1967, 4).

The question is, to what extent this power deficit is influenced by purely quantitative factors and to what extent such factors actually influence a state's foreign and security policy (Goetschel 1998)? Small states may attempt to compensate their traditional quantitative weakness by emphasizing "qualitative" virtues, such as mediation, bridge-building, or other non-coercive means (Rothstein 1968, 26; Liska 1957, 25 ff.). Power may result out of processes and structures such as "bargaining" (Schelling 1980, 2). These power dimensions may of course also be influenced by quantitative power indicators such as military or economic resources. However, such resources will not automatically be transformed into power over outcomes. Bargaining skill and other factors linked to the structure of the negotiation process may well play a decisive role in the result. The term small state may be interpreted as encompassing the systemic role that state leaders see their country playing. A categorization can be established, which differentiates between system-determining, system-influencing, system-affecting, and system-ineffectual states. The corresponding situation must be perceived or internalized by the state concerned (Keohane 1969, 295 f.).

In this context, the continued existence of neutrality provides respective states with a comparative advantage in brokering new ideas in international relations. With their far-reaching historic track record in being both idealistic and realistic, neutral states are well positioned to further advance international norms in highly contested areas of international relations. This point is illustrated with reference to the example of peacebuilding, where it is explained why neutral states are particularly well suited to contributing to norm development in highly sovereignty-sensitive areas (Goetschel 2011b; 2013).

Small states have been used to promote new ideas in order to positively transform the international order. They have acted as innovators and as catalysts of international change. Ideas helped them to limit the relevance of hard power. They worked towards "civilization" of international relations. At the same time, active engagement in debates has provided small states with a "say" in international organizations. This has reinforced their soft power (Busek and Hummer 2004; Jakobsen 2009; Rothstein 1968).

Ideas are particularly crucial for analyzing small states' behavior, as these states have used ideas in order to form the international system according to their interests—assuming the later were in line with a more equity- and law-based international environment. For small states, ideas are both constitutive to their national identity (as they are for other states too) and a crucial foreign policy instrument to achieve their foreign policy objectives. The latter led to the qualification of Western European small states as "norm entrepreneurs" (Ingebritsen 2002). Norm entrepreneurs play a crucial role in promoting the emergence of new norms, because they construct frames of meaning by calling attention to issues (Finnemore and Sikkink 1998, 897). Particularly neutrals have built on the experience they acquired as norm entrepreneurs since the early twentieth century. They show an outstanding combination of credible experiences regarding both the content orientation of their policy and the institutional framework in which this policy was developed. They have been active for decades in confidence-building and violence reduction, following a bottom-up approach and opposing top-down mechanisms, which could infringe on their sovereignty and thereby jeopardize the legitimacy of their neutrality (Goetschel 2011b; Hurd 1999).

Ideas are part of states' national role concepts: they belong to deeply rooted values of the political elite and the population as well as to expectations of third parties (Holsti 1970, 236–239). Role concepts can be seen as methodological tools to capture the links between national identity and foreign policy formulation. They are both constitutive to a state's foreign policy identity and norm setting in respect to its own expected behavior (Aggestam 1998, 11–12).

This article assumes that Western European neutral small states national role concepts have typically included both cognitive and normative ideas. Concerning peace policy, these ideas were mostly reflected in their role concepts' idealistic functions. As will be shown hereafter, the distinction between realist and idealist functions of a role concept, and how different forms of ideas relate to it, can best be described for neutral small states.

HISTORIC ROLE CONCEPTS

Regarding their foreign policy identities, national role concepts deeply rooted historically in neutrality could be found mostly in Ireland, Norway, and Switzerland. Ireland developed a strongly value-based foreign and security policy identity, based on its complex and cumbersome relationship with Great Britain on one hand and on its own economic and social problems on the other. Neutrality became both the corner stone of Ireland's relationship towards Great Britain and of the image, it wanted to cultivate regarding its own role and mission in the world (Devine 2013).

Neither Switzerland nor Norway had a real foreign policy tradition. Both countries developed their diplomatic apparatus at a rather late stage during the second part of the nineteenth century. They basically followed two objectives: first, securing their own survival and second, promoting their national economic development through trade exchanges. When Norway developed its peace policy, it became the core of its foreign policy concept and was closely linked to the role the Norwegian people would have to play. There was an emphasis on neutrality, free trade, arbitration, and international cooperation, as well as emphasis on the peacefulness of the people as opposed to states' behavior. Whereas such discourses in other countries, had to compete with established "Realpolitik," in Norway it became *the* liberal type of foreign policy to be followed as opposed to conventional foreign policy. The positive agency of small people in general and specifically regarding peace was a Leitmotif. Small people had to work for reform or perish. Even after joining NATO in 1949 as a consequence of the German invasion of 1940, Norway maintained the objective of making the world better and more peaceful (Leira 2013).

Switzerland had the strongest focus on neutrality. It followed a "hands off" approach from institutional bonds. An all-encompassing interpretation of neutrality obligations made the latter the corner stone of all major foreign-policy decisions. However, this institutional abstinence did not mean it would not care about the state of peace. The country became home of the International Committee of the Red Cross (ICRC), and it actively promoted the role of Geneva as host of international organizations and conferences. Switzerland also offered its so-called good offices in a great number of international conflicts (Probst 1989). This engagement for the "good" was what the Swiss political scientist Daniel Frei called "Sendungsgedanken" (missionary thoughts) of neutrality (Frei 1966). These activities were seen as complementary to the then very extensive and limiting interpretation of neutrality by the Swiss (Goetschel 1999).

Neither in Sweden nor in Austria, did neutrality have a very long-established anchorage though it became a crucial component of national role concepts during the Cold War. Nonetheless, it became strongly embedded in national discourses of politicians and decision makers (Agius 2011). In both countries, the concept of neutrality was a centerpiece of the ruling social-democratic parties' programs, which stayed in power several decades. In Sweden, its "credible neutrality doctrine" rejected isolationism and provided the bases for the country's active internationalism. It was the platform from which Sweden exported its core domestic values. Sweden saw itself as the "moral conscience of the world" (Agius 2011, 375; 2006). The choice for Sweden was seen to be pragmatic, given its material circumstances, and the Swedish state deployed its resources inward towards state-building rather than continuing expansionist policies (Malmborg 2001; Sundelius, 1989; Agius 2011, 375).

In Austria, smallness and relative weakness were used to construct a sort of national myth that became engrained in Austrian national identity. The idea for neutrality emerged when the country was forced into the status of a small state after decades as a multi- national power block. Neither becoming "small" nor adopting the status of neutrality were deliberately chosen. It was an obligation linked to the State Treaty of 1955. Given the international context of that time, it was the only way for Austria to regain its national sovereignty and keep its territorial integrity. Political leaders of that time managed to turn this "defeat" into a new "opportunity": neutrality became the country's new foreign policy identity (Gebhard 2013).

This is a trait shared by Austria and Finland, which was not deliberately neutral neither, but rather "neutralized." Though it was not formally included in a treaty as in the case of Austria, neutrality in Finland originated with the 1948 Treaty of Friendship, Cooperation, and Mutual Assistance with the Soviet Union. There was an evident material link between both. The term "Finlandisation" was attached to it (Agius 2011, 374). Nonetheless, due to peacekeeping activism since 1956, a strong "peacekeeping power" self-image developed (Vesa 2007). A "moral framework" was established in Finnish international politics with internationalism as a narrative alongside rationalist and pragmatic accounts (Browning 2008, 198–202).

During the Cold War neutral states would not join the European Community (EC). Ireland, which became a member of the EC in 1973, could not be compared to the other neutrals for historic and geopolitical reasons (Devine 2011). Switzerland even refrained from joining the UN for neutrality reasons. Nevertheless, they all contributed to the Conference for Security and Cooperation in Europe (CSCE), later to be known as OSCE, which they perceived as fundamentally democratic and consensus oriented.

This leads to the content of these states' peace policy contributions: Neutral states have participated considerably in promoting specific norms geared towards de-escalation and confidence-building. The most important organization in this regard was the CSCE, where these states were part of the so-called "N+N group" of neutral and nonaligned states. Particularly Finland and Switzerland played an active role there (Palosaari 2013; Renk 1996). Finland, Sweden, Denmark and Norway all contributed to the Nordic bloc, which saw itself as being a security community internally and an active and progressive actor externally—particularly concerning peace and disarmament. The participating countries conceived their security community as a basis for their engagement at the global scale (Wivel 2013; Waever 1992).

Overall, Western European small states and particularly neutral states did not just favor any new idea aimed at control of international peace and security. Their contribution to confidence-building and conflict prevention was widely acknowledged by observers and scholars a like (Fischer 2009; Holst 1985; Renk 1996). There was a clearly visible normative engagement for peace and de-escalation. Neutrality even inspired further normative thinking, such as that of Georg Cohn (1939), who introduced the concept of neo-neutrality in the period between the world wars. Contrary to the tradition of individual abstention inherent in the conventional concept of neutrality, neo-neutrality meant active, collective disqualification of war by neutral states, which included condemning war and adopting sanctions. This differed from merely abstaining from conflict. Even though conceived as a foreign policy concept for individual nation states, the essence of neutrality could be scaled upwards and seen as a possible foreign-policy orientation for a group of states or even for all states. The idea of a defensive link between all neutrals is similar to the objective of reconciling war parties or bringing their hostilities to an end by means of collective action (Frei 1969).

Cultivating their special role on the international scene and the image associated with it helped neutrals justify their policy towards third-party states. They also fostered internal acceptance of neutrality and its role as an identity provider for the population: neutral states distinguished themselves from other states in the way they handled their foreign affairs. They acquired their own foreign and security policy identity. According to it, neutral states, while avoiding traditional interstate military conflicts, make their specific contribution to promoting international peace. As a result, neutral states had their specific way of approaching changes in international relations: while they usually favored reforms aimed at restricting uncontrolled use of force and imposition of interests by sheer power, their support was usually qualified.

Thus, all historic role concepts of Western European small states had clear normative and value-oriented components. Some of these concepts had older and deeper historical roots, others had emerged with the Cold War and partially been imposed by third parties. Western European small states were extremely cautious concerning their entanglement in large powers' politics. Many of them were neutral, most were not members of the EU and most actively participated in UN peacekeeping missions. While they wanted to stay outside the game of power politics, they still wanted to change the rules of the game. They refrained, abstained, or negotiated exceptions. Nevertheless, they also promoted idealistic ambitions regarding transformation of international relations, great power politics, use of power and international arbitration. They showed both realistic and idealistic characteristics in their foreign policy. This was particularly true concerning neutral states: while neutrality's realistic functions made them credible advocates of sovereignty and autonomy, its idealistic function provided them with a track record in "positive reforms" in international relations aimed at reduction of violence and prevention of war. They were keen not to be part of hidden agendas in promoting power-related goals. The type of ideas they promoted were aimed at either preventing war or limiting its negative effects (Goetschel 2011b). Particularly Nordic countries engaged in peacekeeping and export of values to the "global south" were also standing in for their national social policies. This was true for Sweden, and—with slight nuances—for Ireland. Austria too played an important role in trying to bridge the north-south divide and in peacekeeping. Their favored organization was the CSCE, where all neutral states developed impressive and successful activities in regard to confidence and bridge-building between East and West. Normative ideas were solidly anchored in their national role concepts as well as in the peace policies they actually deployed.

POST-COLD WAR ROLE CONCEPTS

With the end of the Cold War, the European and global context changed dramatically. The context for international peacebuilding did as well. Inside Europe, the tensions between East and West ceased to exist and were not replaced by other important tensions, like those, which had marked the last centuries of the continent. The tragic violent conflicts in the Balkans had no serious implications on the general stability of Europe. At the global level, the systematic blockade of the UN Security Council came to an end, and the "golden era" of sanctions and peacebuilding operations began (Luck 2006). An impressive increase in peace and peacebuilding operations could be observed, which had considerable effects on the shape, content, and handling of states' peace engagements. Peace operations developed into exercises of international governance in conflict-ridden countries. New types of peace policies emerged, which did not and could not have existed during the Cold War. New structures were established within national administrations. Their objective was to consolidate resources and handle the administrative and bureaucratic side of peacebuilding (Goetschel and Hagmann 2009). This new context opened the way for new types of ideas and of knowledge transfer in the field of peacebuilding. Parallel to the increase in resources and the multiplication of activities, a qualitative change occurred: technical challenges in the field of peace governance requested problem-solving answers, which were provided by cognitive peacebuilding ideas.

Consequently, the realistic functions of Western European small states' role concepts lost significance. Their survival was not at stake any longer—at least no more than that of larger European states. I will use the same analytical structure as in the preceding chapter, starting with identity and moving on to the institutional setup and content of states' peace policies.

As general trends, all Western European small states strengthened their integration within or cooperation with regional and global organizations. They modified their neutrality, their policies towards NATO and the EU. Many complemented or even replaced their former national role concepts with regional collective objectives and identification. At the policy level, all Western of European small states significantly increased their contributions to military peace operations. Some also became more active in the field of civilian peacebuilding. These changes were not obvious to the public, as little formal changes occurred. None of the neutrals completely rejected neutrality by joining a military alliance such as NATO.

Finland and Sweden switched to the term "alliance-free." They conducted a gradual shift through both policy transformation and adaptation (Ferreira-Pereira 2006; Ojanen 2003; Möller and Bjereld 2010, 364; Rieker 2004). Compared to Sweden, Finland showed a greater readiness towards considering future NATO membership. It also displayed a stronger focus on national defense (Möller and Bjereld 2010, 366). When Austria joined the EU, neutrality remained one of the most discussed issues. However, the country subscribed to all parts of the Common Foreign and Security Policy (CFSP). The significance of neutrality was consistently diminished, stripping it from its political dimensions and reducing it to its military core (Gebhard 2013). Popular survey showed neutrality to have maintained strong support among a majority of the population. But the figures were considerably lower than in Switzerland with a difference of about 20 percent (Haltiner et al. 2007; Reiter 2007). Switzerland was the country most reluctant to relax its conception of neutrality. Even though considerable changes at the operational policy level occurred, the country still claimed to be neutral. It re-installed the concept of "active neutrality" it had been using during 1970s and 1980s (Trachsler 2011, 119–120). Switzerland (and the non-neutral Norway) were the Western European small states, which most considerably strengthened their national civilian peace policy activities. They were also the only two non-EU members. Their engagement became particularly visible concerning their roles in international mediation and facilitation.

Most important changes were triggered through the accession of Austria, Finland, and Sweden to the EU and the latter's development of its CFSP since the Maastricht Treaty. Neutrality remained a corner stone of Austria's national identity and was intensively discussed inside the country. However, regarding the country's external behavior, it was largely replaced by the Austrian contribution to the CFSP (Gebhard 2013). Austria saw itself as a compliant and inconspicuous member state whose foreign policy principles were largely embedded in the EU's CFSP and the UN. The discourse at the international and European level moved away from Austria's special status. Political leaders were keen to underline the country's new focus on the principle of European solidarity and to commit themselves that Austria was not going to obstruct any steps towards further European integration (Schneider 1999).

Swedish foreign policy underwent a strong normative Europeanization. An analysis, taking into account voting behavior in the UN General Assembly and official foreign policy statements in the 1990s, revealed obvious changes comparing them with the policy followed in the 1970s and 1980s, when the country used to be loyal first and foremost to the Third World and to the Nordic community rather than to the EU (Brommesson 2010, 238). Sweden integrated almost its whole peacebuilding activities into the EU and the UN. However, even there it kept its strong engagement for development of international norms, particularly concerning development of a "culture of prevention" and the "responsibility to protect" (Björkdahl 2013). Neutrality was replaced in Finland by a combination of military nonalignment and a strong commitment to the EU's CFSP. There was a change in Finnish state identity from small state neutrality towards member state alignment (Palosaari 2013).

Even though Ireland had already joined the EU in 1973, it had remained a reluctant participant in developing foreign policy and even more of the security policy dimension. This resulted in footnotes to treaty revisions and in negative outcomes of popular referendums due to a perceived lack of safeguards for the country's neutrality (Devine 2011). However, final acceptance of the Lisbon Treaty brought about important changes. Officially, "EU solidarity" has replaced neutrality. Yet the extent of popular support for these developments remains shaky. Meanwhile, the country remains strongly engaged with the UN (Devine 2013).

The new activities became part of revised and extended role concepts. Particularly in case of neutral states, this amounted to important changes and deviations from long-established practices of the Cold War era. While fundamental abstract debates on neutrality proved to be rather difficult, pragmatic policy changes were operated with far less public attention and encountered little political opposition. Western European small states became important players in all kinds of international peace operations and peacebuilding activities. This became most visible with the non-EU members, Norway and Switzerland.

Switzerland has come to see itself as a "peacebuilding champion" (Greminger 2011, 65). It was engaged in mediation processes such as Nepal, Burundi, Armenia/Turkey, Columbia, Uganda, and the Middle East (Greminger 2011, 19–20). It has also developed competence in several thematic peacebuilding clusters such as gender, religion, elections, and dealing with the past to just name of few of them (Federal Council 2011). Similar to Norway, a separate section was established in the Ministry of Foreign Affairs labeled "Human Security Division." However, compared to Norway, peacebuilding enjoys little public support. Politicians and the broader population seem rather untouched by Swiss peace policy. Though institutional and financial framework conditions have improved, the country lacks a strong commitment (CSS: Center for Security Studies 2006, 135–137). In addition, the fact that it is not an EU member was not capitalized upon in a systematic way. Switzerland has been looking for "niches," but this could not replace a coherent long-term strategy. The country encounters costs when it goes its own way (Goetschel and Michel 2009). Switzerland has also reinforced its activities in the military field, but these reforms have remained highly contested. The country's military engagement was not systematically integrated into an overall strategy for peace. This culminated in the 2009 idea of the government to have Switzerland participate in the EU police operation "Atalanta" against pirates in Somalia. Parliamentary rejection of the project was not only a fiasco for the foreign minister but also proof of the lack of coherence in the approach to international peacebuilding, since Switzerland had no other significant peacebuilding engagement in Somalia or in the Horn of Africa at that time. Public support for military peacebuilding remains very low compared to civilian peacebuilding (Swisspeace 2013).

From the EU member countries, Finland was the one that came closest to the activities of Switzerland. Because military peacekeeping had been a corner stone of its peace engagement during the Cold War, changes in military peace operations generated particularly intense debates in this country. Restrictive use of coercive means to fulfil mission mandates became possible. Even the possibility of taking part in missions without UN mandate was discussed. The country's civilian crisis-management activities were developed in parallel. They were seen as bearing some resemblance to the earlier Finnish way of doing peacekeeping in a less military and combat-oriented tradition. They helped bridge the gap between the domestic understanding of traditional identity and new expectations coming from the international level. Most visible became Finland's mediation efforts under the former Finnish president Ahtisaari. The country continued to see itself "being a physician rather than a judge" (Palosaari 2013). Sweden developed a strong focus on conflict prevention. It invested considerable resources in promoting a "culture of prevention" in both the UN and the EU, where it also collaborated with Finland on various initiatives for strengthening the European Security and Defence Policy (ESDP) (Björkdahl 2013). Apart from this institutional engagement, however, it was rather seen as a reluctant peacebuilding actor (CSS: Center for Security Studies 2006, 112–113).

Summing up, the realistic functions of Western European neutral small states role concepts have lost significance since the end of the Cold War. They do not have to fight for their survival any longer—or at least not more than other (larger) Western European states. Nonetheless, this brief comparison has shown that all of these states have kept their idealistic policy dimensions. They still have peace policies, and they all commit considerable resources in these fields. However, when looking at their engagement in more details, some important changes can be observed: All states have shown a considerable increase of institutional involvement with various types of international organizations, mostly the EU, NATO, and the UN. Particularly Austria, Finland, and Sweden who joined the EU in 1995 have replaced part of their national foreign-policy orientation through a "European" one: Solidarity with Europe has replaced the former solidarity dimension of neutrality. The latter was more value-oriented and more global. Ireland has moved into the same direction during recent years. Switzerland and Norway, the two only non-EU members, have reinforced their civilian peacebuilding activities at both the national and international level. They have cultivated their image as peace nations.

When analyzing these changes based on the typology of political ideas, a clear shift from normative to cognitive ideas took place: Western European small states have become loyal and reliable contributors to all kinds of missions and international organizations. They are promoting "best practices," such as Sweden with its engagement for prevention within the EU and the UN. Switzerland (together with the non-neutral Norway) has specialized in its role as facilitators in dialogue processes. Governments are trying to convince their populations to allow their countries to participate in missions with more combat components and less legal restrictions—possibly even without a UN mandate.

Thus, while Western European small states remain very active peacebuilders, the nature of their contributions has changed both institutionally and concerning its content. From an academic point of view, it is interesting to describe and analyze these changes. From a political point of view, it has become more difficult to distinguish what Western European neutral states' peace policies actually stand for compared to other states' peace engagement—at least with the exception of Switzerland (and ironically the non-neutral Norway). Nevertheless, even these two countries dedicate a large part of their peace policies to multilateral and technocratic efforts.

CONCLUSIONS

Describing the two-headed nature of neutral states' national role concepts with both realistic and idealistic functions, I have shown that the relevance of the first category was significantly reduced by geopolitical changes. Except in cases with very old historical roots of peace policies, these changes were joined by a relative loss of the idealistic functions.

With Austria, Finland and Sweden, these changes were significantly enhanced through their accession to the EU. The fact that neither Austria nor Finland had deliberately chosen their status of neutrality also accelerated the process. In the case of Ireland, as with Norway and Switzerland, the historical anchorage of neutrality kept the old role concepts alive and well. The two latter countries not being EU members even allowed them to extend their civilian peacebuilding programs. The foreign policy role concepts of the Nordic countries were also based on their national values of justice and equity reflected in their social models. However, these models were subject to economically driven changes in the last decades. Ireland maintained a strong domestically oriented discussion about neutrality.

The changes within the idealistic dimensions of the respective role concepts can be made visible by differentiating between normative and cognitive ideas, that is, ideas following a logic of appropriateness and ideas following a logic of consequence. Since the end of the Cold War, Western European small states engaging in peacebuilding have been doing this more in a problem-solving perspective based on cognitive ideas. Normative ideas have been losing ground. This was due to the following developments: The OSCE lost considerable significance as an international organization and could no longer provide the same meaningful platform for its engagement as it used to offer during the Cold War. Neutrality itself also had a transforming potential during that time, which it has foregone since then—at least within a European context. Peacekeeping operations represented the cutting-edge type of possible de-escalation in crucial hotspots of international relations. Peace policy, which had almost been an "exclusive domain" of small states, was co-opted by larger states and international organizations alike. "Peace bureaucracies" developed and with them the importance of cognitive ideas in peacebuilding.

These trends were not subject to neutral states influence. However, the fact that certain for them deliberately joined the EU and fully integrated into its CFSP was their own choice. While appeasement took place at their domestic fronts, particularly in Austria and Ireland, the new member states were eager to appear as loyal and unproblematic members towards the outside.

Neutral states have kept very active peace policies. However, the content of their peace engagement changed. To various extents and in different ways, all of the states analyzed have become more operational and more "mainstream." They are still "norm entrepreneurs," but pushing specific agenda points inside international organizations, such as Sweden with issues of prevention, rather than radically questioning established practices including great power politics.

Apart from the strong and visible peacebuilding programs of Switzerland (and non-neutral) Norway and selected activities from Finland in the field of mediation, Western European small states have lost at least part of the substance linked to their branding as "peacemakers." Specialties and innovations, as typical for them in earlier periods, have gone. Engagements for new and cutting-edge initiatives such as R2P, the ICC, or the reform of the UN are no longer their privilege. However, some of them may be linked to one or the other of these initiatives (such as Sweden with R2P or Switzerland with UN reform), NGOs and larger states like Canada, Germany and Japan are playing more important roles.

These developments bear negative consequences at two levels: internationally, most of the political disputes surrounding peacebuilding are due to neglect of the idea's normative dimensions. As was argued elsewhere, Western European small states and particularly neutral ones could play an important role in these debates, being both credible and sovereignty-sensitive. The same norms can be promoted by other actors—possibly with more impact in the short run but on a less sustainable basis due to lack of legitimacy (Goetschel 2011). Particularly after 9/11 and the turn which followed in the perception of peace operations by countries in the global south as part of the "war against terrorism," Western European small states could make use of the trust capital they accumulated in earlier time periods in order to strengthen and enlarge support to peace operations on a selective basis. Following the changes in their peace policy orientations, neutral states lost ground in such non-mainstream activities. Their peace engagements became less distinguishable from those of non-neutral and also of larger states. The demarcation between neutral state peace policies and those of big powers got blurred.

At the national level of Western European small states, the loss of normative ideas' importance compared to cognitive ideas in their peace policies has diminished these policies' anchorage in their foreign-policy identities. Value intense ideas linked to neutrality or to other normative endeavors had explicit or implicit links to these states' self-perception and role expectations, for which cognitive ideas including contributions to multilateral peace governance cannot compensate. This weakens the sustainability of neutral states peace engagement. The history of their idealist engagement accounted for an environment marked by immediate fear of survival and physical threat to their territorial integrity. As this threat has disappeared, neutral states kept their peace policy traditions, but lost the normative ideas out of it. They became peace pragmatists following the mainstream of international organizations and larger states. With the possible exception of the field of peace mediation, where they kept some comparative advantages in certain situations, they lost the initiative to other actors. They remain active, but they have become less special.

Getting back to this papers' original assumption, we conclude that neutral states have become middle powers due to both the changes of the international system and to their increased possibilities to value their foreign policy traditions along the idealist dimension of neutrality. However, the way they have done so varied considerably. According to the argument developed, the impact neutral states exercise on the international system would have been even higher if they had kept it closer to the normative ideas of their idealist dimensions of neutrality. Or put differently: While getting more "usual" international players made life easier for neutral state, it prevented them from exercising a stronger influence.

NOTE

1. The article builds on earlier work of the author: Goetschel 1998; Goetschel 2011a; Goetschel 2011b and particularly Goetschel 2013. A draft version was presented at the Conference "Neutrality from the Cold War to Engaged Neutrality" which took place on October 2, 2015 in Vienna.

BIBLIOGRAPHY

Af Malmborg, Mikeal. 2001. *Neutrality and State-Building in Sweden.* Houndsmills: Palgrave.

Aggestam, Lisbeth. 1998. "Role Conceptions and the Politics of Identity in Foreign Policy." Paper prepared for the third pan-european international relations conference and joint meeting of the ECPR with the ISA, 16–19 September, Vienna.

Agius, Christine. 2006. *The Social Construction of Swedish Neutrality*. Manchester: Manchester University Press.

———. 2011. "Transformed Beyond Recognition? The Politics of Post-Neutrality." *Cooperation and Conflict* 46(3): 370–395.

Björkdahl, Annika. 2013. "Ideas and Norms in Swedish Foreign Policy." *Swiss Political Science Review* 19(3): 322–337.

Brommesson, Douglas. 2010. "Normative Europeanization: The Case of Swedish Foreign Policy Orientation." *Cooperation and Conflict* 45(2): 224–244.

Browning, Christopher S. 2008. *Constructivism, Narrative and Foreign Policy Analysis: A Case Study of Finland*. Oxford: Peter Lang.

Busek, Erhard and Waldemar Hummer (Eds.). 2004. *Der Kleinstaat als Akteure in den Internationalen Beziehungen*. Schaan: Verlag der Liechtensteinischen Akademischen Gesellschaft.

Devine, Karen. 2011. "Neutrality and the Development of the European Union's Common Security and Defence Policy: Compatible or competing?" *Cooperation and Conflict* 46(3): 334–369.

———. 2013. "Ideas and Identities in Ireland's Peace Policy: Centuries of Norm Continuity and Change." *Swiss Political Science Review* 19(3): 376–409.

Federal Council. 2011. *Botschaft über die Weiterführung von Massnahmen zur Förderung des Friedens und der menschlichen Sicherheit 2012–2016*. June 29. Bern.

Ferreira-Pereira, Laura C. 2006. "Inside the Fence but Outside the Walls: Austria, Finland and Sweden in the Post-Cold War Security Architecture." *Cooperation and Conflict* 41(1): 99–122.

Finnemore, Martha and Kathryn Sikkink. 1998. "International Norm Dynamics and Political Change." *International Organization* 52(4): 887–917.

Fischer, Thomas. 2009. *Neutral Power in the CSCE: The N+N States and the Making of the Helsinki Accords*. Baden-Baden: Nomos.

Frei, Daniel. 1966. "Sendungsgedanken der schweizerischen Aussenpolitik." *Schweizerisches Jahrbuch für Politische Wissenschaft* 6: 98–113.

———. 1969. *Dimensionen neutraler Politik: Ein Beitrag zur Theorie der Internationalen Beziehungen*. Geneva: Graduate Institute of International Studies.

Gebhard, Carmen. 2013. "Is Small Still Beautiful? The Case of Austria." *Swiss Political Science Review* 19(3): 279–297.

Gehler, Michael. 2001. *Finis Neutralität? Historische und politische Aspekte im europäischen Vergleich: Irland, Finnland, Schweden, Schweiz und Österreich*. Bonn: Center for European Integration Studies (CEI Discussion Paper C92).

Goetschel, Laurent. 1998. "The Foreign and Security Policy Interests of Small States in Today's Europe." In *Small States inside and outside the European Union: Interests and Policies*, edited by Laurent Goetschel, 13–31. Boston/Dordrecht/London: Kluwer Academic Publishers.

———. 1999. "Neutrality, a Really Dead Concept?" *Cooperation and Conflict* 34(2): 115–139.

———. 2011. "Neutrality." In *International Encyclopedia of Political Science*, edited by Bertrand Badie, Dirk Berg-Schlosser, and Leonardo Morlino, 1697–1700. Thousand Oaks, CA: Sage.

————. 2011. "Neutrals as Brokers of Peacebuilding Ideas?" *Cooperation and Conflict* 46(3): 312–333.

————. 2013. "Bound to be Peaceful? The Changing Approach of Western European Small States to Peace." *Swiss Political Science Review* 19(3): 259–278.

Goetschel, Laurent and T. Hagmann. 2009. "Civilian Peacebuilding: Peace by Bureaucratic Means?" *Conflict, Security and Development* 9(1): 55–73.

Goetschel, Laurent and Daniel Michel. 2009. *Der aussenpolitische Handlungsspielraum der Schweiz als Nichtmitglied der Europäischen Union: ein Blick auf einige Aspekte der Friedensförderung.* Basel: Europainstitut

Greminger, Thomas. 2011. "Die Entwicklung der zivilen Friedensförderung der Schweiz seit 2006." In *Zivile Friedensförderung der Schweiz: Bestandsaufnahme und Entwicklungspotenzial. Zürcher Beiträge zur Sicherheitspolitik 83*, edited by Andreas Wenger, 13–68. Zurich: ETHZ/CSS.

Haltiner, Karl W., Andreas Wenger, Silvia Würmli, and Urs Wenger (Eds.). 2007. *Sicherheit 2007. Aussen-, sicherheits- und verteidigungspolitische Meinungsbildung im Trend.* Zurich: CSS und Militärakademie an der ETHZ.

Holst, Johann J. 1985. *Norwegian Foreign Policy in the 1980s.* Oslo: Norwegian University Press

Holsti, Kalevi J. 1970. "National Role Conceptions in the Study of Foreign Policy." *International Studies Quarterly* 14(3): 233–309.

Hurd, Ian. 1999. "Legitimacy and Authority in International Politics." *International Organization* 53(2): 379–408.

Ingebritsen, Christine. 2002. "Norm Entrepreneurs: Scandinavia's Role in World Politics." *Cooperation and Conflict* 37(1): 11–23.

Jakobsen, Peter V. 2009. "Small States, Big Influence: The Overlooked Nordic Influence on the Civilian ESDP." *Journal of Common Market Studies* 47(1): 81–2002.

Joenniemi, Pertti. 1993. "Neutrality Beyond the Cold War." *Review of International Studies* 19: 289–304.

Keohane, Robert O. 1969. "Lilliputians' Dilemma: Small States in International Politics." *International Organization* 23(2): 291–310.

Leira, Halvard. 2013. "'Our Entire People are Natural Born Friends of Peace': the Norwegian Foreign Policy of Peace." *Swiss Political Science Review* 19(3): 338–356.

Liska, George. 1957. *International Equilibrium.* Cambridge: Harvard University Press.

Luck, Edward C. 2006. *UN Security Council. Practice and Promise.* London, New York: Routledge.

Möller, Ulrika and Ulf Bjereld. 2010. "From Nordic Neutrals to Post-Neutral Europeans: Differences in Finnish and Swedish Policy Transformation." *Cooperation and Conflict* 45(4): 363–386.

Ojanen, Hanna (Ed.). 2003. *Neutrality and Non-Alignment in Europe Today.* Helsinki: The Finnish Institute of International Affairs (FIIA Report 6).

Palosaari, Teemu. 2013. "Still a Physician Rather than a Judge? The Post-Cold War Foreign and Security Policiy of Finland." *Swiss Political Science Review* 19(3): 357–375.

Probst, Raymond R. 1989. '*Good Offices' in the Light of Swiss International Practice and Experience*. Dordrecht: Kluwer.

Reiter, Erich. 2007. *Die Einstellung der Österreicher zu Fragen der Sicherheits- und Verteidigungspolitik und zur EU*. Wien: Internationales Institut für liberale Politik.

Renk, Hans-Jörg. 1996. *Der Weg der Schweiz nach Helsinki: Der Beitrag der schweizerischen Diplomatie zum Zustandekommen der Konferenz über Sicherheit und Zusammenarbeit in Europa (KSZE) 1972– 1975*. Bern: Haupt.

Rieker, Pernille. 2004. "Europeanization of Nordic Security: The European Union and the Changing Security Identities of the Nordic States." *Cooperation and Conflict* 39: 369–392.

Riklin, Alois. 1992. "Die Neutralität der Schweiz." In *Neues Handbuch der schweizerischen Aussenpolitik*, edited by Alois Riklin, Hans Haug, and Raymond R. Probst, 191–209. Bern: Haupt.

Rothstein, Robert L. 1968. *Alliances and Small Powers*. New York, London: Columbia University Press.

Schelling, Thomas C. 1980. *The Strategy of Conflict*. Cambridge: Harvard University Press

Schneider, Heinrich. 1999. "Der sicherheitspolitische Optionenbericht der Bundesregierung. Ein Dokument, das es nicht gibt. Ein Lehrstück politischen Scheiterns." In *Jahrbuch für Internationale Sicherheitspolitik*, edited by Erich Reiter, 419–466. Vienna: E. S. Mittler.

Small, Melvin and J. David Singer. 1973. "The Diplomatic Importance of States, 1816–1970." *World Politics* 25(4): 577–599.

Sundelius, Bengt (Ed.). 1989. *The Committed Neutral. Sweden's Foreign Policy*. Boulder, CO: Westview Press.

Swisspeace. 2013. *Schweizer Friedensförderung geniesst sehr hohen Stellenwert bei der Bevölkerung*. Bern: press release. http://www.swisspeace.ch/fileadmin/user_upload/Media/etc/Media/Media_Releases/2013_Umfrage_def_1Juli2013.pdf.

Thomas, Alastair H. 1996. "The Concept of the Nordic Region and the Parameters of Nordic Cooperation." In *The European Union and the Nordic Countries*, edited by Lee Miles, 15–31. London: Routledge.

Trachsler, Daniel. 2011. *Von Petitpierre bis Calmy-Rey: Wiederkehrende Debatten um die Schweizer Aussenpolitik*. Zurich: ETHZ/CSS.

Vesa, Unto. 2007. "Continuity and Change in the Finnish Debate on Peacekeeping." *International Peacekeeping* 14: 524–37.

Vital, David. 1967. *The Inequality of States: A Study of the Small Power in International Relations*. Oxford: Clarendon Press.

———. 1971. *The Survival of Small States: Studies in Small Power / Great Power Conflict*. London: Oxford University Press.

Wæver, Ole. 1992. "Nordic Nostalgia: Northern Europe after the Cold War." *International Affairs* 68(1): 77–102.

Wivel, Anders. 2013. "From Peacemaker to Warmonger? Explaining Denmark's Great Power Politics." *Swiss Political Science Review* 19(3): 298–321.

Chapter 5

Geopolitics and the Concept of Neutrality in Contemporary Europe

Adrian Hyde-Price

This article examines some of the key implications of the concept of neutrality for European security, particularly in the light of the changing geopolitics of the post-Cold War European security system. It focuses on the tension between neutrality, collective security and solidarity, and draws primarily on the contrasting experiences of Sweden and Finland on the one hand, and Austria, Ireland and Switzerland on the other. It also discusses the option of neutrality for Ukraine.

Neutrality has long been a feature of the European security system. In the context of the East-West confrontation during the Cold War, a significant role was played in the European security system by a group of "neutral and non-aligned" countries. The existence of the "N + N" group—which was formally constituted in February 1974, and which consisted of Austria, Ireland, Switzerland, Sweden, Finland, Yugoslavia and Albania (Makko 2012, 93)—helped mitigate the conflict between NATO and the Warsaw Pact and provided an element of stability to the system. They served as a partial buffer in the military confrontation between the blocs, and some of these countries actively contributed diplomatically and politically to easing East-West tensions and establishing a *modus vivendi* between the two sides, particularly in the context of détente in the 1970s and the establishment of the Conference on Security and Cooperation in Europe (CSCE). With the fall of the Berlin Wall and the opening up of the Iron Curtain, the strategic and political rationale for neutrality fundamentally changed. In the context of a Europe "whole and free" and with the enlargement and deepening of the European Union, neutrality lost much of its former meaning and significance (Sloan 1997). Of the Cold War neutrals, Yugoslavia has broken up and Slovenia and Croatia have joined NATO; Albania joined NATO in 2009; and of the remaining five, all but Switzerland have joined the European Union, and all five have established partnership agreements with NATO. In this context, there is considerable debate as to the relevance and meaning of neutrality. Indeed, Sweden no longer describes itself as "neutral," but rather as "militarily non-aligned."

With the Ukraine crisis, the debate on the issue of neutrality and military nonalignment has become more intense. Russia's illegal annexation of Crimea, its support for violent secessionist groups in eastern Ukraine, and its more confrontational political and military posture towards the Euro-Atlantic community have created a new mood of unease and insecurity across Europe, particularly in those regions of Europe on the new frontline of Europe's "cold peace" with Russia (Granholm 2014). Both Sweden and Finland—both situated on the strategically exposed north-eastern front of the Euro-Atlantic community directly facing Russia—are now investing in new defence capabilities, and have signed a far-reaching agreement for bilateral defence cooperation. Both are also committed to deepening Nordic defence cooperation in the framework of NORDEFCO, and both have signed up to NATO's Enhanced Opportunities Partnership program agreed at the NATO summit in Wales in September 2014. In addition, in both countries, support for joining NATO has grown over recent years, even if formal membership is not on the cards in the immediate future (Ford 2014).

In Austria, Ireland and Switzerland, on the other hand, both political elites and public opinion remain committed to a more traditional understanding of their neutral and nonaligned status. In the case of Austria, its neutrality is embedded in its constitution. For Ireland, neutrality is bound up primarily with the country's troubled relationship with the United Kingdom. Swiss neutrality dates back to the end of the Thirty Years War and is now deeply engrained in the national political culture. More importantly, all three countries are surrounded by a protective wall of NATO member states and are thus insulated from the chill winds emanating from Moscow, which is not the case for either Sweden or Finland.

The deepening interdependence and pooling of sovereignty that have accompanied the European integration process have also exacerbated the tensions, ambiguities and disjunctions that lie at the heart of neutrality: between neutrality and collective security, between national interests and the common good, between state sovereignty and solidarity with others. Neutrality has traditionally been a policy that places the national interest above the common good and the security of others—as Olaf Palme noted in 1970, "The policy of neutrality is primarily based on our own needs. It is our own peace, our own independence and our own security we want to protect (Makko 2012, 85)." The tension between neutrality and collective security first emerged at the time of Peace of Westphalia and was clearly evident in the context of the League of Nations. For members of the European Union today, the key question is whether it is possible—let alone ethical—to be neutral in contemporary Europe in the context of a globalizing international order and a highly interdependent regional security system and what this neutrality signifies in practice. This question is particularly pertinent since the Lisbon Treaty, which includes a legal commitment to "solidarity" with other member states (Article 222) and a Mutual Defence Clause (Article 42:7)—the second of which was formally invoked by France after the terrorist attacks in Paris in November 2015.

The paper considers this question in the light of the different trajectories of the core group of neutral and nonaligned states that took shape in the context of the Cold War: Austria, Sweden, Finland, Ireland and Switzerland. Their different trajectories since the end of the East-West conflict, this paper argues, can best be explained by reference to variations in the sub-regional geopolitical context, in which these states find themselves. Thus, for example, Austria, Ireland and Switzerland have remained committed to a version of "neutrality" because of their relatively benign geostrategic location. Sweden and Finland, on the other hand, have moved away from neutrality to a position of "military non-aligned" primarily because of the more challenging and uncertain security environment in the Baltic Sea region. Theoretically, it is suggested, this foreign policy orientation provides evidence in support of neoclassical realist arguments about the *Primat der Aussenpolitik* and points to the need to combine systemic analysis with domestic level variables.

THE CONCEPT OF NEUTRALITY: A BRIEF HISTORY

Like the food products of H. J. Heinz, neutrality comes in "57 Varieties." An established feature of international politics for centuries, neutrality has been combined with a broad variety of foreign and defence policies—from "absolute passivity" (Sweden's stance in 1864) to an instrumental policy "beyond good and evil" (as defined by the Swedish foreign minister Östen Undén in the 1950s), or to an activist and moralistic internationalism (epitomized by the foreign policy of Olof Palme (Ekengren 2011)). It has also been practiced by both small and medium-sized states, as well as middle and great powers—despite the historical evidence that suggests that, as a security strategy for small states to preserve their national sovereignty and territorial integrity, it has a rather poor track record.

As a general concept, neutrality refers to a state's status of impartiality towards belligerent states in the context of armed conflict, but has different connotations than simply being a non-belligerent. At its core, neutrality refers to a security policy based on the avoidance of mutual defence commitments and a desire to avoid the costs and consequences of participation in war. The legal rights and duties of neutral states were codified in the Second Hague Peace Conference of 1907, which provided the foundations for subsequent international understandings of neutrality, and which remain broadly relevant today. Convention 5 covers land warfare, and convention 13 deals with naval warfare.

The legal status of neutral countries first became an issue in the context of the Thirty Years War, when Hugo Grotius introduced the concept in his work *De Jure Belli ac Paci* (1625): "Those who remain at peace should show themselves impartial to either side in permitting transit, in furnishing supplies to troops and in not assisting those under siege" (Bring 2012, 21). With the Peace of Westphalia that concluded the Thirty Years War, however, the legal status, political legitimacy and morality of neutrality was put into question. This was because the Westphalian peace introduced the embryonic notion of "collective security," whereby all states were accorded a shared responsibility for defending the peace of Europe by taking collective action against aggressors. To remain neutral in the face of clear aggression by one or more states would be to undermine the principle and practice of collective security, putting the national interests of the neutral state above the common good of the regional security system. The same dilemma between neutrality and collective security arose in the wake of the First World War when the League of Nations was established (O'Donghue 2010), and again after the Second World War when the United Nations was created. Thus France wanted all neutral countries excluded from the UN, and when Switzerland sought to join the organization in 1946 while preserving its neutral status, UN Secretary General Trygve Lie responded that "Neutrality is a word I cannot find in the Charter" (Fischer 2012, 29). Nonetheless, Sweden joined the UN in 1946, followed by Austria, Finland and Ireland in 1955. Switzerland finally joined in 2002 after a referendum.

Given the weakness and unreliability of collective security regimes, however, neutrality has remained a persistent feature of international politics. The great powers recognized the permanent neutrality of Switzerland in the Neutrality of Switzerland Treaty signed on November 20, 1815, at the time of the Congress of Vienna, and Belgium neutrality was recognized in 1831 a year after it became independent, although it was not anchored in international law until the Treaty of London signed on April 19, 1839. Luxembourg was recognized as an independent and neutralized principality following a dispute between France and Prussia, as a result of British diplomatic intervention and the 1867 Treaty of London. After the failure of the League of Nations to apply economic sanctions against Italy following its attack on Abyssinia, Switzerland reverted to full neutrality and six smaller neutral states withdrew from the obligation to apply economic sanctions (Sweden, Denmark,

Finland, Norway, Netherlands and Spain). This reflected an emerging legal understanding that collective security would be the primary requirement for members of the League, but that if this failed, then the option of neutrality could be pursued (Bring 2012, 23).

Although sometimes associated with small and medium states, neutrality has also been the foreign policy option for great powers. During the American Civil War, Great Britain issued a Proclamation of Neutrality on May 13, 1861 (without recognizing the Confederacy), followed shortly thereafter by France (Stoker 2010, 96). Subsequently in 1872, the Alabama Claims Arbitration recognized neutrality as a regime of international customary law. Great Britain also declared its neutrality during the Franco-Prussian war of 1870. The United States remained neutral in the First World War until 1917, and was also neutral in the Second World War until Pearl Harbour (although given the clear Nazi aggression in 1939, President Roosevelt asked Congress to modify the neutrality laws passed in the thirties to allow Lease Lend to the United Kingdom). For the great powers, neutrality is an attractive option when they wish to benefit from the mutual weakening of warring rivals, or when the balance of power is not adversely affected.

As a security strategy for safeguarding the independence and territorial integrity of small powers, neutrality has had a patchy record. Belgium was neutral from 1839 to 1914 when it was invaded by Germany. It was neutral again from 1936 to 1940 when it was invaded and occupied by Nazi Germany. Norway was neutral from 1864 to 1940 when it was invaded and occupied by Nazi Germany—an invasion which came as a direct respond to British mining of Norway's territorial waters and an Anglo-British plan to occupy Narvik and interdict the supply of Swedish iron ore to the Third Reich (Lunde 2009). Estonia and Latvia declared their neutrality in 1938, followed by Lithuania in 1939, but all three were occupied and annexed by the Soviet Union in 1940—Soviet Foreign Minister V. M. Molotov declaring that "the time of small nations has passed" (Goodby 2014, 32). Austria was formally neutral from 1920 to 1938, when it was annexed by Nazi Germany. Hungary attempted to become neutral in 1956, but was invaded by the Soviet Union. In the interwar years, Sweden sought to create a bloc of neutral countries in northern Europe as the international situation deteriorated after the Italian invasion of Abyssinia and the failure of the League of Nations to respond. This bloc consisted of Belgium, the Netherlands, Luxembourg, Denmark, Norway, Finland, Sweden and the three Baltic states: by 1940, only Sweden had not been attacked and occupied by either Germany or the USSR. Of twenty neutral countries prior to Second World War, only eight survived more or less unharmed. This negative experience led many formerly neutral countries to join alliances (i.e., Belgium and the Benelux countries, Denmark, Norway and Portugal).

NEUTRALITY AND INTERNATIONAL SECURITY

Like all foreign and security policies, the option of neutrality reflects two sets of pressures—exogenous and endogenous, that is, the external environment and domestic politics. The primary determinants are nearly always exogenous, and reflect the prevailing balance of power in the regional security system. Neutrality reflects a desire by the state in question to avoid the potential risks and costs of war, and a belief that they can stand aloof from great power conflicts because of their geostrategic location and the prevailing configuration of great power relations. In some cases, neutrality can also be a response to defeat in war and/or pressures from neighboring great powers. Endogenous factors reflect a domestic political understanding of exogenous systemic pressures, and in some cases it can be way of managing domestic cleavages (political, ethnic, religious, etc.).

Over time, it is evident that a policy of neutrality can take deep roots in the domestic political culture, becoming a marker of a distinctive national identity. This is evident from the case of Ireland, where referendums on the EU Treaties of Nice and Lisbon were lost in part because of their perceived implications for neutrality. In the case of Austria, neutrality has become an important dimension of national identity, distinguishing the country from its larger neighbor, the BRD, which joined NATO in 1955 (the same year as the Austrian Declaration of Neutrality on October 26, which is now a public holiday). For many Swedes, neutrality is now part of their national identity, as much as Abba, IKEA and meatballs, even though Sweden formally abandoned neutrality in 1992 as it prepared to join the EU. This reflects the legacy of Olaf Palme, who defined Swedish Cold War neutrality with a sense of moral purpose. Swedish neutrality was thus imbued with a sense of moral goodness and superiority it did not have before, and the feel-good effect was very appealing to both the public and the politicians. Neutrality soon became something of a national meta-ideology, and it blended with modernity and the welfare state to become part of the national identity. To be Swedish was to be neutral, to be neutral was to be good, thus, it was good to be a Swede (Dalsjö 2012, 144).[1]

Given the anarchic, self-help character of the international system, characterized by enduring security competition and populated by a diverse range of states—including predatory, opportunistic and power-maximizing great powers—neutrality cannot rely on good faith, which is in short supply, and the benign intentions of others. As outlined above, the historical record on neutrality speaks for itself. To be credible and viable, neutrality depends on one or more of the following conditions:

1. *Being a hedgehog*: in other words, being militarily strong enough to deter potential aggressors by being able to inflict significant costs on an

aggressor ("armed neutrality"). Thus for example Sweden, once it decided to forego the option of developing its own nuclear deterrent (Jonter 2001), developed a military capacity—based on a substantial domestic defence industrial base—for what was termed "marginal deterrence," that is, the ability to resist an armed invasion by the Warsaw Pact long enough for military assistance to arrive from the United States and NATO—for which it actively and secretly prepared (Dalsjö 2006).

2. *Having Powerful Friends:* for smaller states that lack the resources and wherewithal to develop sufficient military capability to become "hedge-hogs," a second option is having powerful friends who provide reliable security guarantees. This was the case with Belgium, which felt confident with the security guarantees it received from the United Kingdom and France—although this was ultimately not sufficient to prevent its invasion and occupation.

3. *Accommodation:* accommodating to the many of the demands and expectations of threatening great powers in order to avoid unnecessarily antagonizing them. This was the approach of Finland during the cold war, for which the term "Finlandisation" was coined (Goodby 2012, 34). Another, more derogatory term would be "appeasement," although the strategic logic of this approach has been obscured by its association with the legacy of Munich and the betrayal of Czechoslovakia.

4. *Hiding:* this is an option available to neutral states situated in territorially inaccessible or strategically marginal locations, such as Switzerland or Ireland. In the nineteenth and early twentieth centuries, the Scandinavian countries also believed they were relatively immune from the power struggles in central Europe, given the peripheral location of Scandinavia on the northern fringes of the continent. This kept them out of the First World War, but by 1939–1940, the strategic importance of Swedish iron ore for the German war economy, combined with the possibilities for maritime operations of Norway's long coastline along the North Atlantic, made Scandinavia the focus of geopolitical attention for both the Allies and the Reich (Lunde 2009, 6).

5. *Free-riding:* the final option is particularly attractive to states insulated from a potential aggressor by being surrounded by friendly states who are able to defend and deter themselves militarily, perhaps by being members of a collective defence alliance. This is an attractive option for states that wish to avoid the costs of a credible military defence capability and avoid the risks of a potential war.

It is therefore apparent that neutrality is a concept that is infinitely malleable, flexible and adaptive. Neutral states tend to like chameleons, adapting their foreign and security policies to the geopolitical context and the prevailing balance of power. This is sometimes forgotten in some formerly neutral

European states that tend to look back with a sense of nostalgia to the lost days of moral clarity that neutrality seemed to provide in context of the East-West conflict. But this ignores the constraints and ethical dilemmas that all neutral countries have had to make. As Thomas Fischer notes:

> Under the ideological Cold War circumstances there has always been a clear price-tag attached to neutrality in Realpolitik. All the neutrals had to compromise to a greater or lesser extent in the political, military and economic dimensions to find acceptance of their neutrality with the great powers and to safeguard the necessary room to manoeuvre between the blocs. (Fischer 2012, 34)

The need to make accommodations and concessions has meant that neutrality has had to be flexible and adaptive. In some cases, neutrality has been combined with an active and engaged internationalist policy; at others with a more passive and quiescent one. It has also been compatible with membership of a variety of international organizations, from the League of Nations to the European Union—or none, as in the case of Switzerland until it joined the UN in 2002. It is also compatible with functional military cooperation with other countries or a military alliance—such as NATO's Partnership for Peace program. Finally, it is compatible with a variety of different approaches to defence procurement, from developing a strong domestic arms industry (which is usually combined with an entrepreneurial approach to arms exports), to buying from one country or alliance, or balancing arms purchases from rival camps (Finland during the Cold War).

NEUTRALITY, STATES AND THE INTERNATIONAL SYSTEM

For the states concerned, and for the international system more widely, neutrality has a number of costs and benefits. For neutral states themselves, neutrality offers a number of benefits: first and foremost, it provides a way of avoiding the costs in blood and treasure of involvement in war, while preserving its sovereignty and independence. Thus in the case of Norway in the First World War, "Although the country had to endure severe blockade measures and the war involved great costs to the Norwegian population, Norwegian companies, industrialists, and shipping magnates reaped huge economic benefits" (Lunde 2009, 6); second, for those with powerful friends, or those that can "hide" or "free-ride," it offers the option of low defence spending, thereby keeping taxes low or spending more on welfare, education, health, etc.; finally, it can give a neutral state more space and opportunities for diplomatic maneuvring in the spaces between the great powers or rival alliance systems, thereby allowing them to raise their international profile and "punch above their weight."

On the down side, neutrality can have significant costs and negative consequences for individual states: first, in a self-help international system, neutral states can find themselves exposed and vulnerable, without credible security guarantees, which was the great fear of the new democracies in East Central Europe after the end of the Cold War and the primary reason why they pushed hard for NATO membership rather than accepting the neutral status that Russia hoped they would adopt after the collapse of the Warsaw Pact; second, neutral states often have to keep their heads down and accommodate themselves to the interests of neighboring great powers, as noted above; finally, neutral states will have no significant input into the debates and decisions of alliances, which can lead to them being marginalized when it comes to decisions about security policy, humanitarian intervention or peace support operations. This is a particular problem if the alliance in question plays a key role in security governance and collective milieu shaping in the region or internationally, and the neutral state has sought to develop functional military cooperation with it. Thus in the case of NATO, neutral states that are active in the Partnership for Peace program, or which have participated in NATO operations in the Balkans, Africa or Afghanistan, have found that they share the costs of the operations in question, but only have a limited involvement in decision-making.

For a regional security system, or the international system more generally, the existence of neutral states can also have both costs and benefits. Firstly, as Hedley Bull argued, neutrality has been one of the ways in which the international society of states has sought to contain and restrain the destabilizing impact of war. By codifying the rights and duties of neutrals (primarily through the Hague conventions), international society has sought to restrict the spread of war and reduce its potential for creating "a state of pure enmity or war of all against all" (Bull 1977, 188). Second, the existence of one or more neutral states in a security system can provide a useful buffer in relations between rival great powers or alliance systems, providing a cushion that can absorb and ameliorate security competition in the system as a whole (as with Sweden and Finland in the context of the Cold War "Nordic balance"). This can help reduce the dichotomies of security competition between rival groups of states by allowing neutral states to raise other policy options, and creating the possibility of disputed territories becoming neutral (as with Austria in 1955, but not Hungary in 1956 or Czechoslovakia in 1968). Thirdly, neutral states can play a mediating role between rival alliances or great powers within international organizations (in the CSCE or the UN during the Cold War) and facilitate diplomatic interaction between them, both by providing the venue for talks on "neutral ground" (as with Stockholm, Helsinki or Vienna) and facilitating those talks.

On the other hand, the existence of neutral states in a security system can have some significant costs and disadvantages. Firstly, neutral states in a buffer zone of geostrategic importance can become a target for major powers seeking opportunities for influence in this region, as with Finland and the Baltic States in 1939–1940, or Norway in 1940. This is particularly so if neutrality is not combined with a credible defence and deterrent capability. Thus in the case of Norway in 1940, "the poor state of its defences, when compared to a generation earlier, served as an invitation to violate the country's neutrality. Both the German and the British leaders viewed the Norwegian military as a minor obstacle to their plans" (Lunde 2009, 10). Second, the existence of neutral states can also complicate allies' defence planning and provide opportunities for ruthless predator states with aggressive intentions—as with the case of Belgium, Holland and Luxembourg in 1939–1940, where their desire to maintain their "neutral" status in the context of the war between Nazi Germany and the allies made effective defence planning much more difficult. As James Holland notes, the desire of three neutral Benelux countries to stay out of the war "was wishful thinking of the highest order," and ignored the strategic situation along the Western front in 1939–1940, which meant that:

> It was therefore a reasonable bet that Belgium—at the very least—would be fought over. Had these countries allowed Allied troops in earlier, then it might have been possible to create a much stronger and unified line while there was still time. This was not to be, however. Both King Leopold of Belgium and his Government and Queen Wilhelmina of the Netherlands and her Government stolidly stuck to their neutral stance, accepting Hitler's assurances that their neutrality would be respected. (Holland 2015, 107–108)

Third, the existence of a significant number of neutral states within a security system makes the construction of a robust system of collective security much more problematic. One or two peripheral neutral states within a system—such as Switzerland or Ireland—is not a major problem, but if the principle of neutrality is more widely adopted, then a credible and effective system of collective security becomes much more difficult to establish. Thus the neutrality of Norway and Sweden in 1939–1940 prevented the Western democracies from aiding Finland during the Winter War when it was attacked by Nazi Germany's ally, the Soviet Union. Finally, neutrality can be used by some states as an excuse to become free-riders within the system, allowing them to benefit from the public goods provide by major powers or alliances without sharing any of the costs. This can have a corrosive effect on the development of a security community, undermining the sense of political solidarity that an effective security community requires.

NEUTRALITY IN THE POST-COLD WAR
EUROPEAN SECURITY SYSTEM

With the end of cold war bipolarity, the former grouping of neutral and non-aligned states has been reconfigured. Yugoslavia has broken apart, and Albania has joined NATO. This has left a group of five neutral and nonaligned states in Europe: Austria, Finland, Ireland, Sweden and Switzerland. There are also a number of minor neutrals, including Liechtenstein and the Vatican City, as well as Malta and Cyprus. In addition, there are a number of newer neutral countries in the Balkans and post-Soviet space. These include Serbia, Moldova, Turkmenistan and Ukraine.

In 2007 the Serbian National Assembly introduced a resolution on the "Protection of Sovereignty, Territorial Integrity and Constitutional Order of the Republic of Serbia," article 6 of which declared that Serbia is "in relation to existing military alliances a neutral country from a military aspect" (Timon 2011). Serbia has a Partnership for Peace agreement with NATO, signed in 2006, and public opinion remains skeptical of joining the alliance with which it fought a war in 1999. But with Montenegro due to join the alliance at the Warsaw summit in July 2016, there is a growing debate whether Serbia will continue to hold to its policy of neutrality.

Moldova declared its "permanent neutrality" in Article 11 of the 1994 Constitution, but this has not been recognized by any other country. Moldova joined NATO's Partnership for Peace program in 1994, but the continued presence of the Russian 14th Army at Bendery in the break-away Transnistria region means that Moldova is wary of moving closer to NATO. Turkmenistan is another post-Soviet successor state that declared its "permanent neutrality" in 1995, which is recognized by the UN. Turkmenistan itself is militarily very weak and unable to effectively defend itself, and had come under growing Russian pressure to accept closer security cooperation with Moscow. However, Turkmenistan has resisted this pressure, and its leadership has spoken of its admiration for the neutrality of Switzerland and Austria, while at the same time having one of the most authoritarian and repressive governments in the regime (Bohr 2016).

The country of greatest geostrategic importance in the "lands between" Germany and Russia is Ukraine (Hyde-Price 2007). Ukraine is therefore the country that epitomizes the dilemmas, difficulties and/or potentialities of neutrality for Ukraine itself, and for the European security system more generally. Ukraine's foreign and security policy reflects both its geopolitical location between NATO countries in the West and Russia in the East (including a major Russian naval base at Sevastopol) and its weak national identity, which included a 10 million strong Russian community after independence. Given these external pressures and domestic cleavages, Ukraine adopted a policy of independence in 1990: in its Declaration of Sovereignty of July 1990, it stated that it had "the intention of becoming a permanently neutral state that does not participate in military blocs and adheres to three nuclear free principles" (Article 9). Ukraine therefore did not join the Russian-led Commonwealth of Independent States established in Tashkent in May 1992, although it did become the first of the Soviet successor states to sign a Partnership for Peace agreement with NATO in February 1994. Later in 1994, at the CSCE summit in Romania in December, Ukraine pledged to accede to the Non-Proliferation Treaty as a non-nuclear weapon state in the Budapest Memorandum, which was signed by the United States, the United Kingdom and Russia. This reiterated existing multilateral commitments found in the Helsinki Final Act and the UN Charter, but did not include the firm legal commitments to Ukrainian sovereignty and territorial integrity that Kiev had hoped for.

The issue of Ukrainian membership of NATO continued to be politically controversial domestically, and public opinion polls consistently showed limited support for this change in security policy. Nonetheless, in 2002 President Kuchma announced that Ukraine would seek to join the alliance. The Orange Revolution in 2004 brought to power President Viktor Yushchenko, who was a keen supporter of NATO membership, and in 2008 Ukraine requested a NATO Membership Action Plan (MAP), which is the first step on the road to membership. The issue of NATO membership was raised at the time of the Bucharest NATO summit in April 2008, but met strong opposition from European NATO members, led by France and Germany. Formally, NATO maintained its position that alliance membership was the sovereign decision of the country concerned, which then had to meet NATO's criteria. Although the Bush administration was a keen advocate both NATO membership for both Ukraine and Georgia, within the alliance's European members there was a widespread recognition that offering membership to these two countries would be unnecessarily provocative to Russia, and would create enormous difficulties in making Article V security guarantees credible. Effectively, the issue of membership was therefore shelved.

With the Ukrainian Presidential election of 2010, the newly elected President Viktor Yanukovych declared that Ukraine would remain a "European, non-aligned state," and would not seek membership of the alliance. This was formally re-affirmed in a law passed by the Ukrainian parliament in May 2010, which excluded the option of "integration into Euro-Atlantic security and NATO membership," but maintained the strategic goal of "European integration" through closer ties with the EU in the framework of the European Neighbourhood Policy (ENP) and the Eastern Partnership. This remained the policy of the Ukrainian government up and beyond the Euromaidan demonstrations that started in late 2013, with the policy of nonalignment being reaffirmed by the new government of Arseny Yatseniuk that came to power after Yanukovych fled to Russia in February 2014.

This policy of nonalignment and neutrality was cast into question after the Russian annexation of Crimea in March 2014, and its support for armed separatists in eastern Ukraine. Russia's territorial aggrandizement and its waging of hybrid warfare against the Kiev government have precipitated a fundamental change in Ukraine's understanding of its geostrategic interests. After new elections in October 2014, the government decided that Ukraine's security and sovereignty could not be achieved by maintaining nonalignment. On December 23, 2014, therefore, the *Rada* (the Ukrainian parliament) voted to drop its nonaligned status, and the government formally declared its intention to seek NATO membership. Public opinion in Ukraine now suggests growing support for alliance membership, as the only effective way to ensure the country's security and sovereignty. President Poroshenko has recently announced an intensive six-year program to prepare Ukraine for NATO membership, providing a breath-space for NATO member states to debate and reflect on the consequences of taking such a momentous political decision with far-reaching military and strategic implications.

For both Ukraine and the European security system, therefore, Russia's violations of the fundamental principles of the Helsinki Final Act and the 1990 *Paris Charter for a New Europe* have been a "game-changer." Beginning with the Euromaidan demonstrations in late 2013 which led to the fall of President Yanukovych, a series of dramatic developments have unfolded which have transformed the climate of European security—most significantly, Russia's pioneering use of "hybrid warfare" for territorial aggrandizement, the shooting down of MH17 over eastern Ukraine, and the simmering violence in the Donbass. Not surprisingly therefore, NATO Secretary General Anders Fogh Rasmussen noted in March 2014 that the Ukraine crisis presented "the gravest threat to European security since the end of the Cold War" (Rasmussen 2014). In terms of Europe's security environment, the Ukraine crisis has not just been a passing storm, but full-blown climate change. UN estimates put the number of dead at over 9,000 by the end of 2015. Many more have been wounded, displaced and psychologically damaged. As the NATO Summit Declaration of September 2014 noted, "Russia's aggressive actions against Ukraine have fundamentally changed our vision of a Europe whole, free, and at peace."

In this new and much harsher geopolitical context that arguments for and against the neutrality of Ukraine must be assessed. At the time of its birth, Ukrainian neutrality provided a way of managing the lack of national identity and domestic cleavages of ethnicity and language, by avoiding choosing between Europe and Russia. With Russia's dismemberment and destabilization of Ukraine, however, the political weight and influence of the Russian minority community has declined, creating a growing political constituency for NATO membership. At the same time, neutrality is now increasingly seen as a failed policy within Ukraine, and support for closer cooperation with both the EU and NATO has grown. To impose neutrality on Ukraine in this context, as part of a political rapprochement with Russia, and without the return of annexed territory seized by armed force, would be viewed as a vindication of Russian aggression and acceptance of its great power dominion over the "lands between." Although there are still many voices in the Euro-Atlantic community advocating Ukrainian neutrality (Kissinger 2014; Mearsheimer 2014), the window of opportunity for such a cooperative solution to the Ukraine crisis on Russian terms has passed (Budjeryn 2016).

At the same time, there is little stomach within NATO for Ukrainian membership. Providing Ukraine with Article V security guarantees would be a defence nightmare for NATO member states, and would require a major relocation of US troops and equipment to Central and Eastern Europe. The most likely outcome, therefore, is a gradual strengthening of functional military cooperation between NATO and Ukraine, combined with Western aid and support in building up credible military forces capable of securing Ukraine's sovereignty and deterring Russian military intervention. Although Ukraine will not be a position to mount an effective defence against a determined Russian invasion for some time, with Western aid it might be able to contain the Russian-backed secessionists in the Donbas, and raise the costs of further Russian aggression, thereby making the option of full-scale intervention less attractive.

Thus as a solution to the Ukraine crisis, the option of neutrality for Ukraine is now increasingly less likely, and provides no solution to the conundrum of managing a recidivist Russia willing and able to use coercive military power to support its assertive foreign policy objectives. Viewed in this light, Putin's opportunistic land-grab can be seen to have led Russia into a strategic dead-end: Russia has "lost" Ukraine; "lost" Germany as a partner in modernization, alienated the EU, its main trading partner, revived deep-seated and historically rooted fears of Russian power and intentions throughout Eastern and Central Europe, and pushed the formerly neutral countries in the Baltic Sea region, Sweden and Finland, closer towards NATO. As EU sanctions begin to bite, and Russia's structural economic problems deepen, the annexation of Crimea and hybrid warfare in the Donbas appears to be singularly counter-productive for the long-term economic and political interests of the Russian Federation.

GEOPOLITICS AND THE BALTIC SEA REGION

The chill winds blowing from the east have been felt with particular concern in the Baltic Sea region, which now constitutes the new frontline of the

"Cold Peace" between the Euro-Atlantic community and Russia. Hopes that the Baltic region could become a key buckle for a Europe "whole and free," providing a venue for new forms of cooperation and integration between Russia and the rest of Europe, have faded. The steady increase in security competition between Russia and the West over the last decade or more has created a "new normal" in the Baltic Sea region, characterized by regular and repeated Russian incursions into the airspace and territorial waters of its neighbors in this area, and aggressive large-scale military exercises, including a mock nuclear attack on Warsaw (Wieslander 2015).

The cumulative effect of these adverse strategic, political and military developments has been to accelerate the strategic reorientation of Swedish and Finnish security policy that began in the 1990s. As *The Economist* magazine noted in June 2014, "Sweden and Finland stopped being neutral years ago" (Charlemagne 2014). They have developed an enhanced partnership with NATO, and now actively participate in the full range of NATO exercises and operations. "The two Nordic countries are thus more willing participants in the transatlantic alliance than several full members."

This is particularly the case with Sweden. Having joined the Partnership for Peace scheme in 1994, Sweden has forged very close cooperation with the alliance—to an extent unthinkable in the Cold War. Swedish units and officers participate extensively in NATO training exercises, which has had a critical impact on Swedish military doctrine and strategic culture (Huldt 2005, 43; Wyss 2011). By 2012 for example, Sweden had participated in forty-two NATO exercises, thirteen of them taking place in Sweden (Herolf 2013, 6). In November 2013, Sweden participated in NATO's Article V military exercise in Poland and the Baltic states (Operation *Steadfast Jazz*), signaling a "soft" commitment to the defence of its EU allies and NATO partners. In addition, Sweden contributes to the NATO Response Force, which has familiarized the Swedish military to some very advanced and "high-end" operational doctrines and procedures.

Sweden's consistent participation in major NATO operations in the Balkans, Afghanistan and Libya marks its out as one of the most active and engaged of NATO's partners. As noted above, Sweden is more active in NATO operations than some long-serving NATO members (Cottey 2013), underlying the extent to which Sweden's formal policy of military non-alignment has been accompanied by ever closer cooperation with NATO. "NATO," the former Swedish prime minister Fredrik Reinfeldt argued, "is central to security and stability in Europe" (Reinfeldt 2014). Tellingly, Sweden has committed more troops to NATO-led operations than to EU ones, and has taken part in all NATO operations with a UN mandate (Aggestam and Hyde-Price 2016). The commitment to Afghanistan has been one of the most significant in terms of the difficulty and complexity of the military mission, and presented the Swedish army with the new challenge of going beyond stabilization and peace support operations and developing a capability for counter-insurgency (Allen 2010). If Afghanistan was important for the Swedish army, Operation *Unified Protector* in Libya was equally important for its air force. This was the first international operation of the Swedish air force in more than fifty years, and provided invaluable lessons on both interoperability with NATO, and the capabilities and potential of the JAS 39C Gripen (Hellenius 2014).

Sweden's quiet revolution in its security orientation is the result of a series of mutually reinforcing developments. On the one hand, it reflects the working out of the tension between neutrality and collective security noted above. The Swedish government formally dropped its neutral status in 1992 in preparation for EU membership and demonstrated its willingness to contribute actively to European security by participating in UNPROFOR in the Balkans (Johansson 1997; Brommesson 2010). This experience of operating alongside NATO peacekeepers in UNPROFOR helped it realize that it was a "stakeholder in the European security order, together with others, and that the problems had to be tackled together with others as well" (Dalsjö 2012, 151).[2] Sweden has subsequently taken part in every CSDP military operation, and served as the Framework Nation for the Nordic EU Battlegroup three times (2008, 2011 and 2015). In 2007, the policy of military nonalignment was complemented by a commitment to seek "security in cooperation with others," although the full implications of this were not explicitly spelled out. Nonetheless, this shift towards security cooperation with others was further deepened in the context of the EU's "Solidarity Declaration," which was included in the 2009 Lisbon Treaty. This was followed by a unilateral "Solidarity Declaration" by the Swedish government contained in the 2009 Defence Bill. This included two revolutionary announcements, made with very little fanfare or public debate: the first was that Sweden would not remain passive if a disaster or an attack should afflict another EU member state or Nordic country, and that Sweden expected these countries to reciprocate; and second, that the Swedish armed forces should be able to both give and receive military assistance (Swedish Ministry of Defence 2009, 140).

The second significant development was changing attitude towards NATO. Revelations of Sweden's secret Cold War cooperation with the United States and NATO put the whole issue of "neutrality" into a very different perspective (Bjereld and Möller 2016), while participation in the Partnership of Peace program and the Partnership Planning and Review Process encouraged growing interoperability and the adoption of NATO standards and procedures. The re-establishment of the independence of the three Baltic republics after the disintegration of the USSR also led to a debate on how best to ensure their future survival and territorial integrity. The Swedish government soon came to the conclusion that the best solution, "both for the Balts and for Sweden, was for NATO to underwrite the Balts security" (Dalsjö 2012, 150). With the hollowing out of Sweden's defence capabilities as a result of a steady shrinkage of the defence budget from the early 1990s onwards, it was also clear that the Swedish armed forces could no longer mount an effective defence of Swedish territory in the event of an armed attack, and that a policy of "armed neutrality" (the "hedgehog option") was no longer possible. In this situation, Sweden has sought to build closer security and defence cooperation with its Nordic neighbors, and with other EU member states and NATO partners—most importantly, the United States.

Finally, Swedish security and defence planning has focused increasingly on the Baltic Sea region (Hultquist 2015; Bengtsson 2016). This regional perspective is one of the central pillars of Sweden's "quiet revolution" in foreign and security policy. During the cold war, Sweden championed the cause of self-determination and sovereignty for Third World countries, but kept relatively quiet about human rights abuses and violations of sovereignty in its regional neighborhood. This disjunction between its moralistic stance on North-South relations with its small state realist approach to East-West relations was designed to reassure the Soviets about its neutrality and maintain the "Nordic balance" (Makko 2012). With the end of the cold war, however, this has radically changed. Sweden now defines its own national security interests in terms of the common interests of its Nordic partners and EU neighbors (Brommesson 2016). This new "neighbourhood perspective" was outlined by the Minister of Defence Sten Tolgfors at the Sälen conference on January 17, 2010. Swedish defence policy, he argued, would henceforth have a "new neighbourhood perspective for the Baltic Sea, Norden [the Nordic countries] and the EU," and the Swedish armed forces would be structured and oriented towards the Baltic Sea region on the understanding that "Sweden builds security together with others" (Tolgfors 2010). This approach of building "security with others" has also been manifested in the new commitment to Nordic defence cooperation in the framework of NORDEFCO, as well as bilateral defence agreements with its Nordic neighbors—particularly Finland (Dahl 2014; Forsberg 2013).

Sweden has thus moved a long way from its Cold War policy of neutrality. This quiet revolution in strategic affairs is a result of two sets of pressures: the working through of the tension between neutrality and collective security in the context of EU membership; and its exposure to the shifting geopolitics of the Baltic Sea region and the "new normal" of Russia's assertive military profile. Given that the "hedgehog option" of "armed neutrality" is no longer possible given the hollowing out of its military capabilities after two decades of shrinking defence expenditure, Sweden is now committed to building "security with others," and is actively exploring a range of options to deepen European security cooperation. Nonetheless, tensions and ambiguities remain, particularly between the desire to retain independence and national sovereignty when it comes to providing military support to threatened neighbors and partners, and the ability to both give and receive military aid. What this means in practice is not clear. As Mike Winnerstig has noted, Sweden has undergone a "profound reorientation of its security and defence policy, a lengthy process that started at least 20 years ago." So convoluted and complex is this process that "even seasoned Swedish diplomats have problems delivering a logical, coherent presentation of Swedish security policy to foreign and domestic audiences" (Winnerstig 2012, 35).

This was also the main conclusion to the *Report from the Inquiry on Sweden's International Defence Cooperation* commissioned by the Swedish Ministry of Defence, and presented by Ambassador Tomas Bertelman in October 2014. "The most significant limitations on further development of cooperation in the defence area," he argued, "are imposed by Sweden itself," because of the continuing focus on the national right to decide on operational capabilities for the defence of Sweden's sovereignty and territorial integrity (a legacy of the policy of neutrality). The concept of "security together with others," he noted, contains three defence policy aspects: effectiveness, solidarity and sovereignty. "However, the problem is that the contradiction among the three components continues to grow. The tension between the requirements of effectiveness, solidarity and sovereignty is increasing, and the result is a growing uncertainty about Swedish policy" (Bertelman 2014, 65–66).

CONCLUSION

Neutrality, as we have seen, comes in "57 varieties." It stretches from a passive and isolationist stance at one end of the spectrum, to an engaged and interventionist approach at the other. For countries like Switzerland or Turkmenistan, their neutrality falls closer to the passive and isolationist end of the spectrum. For neutral and nonaligned states that have joined the EU, however, this is no longer a viable option. EU membership now involves a commitment to solidarity, and in a more globalized and interdependent world, a disengaged and isolationist approach is less sustainable. Whether the principle of solidarity with fellow EU member states leads to a clearer commitment to "security together with others" and enhanced partnership with NATO, however, seems to depend primarily on the geopolitical context in which the neutral and nonaligned state is located. Exposure to direct and immediate security competition, the evidence from the Baltic Sea region suggests, tends to lead over time to greater security cooperation and defence integration, especially if the old policy of "armed neutrality" is no longer viable given drastic defence cuts. As neoclassical realist theory posits (Zakaria 1992; Rose 1998; Lobell, Ripsman and Taliaferro (eds.) 2009), security policies are shaped first and foremost by systemic pressures—what Leopold von Ranke termed, the *Primat der Aussenpolitik* (the "primacy of foreign policy"). Nonetheless, how political elites and national decision makers respond to these systemic pressures—and how quickly—depends a number of domestic level variables, including state capabilities, strategic culture and political traditions.

NOTES

1. See also Michael Malmborg, 2001. *Neutrality and State-Building in Sweden.* Houndsmill: Palgrave.
2. See also Gunilla Herolf, 2007. "Overcoming National Impediments to ESDP." In *The North and the ESDP: The Baltic States, Denmark, Finland and Sweden*, edited by Klaus Brummer. Gütherloh: Bertelsman Stiftung; Carl Bildt, 1998. *Peace Journey: The Struggle for Peace in Bosnia.* London: Weidenfeld and Nicolson.

BIBLIOGRAPHY

Aggestam, Lisbeth, and Adrian Hyde-Price. 2016. "'A Force for Good'? Paradoxes of Swedish Military Activism." In *The Oxford Handbook on Swedish Politics*, edited by Jon Pierre, 479–494. Oxford: Oxford University Press.
Allen, Nick. 2010. *Embed: With the World's Armies in Afghanistan.* Stroud: Spellmount.
Bengtsson, Rikard. 2016. "Sweden and the Baltic Sea Region." In *The Oxford Handbook on Swedish Politics*, edited by Jon Pierre, 447–461. Oxford: Oxford University Press.
Bertelman, Tomas. 2014. *International Defence Cooperation: Efficiency, Solidarity, Sovereignty. Report from the Inquiry on Sweden's International Defence Cooperation.* Stockholm: Swedish Ministry of Defence.
Bildt, Carl. 1998. *Peace Journey: The Struggle for Peace in Bosnia.* London: Weidenfeld and Nicolson.
Bjereld, Ulf and Ulrika Möller. 2016. "Swedish Foreign Policy: The Policy of Neutrality and Beyond." In *The Oxford Handbook on Swedish Politics*, edited by Jon Pierre, 433–446. Oxford: Oxford University Press.
Bohr, Annette. 2016. *Turkmenistan: Power, Politics and Petro-Authoritarianism.* Chatham House Research Paper. https://www.chathamhouse.org/publication/turkmenistan-power-politics-and-petro-authoritarianism?dm_i=1TYG,430EO, KV0619,ESTLM,1.
Bring, Ove. 2012. "The Concept of Neutrality: Origins and Challenges. From the Peace of Westphalia to the European Union." *Neutrality in the 21st Century*, 21–28. Belgrade: ISAC Fond 2012.

Brommesson, Douglas. 2010. "Normative Europeanization: The Case of Swedish Foreign Policy Reorientation." *Cooperation and Conflict* 45(2): 224–244.

———. 2016. "The Europeanization of Swedish Foreign Policy and Beyond: On Multiple Roles in Swedish Post-Cold-War Foreign Policy." In *The Oxford Handbook on Swedish Politics*, edited by Jon Pierre, 529–543. Oxford: Oxford University Press.

Budjeryn, Mariana. 2016. "The Reality and Myth of Ukrainian Neutrality." *World Affairs Journal*. http://www.worldaffairsjournal.org/article/myth-ukrainian-neutrality.

Bull, Hedley. 1977. *The Anarchical Society: A Study of Order in World Politics.* London: Macmillan Press.

Charlemagne. 2014. "What Price Neutrality?" *The Economist*, June 21. http://www.economist.com/news/europe/21604586-russia-stokes-fresh-debate-among-nordics-about-nato-membership-what-price-neutrality.

Cottey, Andrew. 2013. "The European Neutrals and NATO: Ambiguous Partnership." *Contemporary Security Policy* 34(3): 446–472.

Dahl, Ann-Sofie. 2014. *NORDEFCO and NATO: "Smart Defence" in the North?* Rome: NATO Defence College.

Dalsjö, Robert. 2006. *Life-Line Lost: The Rise and Fall of 'Neutral' Sweden's Secret Reserve Option of Wartime Help from the West.* Stockholm: Santérus Academic Press.

———. 2012. "From Self-Sufficiency to Solidarity: The Transformation of Sweden's Defence and Security Policies." In *International Symposium on Security Affairs 2012*, edited by NIDS (Japanese National Institute for Defence Studies), 141–160.

Ekengren, Ann-Marie. 2011. "How Ideas Influence Decision-Making: Olof Palme and Swedish Foreign Policy, 1965–1975." *Scandinavian Journal of History* 36(2): 126–129.

Fischer, Thomas. 2012. "European Neutrals in the Cold War." *Neutrality in the 21st Century*, 29–34. Belgrade: ISAC Fond.

Ford, Matt. 2014. "After Crimea, Sweden flirts with joining NATO." *Atlantic Council*, March 13.

Forsberg, Tuomas 2013. "The Rise of Nordic Defence Cooperation: A Return to Regionalism?" *International Affairs* 89(5): 1161–1181.

Goodby, James E. 2014. "The Survival Strategies of small nations." *Survival: Global Politics and Strategy* 56(5): 31–39.

Granholm, Niklas. 2014. A Rude Awakening: Ramifications of Russian Aggression Towards Ukraine. Stockholm: FOI. http://www.foi.se/report?rNo=FOI-R--3892--SE

Hellenius, Björn. 2014. "Griffin takes wing: SAAB JAS 39 Gripen." *Air Forces Monthly* 312: 50–73.

Herolf, Gunilla. 2007. "Overcoming National Impediments to ESDP." In *The North and the ESDP: The Baltic States, Denmark, Finland and Sweden*, edited by Klaus Brummer. Gütherloh: Bertelsman Stiftung.

———. 2013. "European Security Policy: Nordic and Northern Strategies." *International Policy Analysis*. Berlin: Friedrich-Ebert-Stiftung.

Holland, James. 2015. *The War in the West: Germany Ascendent 1939–1941*. London: Transworld Publishers.

Huldt, Bo. 2005. "Swedish Commentator." In *Challenges to Neutral and Non-Aligned Countries in Europe and Beyond*, edited by Emily Munro, 41–46. Geneva: Geneva Centre for Security Policy.

Hultqvist, Peter. 2015. Speech by Minister for Defence of Sweden at seminar *Regional and Global Impact: The Changing Situation in Northern Europe and the Baltic Sea Area*. Paris: Institut Français des Relations Internationales, September 23, 2015. http://www.government.se/speeches/2015/09/speech-by-minister-for-defence-of-sweden-peter-hultqvist-at-seminar/.

Hyde-Price, Adrian. 2007. *The Challenge of Multipolarity: European Security in the Twenty-First Century*. London: Routledge.

Johansson, Eva. 1997. "The Role of Peacekeepers in the 1990s: Swedish Experience of UNPROFOR." *Armed Forces and Society* 23(3): 451–465.

Jonter, Stefan. 2001. *Sweden and the Bomb: Swedish Plans to Acquire Nuclear Weapons 1945–1972*, SKI Report, September.

Kissinger, Henry. 2014. "To Settle the Ukraine Crisis, Start at the End." *The Washington Post*, March 5.

Lobell, Steven/Ripsman, Norrin/Taliaferro, Jeffrey (Eds.). 2009. *Neoclassical Realism, the State, and Foreign Policy*. Cambridge: Cambridge University Press.

Lunde, Henrik. 2009. *Hitler's Pre-emptive War: The Battle for Norway, 1940*. Newbury: Casemate.

Makko, Aryo. 2012. "Sweden, Europe and the Cold War." *Journal of Cold War Studies* 14(2): 68–97.

Malmborg, Michael. 2001. *Neutrality and State-Building in Sweden*. Houndsmill: Palgrave.

Mearsheimer, John. 2014. "Why the Ukraine Crisis is the West's Fault." *Foreign Affairs* September/October: 77–89.

Möller, Ulrika and Ulf Bjereld. 2010. "From Nordic Neutrals to Post-Neutral Europeans: Differences in Finnish and Swedish Policy Transformation." *Cooperation and Conflict* 45(4): 363–386.

O'Donoghue, Aoife. 2010. "Neutrality and Multilateralism after the First World War." *Journal of Conflict and Law Security* 15(1): 169–202.

Reinfeldt, Fredrik. 2014. "Sverige i en globaliserad värld." *Speech at Folk och Försvars rikskonferens*, Sälen January 12.

Rose, Gideon. 1998. "Neoclassical Realism and Theories of Foreign Policy." *World Politics* 51(1): 144–77.

Sloan, Stanley. 1997. "NATO Enlargement and the Former European Neutrals." *CRS Report for Congress* (97–249 F). Washington: Congressional Research Service, Library of Congress, February 18. http://fas.org/man/crs/crs2.htm.

Stoker, Donald. 2010. *The Grand Design. Strategy and the U.S. Civil War*. Oxford: Oxford University Press.

Swedish Ministry of Defence. 2009. "A Useful Defence." *The Swedish Government's Bill*: 140.

Timon, Karolin. 2011. *Neutrality in the 21st Century: Lessons from Serbia.* Belgrade: Belgrade Centre for Security Policy.

Tolgfors, Sten. 2010. "Försvarsförmåga I focus—ett försvarspolitiskt paradigmskifte." *Fölk och Försvars rikskonferens I Sälen*, January 17. Accessed March 16, 2016. http://www.regeringen.se/contentassets/ff30cab3a3b146a98345a22e649ae21b/tal-2006–2010---forsvarsminister-sten-tolgfors.

Wieslander, Anna. 2016. "NATO, the U.S. and Baltic Sea Security." *UI Paper* 3, Stockholm: Swedish Institute of International Affairs.

———. 2015. "A "new normal" for NATO and Baltic Sea Security." *Atlantic Council*, October 5.

Winnerstig, Mike. 2012. "From Neutrality to Solidarity? Sweden's Ongoing Geopolitical Orientation." In *Advancing U.S.-Nordic-Baltic Security Coopertion: Adapting Partnership to a New Security Environment*, edited by Daniel Hamilton, Andras Simonyi and Debra Cagan, 35–47. Washington: Centre for Transatlantic Relations.

Wyss, Marco. 2011. "Military Transformation in Europe's Neutral and Non-Allied States." *The RUSI Journal* 56(2): 44–51.

Zakaria, Fareed. 1992. "Realism and Domestic Politics: A Review." International Security 17(1): 177–198.

Chapter 6

From Helsinki I to Helsinki II?

The Role of the Neutral and Nonaligned States in the OSCE

P. Terrence Hopmann

The Helsinki Final Act, signed on July 31, 1975, as the outcome of negotiations within the Conference on Security and Cooperation in Europe (CSCE), was heavily influenced in its content by the neutral and nonaligned states of Europe. Many of these states saw in the CSCE an opportunity to break down barriers between the two dominant alliance systems in Europe, NATO and the Warsaw Treaty Organization, and to try to override the Cold War divisions with a new normative structure to enhance security in a divided Europe. The CSCE held three major review conferences after the signature of the Helsinki Final Act, all in capitals of neutral or nonaligned countries, namely Belgrade, Madrid and Vienna. With the end of the Cold War, as the major states tended to assign the CSCE, and the Organization for Security and Cooperation in Europe (OSCE) as it was renamed in 1995, a lesser role in European security, many of the neutral and nonaligned states continued to consider it as vehicle in which their views about security issues could be discussed outside of the framework of an expanding NATO and a newly formed Central States Treaty Organization (CSTO). For the most part, the OSCE Chair-in-Office, the most important political post in the OSCE, has been held by neutral or nonaligned states as well as by middle powers that are aligned with a major power bloc. Furthermore, the normative underpinnings of the OSCE remain attractive to neutral and nonaligned states that tend to reject reliance on power politics in international relations that by and large leave less powerful states with little or no influence over matters that concern their vital security, as well as their economic and humanitarian interests. Thus, while NATO, the European Union, and the CSTO have generally been dominated by the major states of Europe and North America, the OSCE remains a vehicle in which the concerns of the neutral and nonaligned may be addressed and in which their normative power may be advanced, in contrast to the military and economic powers that otherwise dominate the international relations of Europe and the North Atlantic area.

THE ORIGINS OF THE HELSINKI PROCESS

The origins of the CSCE may be found in Soviet proposals beginning in the mid-1950s to hold an all European conference to put a political end to Second World War by resolving the "German question" and essentially ratifying the post-war status quo in Europe. The United States and most of its NATO allies were opposed to a conference with such a vague "political" agenda, preferring instead to hold a conference between NATO and Warsaw Pact states dealing with "hard" arms control in Europe, and their opposition was reinforced by the intervention of Soviet troops in Czechoslovakia in 1968 to suppress the internal reforms of the "Prague spring." In April 1969, neutral Finland offered to host a preparatory conference on European security in Helsinki, and increasingly the neutral and nonaligned countries of Europe, along with some Western European members of NATO, began to support the idea of such a meeting, contrary to the expressed preferences of US leaders. The Warsaw Pact proposed that the agenda of such a meeting should emphasize security matters, including recognition of existing borders and nonaggression, along with scientific and technological cooperation. Movement towards the convening of a European security conference gained further momentum in 1970 with West Germany's "Ostpolitik," and the resulting agreements between West Germany and both the Soviet Union and Poland over the political status and borders of East Germany, and this was further reinforced by the Four Power agreement on Berlin in 1971 (Dean 1987, 103).

NATO responded to the Finnish proposal and to the Warsaw Pact's ideas regarding the agenda for a European security conference by suggesting that the conference should consider prior notification of military maneuvers in the security realm, while emphasizing that it should also include a "human dimension" with a focus on freer movement of people and ideas across the Cold War divide. The United States was especially reluctant to enter into a vague political negotiation that might ratify the European status quo, especially because US leaders perceived that the Warsaw Pact possessed a significant quantitative superiority in troops and armaments in the Central European region. Nonetheless, when President Richard Nixon and Soviet General Secretary Brezhnev met in Moscow in May 1972 to sign the SALT I Treaty, tentative agreement was reached to open preliminary talks on conventional forces in Central Europe in exchange for beginning preliminary talks in Helsinki on broader European security issues as proposed by the government of Finland (Dean 1987, 105). As the initiative for the conference had come from Finland, Europe's neutral and nonaligned states also enthusiastically responded to the call to come to Helsinki, even though they were not included in the "hard" arms control negotiations on MBFR that began at about the same time in Vienna.

The CSCE negotiations opened with a foreign ministers' meeting in Helsinki on July 3–7, 1973. At the opening there were thirty-five delegations present, including two North American countries—the United States and Canada—plus almost all states of Europe big and small, including the Soviet Union and the Holy See. The sole exceptions were Albania, which at that time followed a policy of self-isolation from international organizations, and Andorra, a micro-state in Western Europe that entered both the UN and the OSCE only in 1996. The participating states tended to coalesce into three major groups: (1) The Warsaw Pact, led by the Soviet Union; (2) the NATO/ European Community group; and (3) a Neutral and Nonaligned Group, which comprised all remaining states including Yugoslavia, with the exception of Spain (still governed at that time by its fascist dictator, Francisco Franco), which refused to participate with any group. In addition, caucuses were formed on several issues by both the Nordic countries and a Mediterranean group, and a special Berlin group emerged consisting of the four "great powers," the former Second World War allies, focused on issues involving the status of divided Berlin and Germany (Maresca 1995, 18–21).

The working phase of negotiations began in Geneva on September 18, 1973, and continued until July 25, 1975. During this phase, issues were grouped together into three major substantive "baskets," which also were reflected in the eventual agreement: Basket I dealt with security issues, especially military confidence-building measures; Basket II dealt with cooperation in economic, scientific and technical fields; Basket III treated the "human dimension" including freer movement of peoples, communications, and tourism across national boundaries, especially bridging the East-West divide in Europe. Of special importance as well was the decision rule adopted for the conference, namely that all decisions would be taken only by the consensus of all participating states, in the words of the "final recommendations" on procedures, "understood to mean the absence of any objection expressed by a Representative and submitted by him as an obstacle to the taking of the decision in question" (Lehne 1990, 3–4). With a few notable exceptions, this has been the operative decision rule in the OSCE ever since, formalizing at least in principle the sovereign equality of all participating states, large and small, allied and neutral.

The preparatory talks that took place in Dipoli, just outside Helsinki, included all of the European neutral and nonaligned states. The core group was composed of four formally neutral European states—Austria, Finland, Sweden, and Switzerland—plus Yugoslavia, which at the time was among the leaders of the global Group of 77 or "non-aligned" bloc. It also included Cyprus, Malta, Liechtenstein, and the Holy See. Spain did not participate in any bloc, as noted above. As John Maresca, a member of the US delegation at the original Helsinki negotiations, writes:

> The neutral group had similar views of several issues. Being left out of the negotiations on force reductions in Vienna, they were eager to enhance and broaden the military content of the CSCE. They were also generally favorable to an early, successful conclusion to the Conference and an elaborate follow-up mechanism that would provide them with a forum for multilateral consultations on European issues. Their cohesiveness on these issues was surprisingly strong. (Maresca 1995, 21)

In a study of the drafting of the final text of the Decalogue and Basket One (Security Measures) of the Helsinki Final Act, this author was able to identify that about 33.7 percent or one-third of the text was initiated by members of this neutral and nonaligned group, well out of proportion to their size and power rankings among the thirty-five participating states. Interestingly, by far the largest contribution came from Yugoslavia, which alone contributed about 20 percent of the overall text; Yugoslavia submitted the original draft of the largest portion of the text of any participating state, followed closely by the Soviet Union (Hopmann 1978, 141–177).[1] Interestingly, one Warsaw Pact state, Romania, also frequently diverged from its allies and supported positions advocated by the neutral and nonaligned participants, while also making major contributions of its own to the final text.

The original CSCE negotiations culminated in a summit conference of heads of state from all thirty-five countries in Helsinki on July 31–August 1, 1975, at which the Final Act was signed. The Helsinki Final Act, first and foremost, contains the "Decalogue," ten principles that should govern interstate relations: (1) sovereign equality of states, (2) refraining from the threat or use of force, (3) inviolability of frontiers, (4) territorial integrity of states, (5) peaceful settlement of disputes, (6) non-intervention in internal affairs, (7) respect for human rights and fundamental freedoms, (8) self-determination of peoples, (9) cooperation among states, and (10) fulfillment of obligations under international law.[2]

This normative regime has had a profound impact on the security situation in Europe ever since 1975. Some commentators have even concluded that it played a significant role in undermining the legitimacy of the communist governments throughout Central and Eastern Europe, where governments signed agreements that they clearly had no intention of implementing in fields such as human rights. It certainly inspired the formation of a wide variety of human rights movements in Central and Eastern Europe, such as

Charter 77 in Czechoslovakia and Solidarity in Poland, which lobbied their governments to observe their commitments undertaken when they signed the Helsinki Final Act. In the final analysis, a network of informal domestic and transnational alliances emerged across Eastern Europe and the Soviet Union that "weakened the institutions, drained the resources, and delegitimated the arguments that sustained repressive, one-party rule" (Thomas 2001, 284). From the perspective of the neutral and nonaligned participants in Helsinki, it attenuated many of the most intense conflicts of the Cold War and paved the way for its eventual demise, far sooner than anyone envisioned at the time the Final Act was signed in 1975.

KEEPING THE CSCE RELEVANT: THE ROLE OF THE NEUTRAL AND NONALIGNED STATES AFTER HELSINKI

One of the major accomplishments of the neutral and nonaligned group was to insure that there would be a series of follow-on conferences to review progress in the implementation of the Final Act and to consider new provisions to strengthen security in Europe, in spite of considerable reluctance on the part of most NATO states. Both the United States and the Soviet Union were skeptical about extending the process in this way. Support for the CSCE in the United States waned after the Helsinki Summit, and the Soviet Union, having achieved its goals regarding the affirmation of European frontiers, was also concerned about where further extension of the CSCE process might lead. Among the Warsaw Pact states only Romania demonstrated much support for the long-term extension of the CSCE process, but in fact they had been way out in front of the Soviets throughout the entire Helsinki negotiation process in an effort to establish their independence from Soviet domination of the bloc.[3]

Therefore, the primary impetus to include a provision for a series of follow-on conferences came from the European neutrals and nonaligned, who favored converting the CSCE into a continuing series of conferences both to evaluate implementation of the Helsinki Final Act and to decide upon additional measures to promote the goals of security and cooperation in Europe.

Fittingly, Belgrade was selected as the site of the first such conference held in 1977. Although this meeting did not produce any major substantive agreements, it provided a thorough review of the early implementation of the Helsinki commitments. The Belgrade conference, and the second conference in Madrid, tended, however, to be diverted by various conflicts along traditional Cold War lines. Indeed, the administration of President Jimmy Carter, which entered the White House in 1977, saw in the humanitarian provisions of the Final Act an opportunity to criticize the human rights performance of communist regimes. Although Western European governments, especially the West German government of Helmut Schmidt, were less inclined than Washington to use the Final Act as a kind of political club with which to bash the Soviets for their poor human rights record, they nevertheless generally supported the United States in this endeavor, even if reluctantly at times (Leatherman 2003, 197).

Thus the first CSCE Review Conference in Belgrade in 1977–1978 was characterized largely by rhetorical attacks and counterattacks, with Western governments criticizing the human rights performance of the communist bloc countries, while the latter accused the West of blatant interference in their internal affairs. Ambassador Arthur Goldberg, a former US Supreme Court justice who headed the US delegation in Belgrade, led this attack vigorously in a conference during which direct East-West negotiations were kept to a minimum. In response, human rights activists in a number of communist states in Central and Eastern Europe formed Helsinki Committees to pressure their governments to live up to the principles that they had endorsed at Helsinki. Not surprisingly, one consequence of the abuse heaped upon the Soviet government at Belgrade was a diminished enthusiasm for the Helsinki process in Moscow and other East European capitals, especially as dissidents within their own countries used the Helsinki Final Accords as a standard against which the performance of their own governments might be measured.

A subsequent meeting in Montreux, Switzerland on the Peaceful Settlement of Disputes also became stymied by the competing conceptions between the two Cold War blocs, with the Western bloc calling for compulsory third-party mediation in interstate disputes whereas the Eastern states preferred direct consultations between parties to a dispute. A second expert conference was convened in Valletta on the insistence of Malta to discuss cooperation in the Mediterranean region, and it too concluded with a vague and general agreement on enhancing cooperation in the Mediterranean region. Finally, a Scientific Forum was held in Hamburg in 1980 among scientists rather than diplomats. While it advanced some ideas about enhancing cooperation among scientists working on common problems in the region, it too was confronted with serious conflicts along Cold War lines.

The second follow-on meeting began in Madrid in 1980, after the death of Franco had enabled Spain to join with the neutral and nonaligned group; it lasted for more than three years. At the outset, it too was stalemated by the intensified debate over human rights and non-intervention in internal affairs. By the end of 1979, détente had all but faded following the Soviet invasion of Afghanistan, the refusal of the United States to ratify the SALT II Treaty, and in 1981 General Jaruzelski imposed martial law in Poland in response to the rise of the Solidarity movement in that country, a movement that had taken inspiration in part from the principles enshrined in the Helsinki Final Act (Thomas 2001, 204–205). The new US administration of President Reagan took an even stronger anticommunist stance than its predecessor, fully repudiating the policy of détente and all it represented. Western governments in Madrid refused to move forward on proposals to reinforce confidence-building measures and other provisions to increase security until the situations in Poland and Afghanistan were resolved to their satisfaction and until the communist governments improved their general human rights performance.

However, Western European and neutral and nonaligned governments put increased pressure on the United States to try to promote some areas of cooperation across the Cold War lines. Finland took the lead in trying to balance the principles of the Helsinki Decalogue with the desire of Western European countries to move forward on confidence and security-building measures (CSBMs) (Leatherman 2003, 212). Therefore, eventually the Madrid conference was able to discuss ideas for strengthening CBMs and to establish machinery for the peaceful resolution of disputes. Of particular significance was the adoption of a mandate for negotiations under CSCE auspices in Stockholm, officially known as the Conference on Confidence- and Security-Building Measures and Disarmament in Europe (CDE). In addition, working meetings were set up to deal with human rights and fundamental freedoms in Ottawa, human contacts in Bern, the peaceful settlement of disputes in Athens, cultural contacts in Budapest, and Mediterranean security issues in Venice. While few actual decisions were taken in Madrid, the CSCE process at least regained some momentum due in no small part to the efforts by neutral and nonaligned states. In spite of these modest accomplishments, however, the collapse of détente in the immediate aftermath of the signing of the 1975 Helsinki Final Act meant that the CSCE over the ensuing decade generally fell short of the vision and goals that had inspired the process in its formative years.

The political climate in East-West relations began to change rapidly after Mikhail Gorbachev assumed the position of general secretary in the Soviet Union. This new spirit was clearly reflected in the Stockholm conference on expanded CSBMs, which became a forum in which many of Gorbachev's ideas about "new thinking" began to take shape. The CDE announced a breakthrough in arms control in Central Europe, including significant measures that permitted international observation of military maneuvers inside the Soviet Union west of the Urals. The momentum created by the CDE carried through into the third CSCE follow-on conference that began in Vienna on November 4, 1986. The Vienna conference, which lasted until January 1989, became a venue for the rapidly changing political scene in Central and Eastern Europe to play out, and the European security framework began to adapt to the new environment even before the definitive end of the Cold War.

Virtually all baskets of the Helsinki Final Act were strengthened, and numerous conferences were spawned to deal with the rapidly changing security environment.[4] When the Vienna follow-on conference opened, East-West relations were embroiled in an intense crisis, and its conclusion came at a time when the Cold War was clearly coming to an end.

With regard to Basket I issues, the successful conclusion of the Stockholm Conference on Disarmament in Europe paved the way for a new mandate on confidence and security-building measures that especially would constrain independent activities involving air and naval units not covered in previous agreements. In addition, the moribund talks between NATO and the Warsaw Pact on Mutual and Balanced Force Reductions (MBFR) were reinvented, given a new mandate under the title of the Conventional Forces in Europe (CFE), and linked more closely to the CSCE process. The Vienna document also pointed to the significance of terrorist threats, and it called on the participating states to cooperate in preventing terrorists from seeking refuge on their territory, from crossing international boundaries, to demonstrate firmness in responding to demands of terrorists, and to vigorously prosecute terrorists who were captured on their territory or to extradite them to the country where their acts were committed. The results on Basket II issues were quite modest, calling for increased cooperation in trade and creating some environmental regulations concerning the pollution of major international waterways and measures to respond in the event of environmental catastrophes, adopted in the wake of the crisis at the Soviet nuclear facility at Chernobyl, in the Ukraine.

The most significant accomplishments of the Vienna meeting, however, undoubtedly came in the "human dimension." At its very outset, Soviet Foreign Minister Eduard Shevardnadze surprised those in attendance by proposing a special CSCE conference on humanitarian issues to be held in Moscow, suggesting as well that the CSCE provided the institutional foundation for what he described as a "common European home" extending across its entire territorial span (Thomas 2001, 238). Consequently, the *Concluding Document* proclaimed that issues of human rights are a fundamental component of international security and thus constitute a responsibility of the entire group of states and do not fall exclusively within the "internal affairs" of the state:

> They also confirm the universal significance of human rights and fundamental freedoms, respect for which is an essential factor for peace, justice and security necessary to insure the development of friendly relations and cooperation among themselves, as among all States (CSCE 1989, 6).

This language in effect legitimized the discussion and monitoring of human rights behavior as an appropriate activity of the CSCE, and no longer could participating states claim with credibility that international involvement in issues concerning the human rights of their citizens represented a violation of sovereignty, specifically of the principle of non-interference in the internal affairs of states.

From a more practical point of view, however, perhaps the most important innovation adopted in January 1989 in Vienna emphasized freedom of movement across state boundaries, found in Paragraph 20 of the Concluding Document:

– The participating States will respect fully the right of everyone
– to freedom of movement and residence within the borders of each State, and
– to leave any country, including his own, and to return to his country (CSCE 1989, 9).

This provision had a tremendous impact on world history in just a few short months after its adoption. In September 1989, thousands of East German tourists in Hungary refused to return home and demanded instead to be allowed to cross the border into Austria and eventually to make their way to West Germany. On September 11, the government of Hungary agreed to let these individuals enter Austria, contrary to a bilateral treaty with the GDR, referring specifically to their commitments under the Vienna CSCE document that took precedence over their bilateral treaties. This began the flood of emigration across the former "Iron Curtain" that resulted two months later in the breach of the Berlin Wall on November 9, 1989, generally thought to be the signal event marking the end of the Cold War. What has not been sufficiently noted in most accounts of these events, however, is the significant role of the CSCE's normative principles in providing both an impetus and a rationale for decisions taken by governments such as the one in Budapest that spelled the end of the division of Europe into two hostile camps.[5]

In short, the normative principles that had been promoted in Helsinki by the neutral and nonaligned group, that some other governments had accepted with little or no intention to implement in practice, were often turned against those governments in the aftermath of the Vienna Follow-on meeting, and governments that had paid little heed to these principles suddenly found themselves out of office. As summarized by Stefan Lehne, who served in the Austrian delegation at the Vienna meeting:

Beginning in the late 1970s and throughout the 1980s the human rights element of the CSCE helped to undermine the apparent stability of Eastern Europe. It aggravated the legitimacy crisis of Eastern regimes, which had accepted Principle VII but were unwilling and unable to abide by it. At the same time it legitimized and stimulated the political opposition, which could now base its demands on international commitments signed by the governments. Last but not least Western criticism of human rights violations in CSCE fora increased the political costs of Eastern repression and afforded the opposition in these countries a certain amount of protection. (Lehne 1990, 185)

It would be difficult to envision another historical event in which normative principles adopted by an international institution had such a significant impact on actual political life and indeed changed the course of history. This also contradicts the frequent assertion that normative principles adopted by states for cynical purposes are automatically either worthless or worse yet harmful. A developing civil society in Central and Eastern Europe held their governments to the standards to which they had subscribed, and in this case at least the underpinning given to popular protest by the power of these normative principles in the end proved to be stronger than the repressive instruments of state power. As Daniel Thomas concludes:

> ... the salience of human rights norms and the mobilization of domestic and transnational human rights movements were critical to the demise of Communist rule in Eastern Europe and the Soviet Union. Neither the structural contradictions of the party-state and centralized planning nor generational changes in the Soviet leadership would have brought about the largely peaceful and rights-protective political transitions of 1989 without the changes in international norms and state-society relations connected to the Helsinki Final Act. Over time, the human rights norms established at Helsinki affected both the behavior of state actors and the fundamental constructions of self-interest and identity that shape behavioral choices. (Thomas 2001, 255)

FINDING A NEW ROLE FOR THE NEUTRAL AND NONALIGNED STATES AFTER THE COLD WAR

With the fall of the Berlin Wall on November 9, 1989, the CSCE began a rapid process of transformation to respond to the new post-Cold War security situation in Europe. Suddenly the possibility of creating a genuine system of "cooperative security" on the European continent appeared to be feasible. In principle, cooperative security seeks to replace competition among opposing blocs with a genuinely cooperative set of relations, in which the security of all states is insured by cooperation among them. Rather than relying on a classical balance of power or fixed alliances, cooperative security assumes that security is indivisible. Rather than being directed against external enemies, it seeks to provide guarantees against a breach of the peace by one of the community's own participating states. Rather than relying on pre-existing alliances, it seeks to respond flexibly and collectively to efforts by any one state or a small group of states to violate the principles, norms, and rules established by the collective action of all participating states.

In other words, the immediate post-Cold War vision included the possibility of a CSCE no longer divided into three groups—West, East, and Neutral/Non-aligned—but instead united to maintain cooperative peace and security within the large European region covered by the CSCE. It thus changed from a regime based on mutual confidence-building and transparency between two competing blocs into a cooperative security regime covering the entire European region "from Vancouver to Vladivostok." This view was most clearly articulated by the neutral and nonaligned participants, now joined by the new leadership that emerged in Central Europe following the collapse of communism. Most directly, in March 1990 Czechoslovakia's foreign minister Jiri Dienstbier proposed to replace the existing system of competing alliance systems with a collective security system based on the CSCE. Even earlier, Polish prime minister Tadeusz Mazowiecki proposed creating a Council of European Cooperation to coordinate policy in the entire CSCE region. And even in the Soviet Union, Foreign Minister Shevardnadze called for the creation of a new order based on a system of collective security and built around the CSCE, while Mikhail Gorbachev referred to the CSCE as the foundation for his conception of a "Common European Home."

This enthusiasm for the CSCE, however, was not so widely shared in the West, as the United States responded cautiously, fearing competition with NATO, while several Western European countries, especially France under François Mitterand, seemed to prefer focusing upon the enlargement of the European Union as the primary foundation for a post-Cold War European security structure. At its summit in London in July 1990, however, the NATO heads of state did recognize explicitly that the new security situation in Europe would require that the CSCE develop a permanent institutional structure to replace the series of conferences and follow-on meetings that had constituted the only institutionalized format for the CSCE prior to 1990.

These changes also posed dilemmas for Europe's neutral and nonaligned states that had long advanced the concept of active neutrality, based on the assumption that "their only real security threat was the threat of being caught up in a conflict between the two military alliances," whereas with the end of the Cold War they confronted the challenge that the "new security picture" would present to "the very concept of neutrality" itself (Kruzel 1990, 31). Among other difficult questions was what would happen to neutrality if a new European security order emerged around the CSCE, somehow managing to supplant the Cold War system of competing alliances; it was hard to imagine what neutrality would mean if there were no longer competing alliances between which it was necessary to maintain a distinct policy of neutrality. On the other hand, if NATO and the EU not only survived but expanded both their activities and their geographic scope, too great an emphasis by the neutrals on the CSCE as the foundational pillar for European security could leave them out in the cold if the cooperative security order failed to materialize. This dilemma grew even stronger as the CSCE first began to strengthen its normative foundations and its capacity to act in promoting security and cooperation, but subsequently proved incapable of producing a fundamental change in the European security order. In short, the neutrals and nonaligned simultaneously supported the further development of the CSCE, while keeping options open to respond to the very real possibility that the European security structures preferred by the major powers might move in a different direction, leaving vestiges of the old order based on new forms of balance of power politics.

In the early 1990s there was reason for optimism that the CSCE might provide a viable foundation of a radically transformed European security architecture. Two major documents were produced by the CSCE in the first year after the end of the Cold War that fundamentally changed the normative and institutional structure of European security. The first of these was a report of an expert meeting held in Copenhagen in June 1990 on the human dimension of security. It reflected the essential features of democratic practices, often articulated by the neutral and nonaligned states and by some Western states, and attempted to apply them to the entire continent. Specifically, it called for free elections open to outside observation leading to representative governments in all CSCE states, equality before the law, pre-eminence of the rule of law, freedom to establish political parties, and assurances about the rights of accused persons. In effect, it enacted a code of democratic procedures to guide all member states, noting "that vigorous democracy depends on the existence as an integral part of national life of democratic values and practices as well as an extensive range of democratic institutions" (U.S. Commission of Security and Cooperation in Europe 1990, 14). It also expanded and gave substantive content to many of the human dimension principles contained only in general terms in previous CSCE documents. Among the most important of these were the right of peaceful assembly, the complete prohibition of torture under all circumstances including in times of war, progress in eliminating capital punishment through abolishing the death penalty in all participating states, protection of the right of conscientious objection to military service, insuring rapid issuance of visas and other documents to facilitate movements of peoples across international borders, and broad protection of the rights of national minorities to participate fully in political life without restriction (U.S. Commission of Security and Cooperation in Europe 1990).

The second major document was the "Charter of Paris for a New Europe" signed at a summit meeting held November 19–21, 1990. In its preamble, the Paris charter announced the opening of a new era for European security, based on a reaffirmation of the Helsinki Decalogue:

Europe is liberating itself from the legacy of the past. The courage of men and women, the strength of the will of the peoples and the power of the *ideas* of the Helsinki Final Act have opened a new era of democracy, peace and unity in Europe. (U.S. Commission of Security and Cooperation in Europe 1990, 13)[6]

In addition to reaffirming the "acquis" of the CSCE from the Helsinki Final Act through the various follow-on conferences and expert meetings, the Charter of Paris began the formal institutionalization of the CSCE. Having met as an itinerant series of conferences, moving from site to site without permanent headquarters or secretariat, the Paris meeting established a secretariat in Prague (moved to Vienna in 1993). In addition, a Conflict Prevention Center (CPC) was created in Vienna, an Office for Free Elections (subsequently renamed the Office for Democratic Institutions and Human Rights—ODIHR) was set up in Warsaw, and a Parliamentary Assembly, made up of parliamentarians from all participating states, was created with headquarters in Copenhagen. Regular meetings were to be held at the level of foreign ministers annually, summit meetings of heads of state were to be held biannually[7], and a Committee of Senior Officials (later replaced by the Permanent Council) would meet as needed to conduct all business between the annual and biannual meetings at the highest political levels. In short, after Paris the CSCE began to take on most of the traditional features of an established international organization rather than a series of ad hoc meetings about security issues.

Central to the new organization of the CSCE was the primary political role to be played by the Chairman-in-Office (CiO), organized in a troika system with the incoming chair, current chair and past chair all taking the leadership as the major political actors within the CSCE/OSCE. Between 1991 and 2017, twenty-seven countries (including three repeating chairs) have served as CiO. Seven of these chairmanships have been held by formally neutral participating states (in spite of the fact that all but Switzerland have entered the European Union but not into NATO), and another seven chairmanships were held by countries that at the time were nonaligned, although five of these entered NATO after serving as OSCE chairman-in-office. Even among the aligned CiO's, all but Germany (which served as the first CiO in 1991 and assumed a second term in 2016) came from among the European "middle states" such as Denmark, Norway, Belgium, and the Netherlands. This further suggests the desire of the European neutrals and nonaligned not to have the organization dominated by any of the traditional "great powers," and none of the four UN Security Council permanent members that also participate in the OSCE have ever served in a major political position in the OSCE.

The decade after the end of the Cold War, from 1991–1999, proved to be the most productive years for the OSCE. Confronted with conflicts appearing in numerous locations throughout the former Soviet Union and the former Yugoslavia, the CSCE/OSCE responded in the decade of the 1990s by opening eleven "missions of long duration" and five other "field activities" that engaged in various roles from conflict prevention, through mediation of cease-fires, to post-conflict peacebuilding.[8] Furthermore, this was generally a unique period of relative consensus among the participating states, in which bloc memberships faded in importance and substantial cooperation was achieved to address the many conflicts that appeared in Central and Eastern Europe after the end of the Cold War. Although neither the Russian Federation nor the United States tried to dominate the organization, both were generally supportive of its many activities related to promoting peace across the European continent. At the same time, the neutral and nonaligned states stepped up to take a leading role in most CSCE/OSCE institutions, supported by many western European states that also belonged to NATO and the EU.

During this time, however, NATO and the EU began their rapid enlargement to the east, which not only brought many former socialist bloc countries into one or both institutions, but also integrated most of the Western European neutral and nonaligned states (with the notable exception of Switzerland) into the EU and/or NATO. This, of course, raised the question of whether new EU member states like Austria, Sweden, and Finland could still reasonably be considered to be formally neutral, even though their neutrality had for many decades existed alongside a distinctly western orientation; however, their integration into a "common foreign and security policy" with aligned states raised questions about the compatibility of this move with formal neutrality, the Treaty of Lisbon's special provisions notwithstanding. During this period Moldova's 1994 Constitution proclaimed its neutrality in Article 11; Ukraine adopted a policy of neutrality, enshrined in its 1996 constitution (which it later renounced in 2014, following the Russian annexation of Crimea and the opening of violent conflict in eastern Ukraine); Belarus joined the Non-Aligned Movement in 1998; and Serbia's National Assembly declared a policy of armed neutrality in 2007 and became an observer state in the Non-Aligned Movement; Armenia, Bosnia and Herzegovina, Kazakhstan, Kyrgyzstan, Montenegro,[9] Tajikistan, and Ukraine among OSCE participating states have also become observers in the Non-Aligned Movement.

NEUTRAL ROLES IN THE OSCE IN THE TWENTY-FIRST CENTURY

Consensus within the OSCE began to decline towards the end of the twentieth century, and the years 1999–2000 marked a dramatic shift in the centrality of the OSCE in the security policies of many participating states. Several major events largely accounted for this change:

1. Many of the neutral and nonaligned states, along with former Warsaw Pact member states, joined NATO and/or the European Union, moving the line of demarcation between the two halves of Europe further to the east; most tended to see membership in these two institutions as more central to their security interests than their participation in the OSCE. At the same time, the European Union began to develop its common foreign and security policy that, in at least some respects, seemed to duplicate many of the primary functions of the OSCE.
2. The war in Kosovo in 1999 undertaken by NATO without authorization by either the UN or the OSCE created a precedent that was strongly opposed by the Russian Federation, Serbia, and several other like-minded participating states.
3. OSCE missions in Estonia and Latvia were closed and the mission in Ukraine was downgraded, creating in Moscow the perception that the OSCE was no longer prepared to defend the interests of Russian-speaking minorities in these states. This occurred at a time when the newly arrived Russian President Vladimir Putin sought to enhance Russian engagement in its "near abroad" as a counter to the humiliation felt by many Russians in the decade following the end of the Cold War.
4. The terrorist attacks in New York and Washington on September 11, 2001, significantly altered US security policy away from its focus on Europe and towards the "war on terror," perceived to be emanating largely from the Middle East and Southwest Asia. US military action in Iraq and Afghanistan became the primary foreign policy focus of the administration of President George W. Bush and diverted attention away from European security concerns. Furthermore, the administration of President Barack Obama inherited these engagements throughout these regions that largely prevented it from devoting high priority to security issues in Europe.

The result has been that, in the first decade and a half of the twenty-first century the OSCE declined in importance in the eyes of the major powers concerned with European security, although this trend was partly reversed by the crisis in Ukraine and Crimea beginning in 2014. In the years prior to this crisis, United States policy towards the OSCE might have best been described as "benign neglect." In principle, the OSCE is viewed in positive terms in Washington, especially for its work on issues of human rights, rights of persons belonging to minorities, and ODIHR election monitoring. However, it has also become viewed as largely useless on security issues due both to the inability to achieve consensus on vital issues and the lack of resources available to carry out decisions in the security arena, and the United States has thus relied almost entirely on NATO or on bilateral relations with relevant states to manage its security relationships in Europe, while dismissing the OSCE as a "talking shop" largely incapable of meaningful action on major security issues (Hopmann 2015). At the same time, the Russian Federation adopted a more hostile view of the OSCE, emphasizing its biased focus on issues "east of Vienna" while ignoring similar problems "west of Vienna," its intrusive interference in the internal affairs of states through programs such as human rights support and election monitoring, its failure to defend the rights of ethnic Russians living outside the Russian Federation, and its failure to live up to its promise of creating a Europe that is "whole" and without dividing lines such as those created by NATO and EU enlargement. Therefore, Russia has tended towards a security policy of unilateralism in its dealings with other OSCE participating states and their security interests, largely giving up on efforts to find multilateral solutions to regional problems (Hopmann 2010; Zagorski 2015). Finally, although support for the OSCE is generally greater in Western and Central Europe than in either the United States or Russia, in the eyes of most West Europeans the EU appears to be a more effective mechanism for dealing with foreign and security issues than the OSCE with its intense difficulties in achieving consensus around important policy decisions.

By contrast, many of the smaller states of Europe, including the remaining neutral and nonaligned states, generally remain relatively alone in holding the OSCE in high regard as an institution through which they can advance many of their foreign policy goals. Since the OSCE is not dominated by any of the global superpowers, it remains a forum in which the security concerns of the small neutral and nonaligned states may be addressed, if seldom resolved. It is hardly surprising that such a disproportionate number of senior offices within the OSCE have been held by officials from these countries. Furthermore, the normative "soft power" focus of the OSCE generally fits better with the foreign policy orientation of these participating states, in contrast to the emphasis on "hard power" in the foreign policies of the more powerful states. These more powerful countries see their interests better served by "hard power" military organizations like NATO or the CSTO, or institutions emphasizing mostly economic issues like the EU, although as noted above many of the European neutrals and nonaligned have managed to find a home in the EU without feeling that their neutrality or nonalignment has been drastically compromised. But as frequent intermediaries, they often find that the OSCE offers the potential to serve as a "go between" on conflicts dividing the major powers, especially the United States and Russia, which, in spite of their apparent lack of deep interest in the OSCE, continue to participate in the one institution beyond the United Nations in which they interact alongside Europe's smallest neutral and nonaligned states.

Many of these neutral and nonaligned states would likely welcome a "Helsinki II" that strengthened the capacity of the OSCE to engage in conflict prevention, management, resolution, and post-conflict peacebuilding without being restrained by the threat of a veto by either of the major powers that sit on the periphery of the core European region. In short, the OSCE remains a vehicle in which the concerns of the neutral and nonaligned states may be addressed and in which their normative power may be advanced in contrast to the military and economic powers that otherwise dominate the international relations of Europe.

NOTES

1. Note that only about 50 percent of the text could be identified as having been proposed by a specific participating state.

2. The text of the Helsinki Final Act may be found at www.osce.org/docs/english/1990–1999/summits/helfa75e.htm.

3. For a further elaboration of Romanian deviations from the general Warsaw Pact line during the negotiation of the Helsinki Final Act see, P. Terrence Hopmann, 1978. "Asymmetrical Bargaining in the Conference on Security and Cooperation in Europe," *International Organization* 31(1): 169, 172–75.

4. For a comprehensive analysis of the Vienna CSCE follow-up meeting authored by a member of the Austrian delegation, see Stefan Lehne, 1990. *The Vienna Meeting of the Conference on Security and Cooperation in Europe, 1986–1989: A Turning Point in East-West Relations.* Boulder: Westview Press.

5. As noted previously, the one notable exception is Daniel Thomas' book: Daniel Thomas, 2001. *The Helsinki Effect: International Norms, Human Rights, and the Defense of Communism.* Princeton: Princeton University Press.

6. Italics added.

7. This alternation of summit conferences and ministerial meetings continued regularly through 1999. Beginning in 2000, however, only ministerial meetings have been held, due mostly to the unwillingness of heads of state from the major powers to attend.

8. For a summary of the work of these field activities established in the 1990s see, P. Terrence Hopmann. 1999. *Building Security in Post-Cold War Eurasia. The OSCE and U.S. Foreign Policy.* Washington, DC: United States Institute of Peace.

BIBLIOGRAPHY

Conference on Security and Cooperation in Europe (CSCE). 1990. *Charter of Paris for a New Europe.* Paris.

———. 1989. *Concluding Document of the Vienna Meeting 1986 of Representatives of the Participating States of the Conference on Security and Co-operation in*

Europe, held on the basis of the provisions of the Final Act relating to the follow-up to the Conference. Vienna.

Dean, Jonathan. 1987. *Watershed Europe: Dismantling the East-West Military Confrontation.* Lexington, MA: Lexington Books.

Hopmann, P. Terrence. 2015. "The United States and the OSCE after the Ukraine Crisis." *Security and Human Rights* 26(1): 33–47.

———. 2010. "Intergovernmental Organizations and Non-State Actors, Russia and Eurasia: The OSCE." In *Key Players and Regional Dynamics in Eurasia,* edited by Maria Raquel Freire and Roger E. Kanet. Houndsmill. UK: Palgrave Macmillan, 238–270.

———. 1999. *Building Security in Post-Cold War Eurasia. The OSCE and U.S. Foreign Policy.* Washington, DC: United States Institute of Peace.

———. 1978. "Asymmetrical Bargaining in the Conference on Security and Cooperation in Europe." *International Organization* 31(1): 141–177.

Kruzel, Joseph. 1990. "The European Neutrals Face the 1990's." In *The Helsinki Process and the Future of Europe,* edited by Samuel F. Wells. Washington, DC: The Wilson Center Press.

Leatherman, Janie. 2003. *From Cold War to Democratic Peace: Third Parties, Peaceful Change, and the OSCE.* Syracuse, NY: Syracuse University Press.

Lehne, Stefan. 1991. *The CSCE in the 1990s: Constructing European Security and Cooperation.* West Lafayette, IN: Purdue University Press.

———. 1990. *The Vienna Meeting of the Conference on Security and Cooperation in Europe, 1986–1989: A Turning Point in East-West Relations.* Boulder, CO: Westview Press.

Maresca, John J. 1995. *To Helsinki: The Conference on Security and Cooperation in Europe, 1973–1975.* Durham, NC: Duke University Press.

Thomas, Daniel C. 2001. *The Helsinki Effect: International Norms, Human Rights, and the Defense of Communism.* Princeton, NJ: Princeton University Press.

U.S. Commission on Security and Cooperation in Europe (CSCE). 1990. *Document of the Copenhagen Meeting of the Conference on the Human Dimension of the CSCE.* Washington, DC.

Zagorski, Andrei. 2015. "Russian Views of the OSCE and the 2016 German Chairmanship." *Security and Human Rights* 26(1): 25–32.

Chapter 7

Neutrality for Peace

Switzerland's Independent Foreign Policy

Christian Nünlist

At first sight, Swiss foreign policy seems to be unchanging, enduring, and even anachronistic. In the twenty-first century, Switzerland is still bound to permanent neutrality. Unlike other former European neutrals, Switzerland did not become a member of the EU in the 1990s. Opinion polls show that more than 95 percent of the Swiss population wishes to abide by neutrality (Tresch and Wenger 2015, 115).

At the same time, Swiss foreign policy has changed dramatically since 1990. The traditional policy of strict neutrality has been replaced by a less absolute version displaying more solidarity. Today, neutrality is only rarely legally applied, because interstate wars have largely been superseded by intrastate civil wars. Since 1990, regular Swiss Foreign and Security White Papers have promoted an active foreign policy. As a result, numerous aspects of Switzerland's foreign policy have evolved, including its participation within the UN, the Organization for Security and Cooperation in Europe (OSCE), and NATO's Partnership for Peace (PfP).

In the twenty-first century, Switzerland continues to be a global leader in science and research, and the country ranks among the leaders in terms of economic power, innovation and competitiveness, infrastructure, legal certainty, political stability, standard of living, global interdependence, and openness as well as image. Thus, Switzerland's "soft power" is remarkable—and that raises expectations among the international community that Switzerland as a solution-oriented, medium-sized European country should actively contribute to finding solutions to current foreign and security policy challenges.[1]

The break off of diplomatic relations between Saudi Arabia and Iran in early 2016 and Switzerland's assumption of the respective protective power mandates demonstrate the continued international need for good offices provided by neutral Switzerland.[2] In a more fragmented and polarized world, the demand for Swiss bridge-building between conflict parties has increased in recent years. Geneva remains a center of numerous important global summits and conferences seeking diplomatic solutions for key international conflicts. Civilian peace promotion has become a new key focus of Switzerland's foreign policy. Switzerland also emphasizes the interface between peace and security in development cooperation, particularly in fragile contexts.

The case of contemporary Swiss foreign policy demonstrates that neutrality is not automatically an obstacle to international cooperation. An independent diplomacy can provide very useful services to mediate and deescalate international conflicts. "Modern neutrality" (Gärtner 2011, 477f.) is far removed from free-riding, and neutral states are well-placed as "brokers of peacebuilding ideas" (Goetschel 2011) to make meaningful contributions in finding multilateral solutions to current global challenges.

SWISS NEUTRALITY: GHOST FROM THE PAST

Neutrality has a long tradition as a dominant principle of Swiss foreign policy. Supposedly, Switzerland's reticence in foreign-policy matters was a direct outcome of the defeat of the Confederates at the Battle of Marignano (1515), though it was not fixed in writing until 1674 (Bonjour 1965; Riklin 1992). However, historical research holds that the date of 1515 as the beginning of Swiss neutrality is a myth. It was only after Europe was reorganized after the Napoleonic Wars that the formal recognition by Austria, France, Great Britain, Russia, and Prussia in the Act of Paris of November 20, 1815, leveraged Swiss neutrality. From that moment, neutral Switzerland was established as an impartial fixed pole amid rivaling European great powers, offering a neutral space for hosting international meetings and seating international organizations (Rosin 2014, 15). Neutrality proved to be valuable in the European conflicts of the nineteenth century and the two world wars in the twentieth century. Therefore, the Swiss government decided in 1945 to continue to adhere to permanent armed neutrality. As a consequence, Switzerland remained aloof from the UN, European integration, and NATO.

In discussing the concept of neutrality, the legal dimension must be distinguished from the political dimension. On the one hand, the law of neutrality establishes specific rights and obligations of a neutral country in case of a war between third countries. The territory of neutral powers is inviolable. Neutral states have to treat warring parties equally. They are prohibited from engaging in arms sales to warring powers. On the other hand, neutrality policy compasses all voluntary measures that will prevent a neutral country from being drawn into a conflict and that will strengthen and protect the law of neutrality. A permanently neutral country like Switzerland should not join a military alliance in peacetime, and no foreign military facilities should be established on its territory (Fischer 2009, 30).

After the end of Second World War, international recognition of Swiss neutrality sank to a low point. Having come out of the war unscathed, Switzerland not only earned disrepute from being seen as a war profiteer. In the evolving UN system, there seemed to be no place for neutral aloofness. UN Secretary General Trygve Lie famously rejected Swiss efforts to negotiate a membership with a special status of Swiss neutrality at a press conference in Berne in August 1946 with laconic words: "Neutrality is a word I cannot find in the Charter" (Trachsler 2008, 15). Thus, after 1945, Switzerland was politically isolated in the international system. With difficulty, the Swiss government managed to improve relations with the two new superpowers, the United States and the Soviet Union. But the escalating East-West conflict soon paralyzed the UN and allowed neutral Switzerland again to provide good offices to the international system. Swiss foreign minister Max Petitpierre coined the slogan of "neutrality and solidarity" for Swiss foreign policy doctrine in the Cold War. Switzerland was able to continue a policy of neutrality until 1989 (Spillmann 2001, 34–38; Trachsler 2011, 59–75).

Nevertheless, it was never questioned that strictly anticommunist Switzerland was firmly anchored in the Western camp—not only geographically, but also culturally and economically. The conceptual basis for Switzerland's policy of neutrality during the Cold War was defined in the "Bindschedler doctrine" of 1954. This dogma, according to which politics and economics could be clearly demarcated, allowed Switzerland to join "apolitical, technical" international organizations while abstaining from "political" organizations for neutrality concerns (Möckli 2000, 254–266).

In practice, however, the Swiss government found pragmatic ways, partly under strict secrecy, to break out of the tight corset of an integral neutrality policy, and to morally position Switzerland clearly within the West. For example, Switzerland participated in the Marshall Plan to rebuild Western Europe in 1947. After 1951, Switzerland also took part, under intense US pressure, in the Western export control regime (COCOM) of strategic goods to the Eastern bloc. The secret agreement, which was made public only in 1987, clearly violated the right of neutral states to conduct free trade with all countries in peacetime (Schaller 1987).

Informal secret contacts of senior Swiss military and political leaders with high-ranking representatives of NATO countries—in particular British Field Marshal Bernard L. Montgomery from 1949 to 1958—certainly exhausted the room of maneuver for neutrals to enter into preliminary military agreements for the event of war. For example, the Swiss Army apparently arranged concrete contact points with Italian and French NATO forces to be used in wartime in 1951–1952 (Mantovani 1999, 95–113; Fuhrer 2005).

Overall, however, Swiss foreign policy during the Cold War remained decidedly apolitical and consciously economically dominated, despite humanitarian and peace policy gestures. This foreign policy abstinence significantly differed from other neutral European countries like Sweden, Finland, or Austria, which all were UN members and repeatedly pointed the finger from a moral high ground, criticizing for example the US war in Vietnam or South Africa's apartheid regime. In contrast, Swiss foreign policy limited itself "to the humanitarian role of a helpful Samaritan and a diplomatic postman" (Kunz and Morandi 2000, 67).

An important milestone for a more active foreign policy was the first Swiss White Paper on Security Policy in 1973, which called for a combination of a passive defense policy with an active, flexible foreign policy. However, with the exception of Switzerland's successful participation in the Conference on Security and Cooperation in Europe (CSCE), Swiss security policy overall remained passive and dominated by an autonomous military and defense policy. An ideologically inflated neutrality doctrine prevented the implementation of an active foreign policy promoting peace and security (Spillmann 2001, 117–146). In 1986, the Swiss electorate overwhelmingly rejected the proposal advanced by government and parliament that Switzerland should join the UN.

NEUTRALITY IN TRANSITION: THE GOLDEN 1990s

The end of the Cold War was a turning point, not least for Swiss foreign and neutrality policy. The tension between an export-oriented foreign trade policy and a value-oriented foreign policy was rebalanced. Swiss foreign policy became more active, more solidarity-minded, and more participatory than before 1989.

The transition from integral to differential neutrality can be precisely dated: On August 7, 1990, after a conference call during the summer holidays, the Swiss Federal Council imposed economic sanctions against Iraq, following UN Security Council Resolution 661 of August 6, 1990. Iraq's occupation of Kuwait was assessed differently than previous situations, where Switzerland had strictly adhered to neutrality law. The Swiss government now argued that Iraq had blatantly violated most fundamental norms of international law and that for the first time the international community was united in its reaction. For Switzerland as a small state, the adherence to international law was an overriding interest. The collective security applied in the Gulf War–led Switzerland to rethink its neutrality policy. For the first time, Switzerland, at that time not yet a UN member, fully participated in economic sanctions against a belligerent state, Saddam Hussein's Iraq (Künzli 2008, 147).

Ever since, neutrality and embargoes have been considered to be compatible. In response to serious human rights violations, Switzerland displayed solidarity and joined UN or EU sanctions, among others, against Yugoslavia, Myanmar, Zimbabwe, Uzbekistan, Belarus, Ivory Coast, Sudan, Syria, Yemen, North Korea, or Iran. In all these cases, Switzerland wished to avoid being seen as an accomplice of an internationally isolated and ostracized regime.

The Security White Paper of 1990 anchored international peace promotion as a new foreign policy goal by stipulating that Switzerland should "contribute to international stability, mainly in Europe."[3] The landmark White Paper on Foreign Policy of 1993 reinforced the entanglement of Swiss foreign and security policy. Five new foreign policy objectives were introduced, in addition to the traditional aim of preserving Swiss independence: (1) to relieve poverty and misery in the world; (2) to respect human rights; (3) to promote democracy; (4) to promote the peaceful coexistence of peoples; (5) to conserve natural resources. In the spirit of solidarity, Switzerland wished to shape its security environment through active and preventive peace promotion and through participating in collective security efforts.[4] In an annex on neutrality in the Foreign Policy White Paper of 1993, the new slogan of "security through cooperation" was mentioned for the very first time, albeit somewhat hidden, before becoming the prominent title of the Security Policy White Paper in 1999 (Spillmann 2001, 162f.).

This time, the Swiss government was more successful than it had been after 1973 in actually implementing the noble intention of a more active foreign policy. In particular, the decisions to assume the chairmanship of the OSCE in 1996, to participate in the NATO PfP initiative (1996), and to take a more active part in international arms control efforts meant that Swiss foreign policy contributed to enhancing peace and stability in Europe's neighborhood through multilateral frameworks. At that time, the OSCE was the only security organization in which Switzerland could participate on an equal footing. With electoral and military observers, Switzerland significantly contributed to the success of the OSCE's mission in Bosnia during the Swiss OSCE Chairmanship of 1996. The increased involvement of Switzerland in OSCE activities in the Western Balkans was widely supported domestically because OSCE values coincided with Swiss traditions and with the new peace policy that the government had just conceptually designed (Goetschel 1997).

Switzerland's participation in the PfP in 1996 was a surprising political move. After all, involvement with NATO as a Western military pact was fundamentally incompatible with neutrality, and the Swiss voters had repeatedly rejected the government's course of opening up Swiss foreign policy by voting "no" to a Swiss UN membership in 1986, "no" to joining the European Economic Area (EEA) in 1992, and "no" to contributing a UN Blue Helmet brigade to military peacekeeping in 1994. However, NATO had transformed in the 1990s from a defensive military alliance into a more political instrument for exporting Western values to Eastern Europe and for providing stability and peace in Central and Eastern Europe during the transition years after the end of the Cold War. Therefore, the Swiss government considered PfP participation to be a welcome option for a more active foreign policy without loss of sovereignty, because each PfP participating state could decide the level of cooperation for itself. Switzerland made it clear from the outset that it would remain committed to permanent, armed neutrality. Yet, Swiss PfP participation in fact marked a (modest) rapprochement between Switzerland and NATO, which was intensified in 1999 with the deployment of a Swiss military company (SWISSCOY) to the NATO stabilization mission in Kosovo (KFOR) (Wenger 1997/98; Nünlist 2016).

In the field of international arms control, Switzerland played an important pacesetter role in the negotiation process for a comprehensive ban on land mines from 1994 to 1999. The initiative for the "Ottawa process" originated in a meeting of experts in Geneva in 1994, and a media campaign by the International Committee of the Red Cross (ICRC) helped to raise awareness for humanitarian concerns. Switzerland supported the Canadian initiative to negotiate an agreement outside of established arms control fora from the beginning. In 1997, Switzerland launched a "pilot group" which included (in addition to Switzerland) Belgium, Germany, Canada, Austria, Mexico, Norway, the Philippines, and South Africa—all of them small or medium-sized countries. For Switzerland, it was extraordinary that the government exposed itself internationally so early and decisively (Gerber 1999; Dahinden 1998).

However, in the 1990s, domestic political polarization over the orientation of Swiss foreign policy after the Cold War increased. National conservative forces led by the Zurich wing of the Swiss People's Party (SVP) under Christoph Blocher instrumentalized the myth of neutrality as a vehicle for their vision of a passive and isolationist foreign policy. The geostrategic turning point of the terrorist attacks in the United States of September 11, 2001, reinforced the propensity among a vast majority of the Swiss population to cling to the myth of neutrality (Haltiner 2011, 48ff.)—even if the landmark 1993 White Paper on Neutrality had forcefully argued that neutrality had lost much of its security function in the post–Cold War world.

ACTIVE SWISS FOREIGN POLICY UNDER CALMY-REY AND BURKHALTER

Considering the unfavorable signs of domestic polarization between conservative isolationists and liberal internationalists, foreign ministers Micheline

Calmy-Rey (2003–2011) and Didier Burkhalter (since 2012) innovatively reinvigorated Swiss foreign policy and gave Swiss neutrality a modern face. Under Calmy-Rey, the active foreign policy of the 1990s became more dynamic, ambitious, and visible (Calmy-Rey 2014).

Swiss relations with the EU, however, were set back by ten years. The government concealed the fact that the EU no longer agreed with the bilateralism between the EU and Switzerland. Accordingly, the bilateral path was still perceived among the Swiss population as the best approach for Switzerland's policy towards Europe (Möckli 2011). Since relations with the EU were blocked, in 2005 Calmy-Rey pushed the new idea of strategic partnerships with non-European countries, including the United States, Japan, Brazil, Russia, China, India, South Africa, and Turkey. Thus, Switzerland responded to the trends of a more multipolar world and a shift of the geostrategic center of attention from the West to Asia. Economically, however, Switzerland still remained dependent on good trade relations with EU countries, particularly with its immediate neighbors.[5]

Calmy-Rey's most remarkable achievement was to free Swiss foreign policy from the shackles of its rigid neutrality policy of the past. She linked Switzerland's foreign policy to the active foreign policy of the 1970s and forced a revival of the successful era when Swiss diplomacy in the Helsinki process had successfully mediated between East and West. Calmy-Rey's key concern was civilian peace promotion, and during her tenure at the foreign ministry was able to achieve considerable success in this field. Switzerland served as an impartial mediator between Turkey and Armenia as well as between Russia and Georgia. Swiss diplomats also significantly contributed to peace processes in Burundi, Sudan, Kyrgyzstan, Sri Lanka, and Nepal. Within ten years, the budget of Swiss civilian peacebuilding doubled to CHF 75 million (Greminger 2011).[6] Under Calmy-Rey, Swiss diplomacy substantially mediated in over twenty peace negotiations in fifteen countries—thus actually breaching strict neutrality as understood by traditionalists. The fact that Calmy-Rey's version of an active foreign policy was domestically presented and recognized as active neutrality policy must be considered a success (Möckli 2011).

Calmy-Rey leveraged neutrality as a unique strength that could be advantageous for Swiss foreign policy—just like other features of the country, such as its lack of a colonial past, its federal and multicultural tradition, and its high technical expertise. Neutrality and universality were considered virtues that could aid Switzerland's role as a mediator and bridge-builder between conflict parties. A governmental report on neutrality in 2007 emphasized these benefits when acting as an impartial mediator.[7]

After replacing Calmy-Rey, Didier Burkhalter in early 2012 shifted the focus of Swiss foreign policy back to Europe.[8] For him, Swiss relations with the EU had priority over relations with non-European strategic partners.

For the clarification of institutional questions, Switzerland won time, because the EU was so strongly absorbed by the Euro crisis that for Brussels, the relationship with Switzerland was merely a footnote. At first, Burkhalter succeeded in explaining his EU policy to the partly very skeptical Swiss population, and to gain domestic support for the new policy.[9] However, with the outcome of a referendum "against mass immigration" in February 2014, Switzerland risked jeopardizing the important principle of free movement with the introduction of a new constitutional article to that effect. It brought a temporary halt for Burkhalter's efforts to establish a new, institutionalized base for Switzerland's relations with the EU. Because of the potential withdrawal of Britain from the EU ("Brexit"), the EU was in no mood to compromise with Switzerland on free movement. In addition, Burkhalter and Swiss diplomacy in 2014 were almost completely absorbed by the tasks of the Swiss OSCE Chairmanship and the management of the Ukraine crisis within the framework of that organization. Thus, the EU issue was pushed back in Swiss foreign policy priorities. In 2015, the European refugee crisis reinforced an already prevailing, negative image of the EU. Domestically, a voluntary ceding of sovereignty to the EU was now even harder to sell to the Swiss public.[10]

Strategic developments in Europe's neighborhood confirmed Burkhalter's decision to downgrade the importance of Switzerland's strategic partnerships with non-European countries, even if Switzerland's free trade agreement with China, which entered into force in 2013, was celebrated as an (albeit controversial) success (Lanteigne 2014). However, other newly established partnerships proved to be difficult and delicate. In 2014, the Ukraine crisis led Switzerland to strongly condemn Russia's violation of international law and to put its military contacts with Russia on hold. Switzerland did not join Western economic sanctions against Russia, but at least made sure that Switzerland was not used to bypass Western sanctions (Grätz 2013).[11] The strategic partnership with Turkey, officially launched in 2013, also suffered, with Turkey sliding towards an autocracy and the ruling AKP party growing increasingly intolerant towards the political opposition, public demonstrations, and media criticism (Watanabe 2015).

Burkhalter continued and even upgraded civilian peacebuilding. The Swiss foreign ministry designed, among others, a new regional focus program for dealing with the three unresolved secession conflicts in the Southern Caucasus, a strategy on how to deal with antipersonnel mines, and a strategy for the protection of civilians in armed conflicts.

Initially, Burkhalter largely avoided referring to Swiss neutrality. In speeches, he preferred the word "independent" to describe the special case of Switzerland as a nonmember of EU and NATO. In responses to parliamentary inquiries, however, he has repeatedly made it clear that permanent neutrality has stood the test of time as a guiding principle of Swiss foreign policy and that the conceptual basis of neutrality of 1993 remains valid. The aim of Switzerland's neutral foreign policy was to maximize the advantages and minimize the disadvantages of Swiss "independence"—its nonaligned, neutral status.[12]

Following the experience of his successful tenure as neutral OSCE chairperson, Burkhalter in 2015 in several speeches took up again the old formula of "neutrality and solidarity" of Max Petitpierre (1946)[13]—in a flashback to the ideological romantization of neutrality during the Cold War.

BRIDGE-BUILDING IN THE OSCE

The OSCE Chairmanship in 2014 turned out to be a success story for modern, independent Swiss foreign policy. Didier Burkhalter used the "double impartiality"[14] of Switzerland and the OSCE to mediate in the most important geopolitical conflict in Europe since 1945 and to contribute to de-escalation while maintaining open channels for dialogue between the West and Russia and between the Ukrainian conflict parties. Swiss national conservatives reflexively criticized Burkhalter's policy of active neutrality in the Ukraine crisis in March 2014 as a dangerous interference in a foreign conflict. A daily newspaper even denounced Switzerland as a "useful idiot of Moscow."[15] But ultimately, a large majority of the Swiss population supported Burkhalter's peace efforts in the crisis.[16] In an annual TV gala show, Burkhalter was even voted "Swiss of the Year 2014"—an honor previously bestowed on exceptional athletes such as Roger Federer (2003) or Dario Cologna (2012) rather than politicians.[17]

Switzerland was the very first country to volunteer to chair the OSCE for a second time. As briefly mentioned above, the first Swiss OSCE Chairmanship in 1996 had been dominated by the implementation of the Dayton Agreement of December 1995. In supporting the holding of elections in Bosnia and Herzegovina in the fall of 1996, Swiss diplomacy made a key contribution to the stabilization of the Balkans. Switzerland sent 70 "yellow berets"[18] and 160 experts to the Western Balkans, mostly electoral and human rights observers. Thanks to Switzerland's "good offices," the OSCE assumed a prominent and visible role in consolidating peace after a civil war for the first time (Wenger 1997). The hugely successful OSCE Chairmanship of 1996 put into practice the active peacebuilding policy mentioned in the Foreign Policy White Paper of 1993. Thanks to the OSCE presidency, Switzerland succeeded in ending her self-imposed political aloofness in Europe, after the Swiss electorate had narrowly rejected the country's accession to the EEA in 1992 (Goetschel 1997).

During the second OSCE Chairmanship in 2014, Swiss diplomacy responded very well to the surprising Russian annexation of the Crimea and the rapid deterioration of the Eastern Ukraine situation into civil war. Didier Burkhalter as OSCE Chairman-in-Office invested energy and resources into handling the Ukraine crisis. Consulting with key stakeholders in Moscow, Kiev, Berlin, Paris, and Washington, he played out the OSCE's conflict management tools to the full. Within a few months, the Swiss Chairmanship achieved considerable success. For the first time in over a decade, the OSCE established a large field mission in March 2014. Verification missions under OSCE arms control arrangements demonstrated the value of military transparency and confidence-building measures. Innovative diplomatic ideas included the establishment of international contact groups for dialogue in Geneva, Berlin, and Minsk between Russia, the Ukraine, and pro-Western separatists in Eastern Ukraine, and the negotiation of an (albeit fragile) cease-fire agreement in Minsk (Nünlist 2014).

Foreign voices, including that of German foreign minister Frank-Walter Steinmeier, have unanimously testified to the usefulness of Switzerland's neutrality for her role in OSCE conflict management during the Ukraine crisis.[19] In retrospect, intimate knowledge of OSCE rules was just as important for the success of the Swiss 2014 Chairmanship of the OSCE as the fact that neutral Switzerland could credibly mediate between Russia and the West.

The neutrality of the OSCE Chairmanship was probably most important for the difficult task of obtaining Russia's green light for an OSCE observer mission to Ukraine. In early March 2014, Vladimir Putin still clearly rejected such a role, because he had no confidence in the OSCE. In a personal phone conversation, Burkhalter succeeded in convincing the Russian president that such an OSCE field mission would also protect the rights of the Russian minority in Ukraine. In Switzerland, the OSCE's Special Monitoring Mission (SMM) was hailed as a success of Swiss diplomacy (Nünlist 2014, 48–51).

On May 7, 2014, Burkhalter—acting in his capacity as OSCE Chairman— became the first Western statesman to meet personally with Putin since the beginning of the Ukraine crisis, with the aim of wresting from him first signs of a relaxation of tensions. Thanks to the neutrality principle, the encounter did not become an international or domestic scandal. Already on April 17, 2014, the Swiss foreign policy principles of neutrality and universality had enabled a much-anticipated first meeting between Russian foreign minister Sergei Lavrov and his Ukrainian counterpart Andrei Deshtshiza—even though the Kremlin at the time did not recognize Ukraine's interim government. Within the tradition of "good offices," Switzerland provided the international stage of Geneva as a venue for peace talks. The Geneva talks were moderated by US Secretary of State John Kerry and EU External Affairs High Representative Catherine Ashton. After these talks, Swiss diplomacy introduced a specific, sequential timetable for the de-escalation measures vaguely adopted in Geneva with its "road map" of May 12, 2014: first renunciation of force, then disarmament, then national dialog, and finally the holding of presidential elections on May 25, 2014. Thus, the explosive situation in Ukraine was successfully defused in the second half of May (Nünlist 2014, 44–53).

With Tim Guldimann and Heidi Tagliavini, Switzerland provided the OSCE with two tried and tested diplomats in the Ukraine crisis, both of whom dedicated great personal efforts to arrive at de-escalating steps in the conflict. Both Russia experts had proven their mediation skills in previous crises, including in Chechnya and Georgia. Armed with the credibility of neutral diplomacy, they were also able to perform valuable conciliatory services in the Ukraine crisis. For example, Heidi Tagliavini maintained contact with the pro-Russian separatists in Eastern Ukraine (Nünlist 2014, 53f.).

Switzerland fulfilled her duty as OSCE chair so well that she was overwhelmed with international praise at the OSCE Ministerial Council in Basel in late 2014.[20] Among academics, the idea even briefly emerged that neutral Switzerland could be permanently assigned the annually rotating OSCE Chairmanship (Stern and Svarin 2014; Liechtenstein 2014).

"WEP-5": THE REVIVAL OF THE CLUB OF NEUTRALS

The well-functioning "club of neutrals" (Switzerland, Austria, Sweden, Finland) that had formed during the Helsinki process quickly fell apart after the end of the Cold War. In 1995, Austria, Sweden, and Finland joined the EU and henceforth reduced neutrality to military nonalignment. Interestingly, the European "neutrals" found together again in the context of NATO's PfP. Together with Ireland, they began to build an informal PfP partner group called "Western European partners" (WEP).[21]

The beginning of institutionalized relations with NATO in November 1996 confirmed a clear break in Swiss foreign and security policy. The participation within PfP has become an important element of Switzerland's leitmotif "security through cooperation." Participation in NATO military exercises and the deployment of a Swiss Army contingent ("Swisscoy") to the NATO-led international peace support mission to Kosovo (KFOR) allowed the Swiss armed forces to acquire the ability to work with other military and civilian partners in international peacekeeping operations.

NATO's initially rather loose relationship with its Western European partners was formalized in Berlin in April 2011 as part of NATO's partnership reform. Previously, political consultation in the PfP framework had increasingly lost relevance after several NATO enlargement rounds. NATO seemed to assess its partners exclusively in terms of to their military contribution to NATO-led military operations (Andrey 2010, 87f.). Since 2011, it has been possible for the WEP-5 (Switzerland, Austria, Sweden, Finland, and Ireland) to request meetings with the twenty-eight NATO allies in the flexible format "NAC+WEP5." From time to time, the WEP group of five is expanded to include Malta, thus becoming the "WEP-6."

These WEP-5 consultations with NATO originated during informal lunch discussions that EU members Sweden, Finland, Austria, and Ireland regularly held at the level of deputy ambassadors to NATO at NATO headquarters in Brussels from the mid-2000s—and to which they also invited neutral Switzerland. From 2008 onward, this informal cooperation among the "Western Five" had become so established that the Five as a cohesive group drafted informal non-papers on the development of a value-based NATO partnership policy, which they introduced to NATO in the EAPC framework.[22]

The first official ambassadorial meeting on the basis of "NAC+WEP6" was held on the initiative of the WEP-6 in April 2012. In February 2013, the Swiss Mission to NATO also set up an informal discussion on the situation in Mali and the Sahel region in light of the French military intervention in Mali. Previously, France had deliberately avoided discussing Mali at the NATO Council, because the crisis primarily concerned the EU, and Paris initially did not want to have NATO involved. Interestingly, however, a representative of the French Mission to NATO participated in the Swiss meeting on February 15, 2013, and explained the French position on Mali to about fifty representatives of NATO allies, partners, and the NATO Secretariat.[23] This example clearly demonstrates the advantage of the "good offices" neutral Switzerland can provide even within the Western military alliance. Thanks to the Swiss initiative, the Mali situation was discussed at NATO despite initial resistance from Paris, in a meeting organized by Swiss diplomats in an informal setting. Other WEP-6 meetings in 2013 focused on the security situation in the Middle East and North Africa, NATO missile defense, Afghanistan, Kosovo, and the United States pivot to Asia.[24]

In recent years, Switzerland also exhausted the potential for cooperation with NATO using so-called tiger teams to proactively carry various initiatives into the military alliance. Each "tiger team" is composed of at least one NATO member state and at least one partner state. By using a forerunner of a tiger team (the term was introduced only later), Switzerland succeeded making the "Montreux Document" (2006) the NATO standard for dealing with private security companies in late 2013. Switzerland had triggered this process in 2009 by organizing an EAPC session on the topic and by later forming an informal working group with the United States and the United Kingdom to prepare the issue for NATO. Since November 2013, Switzerland has also been actively involved in a tiger group on "PfP Branding," the aim of which is to transfer the concept of "human security" to NATO. The fact that the NATO Summit Declaration of Wales in September 2014 mentioned "human security" in the paragraphs on NATO partnerships may be considered a first concrete success of Switzerland's efforts in the "PfP Branding" working group. Swiss diplomacy also supports other tiger groups launched by fellow WEP-5 partners, including Austria's efforts on "Protection of Civilians" (POC) and Sweden's commitment to implement UN resolution no. 1325 on women, peace, and security within NATO (Nünlist 2015, 29ff.).[25]

In 2014 and 2015, however, the "club of neutrals" suffered from the impact of the Ukraine crisis and the different responses of Scandinavian (Sweden, Finland) and Alpine countries (Switzerland, Austria), respectively. At its Wales summit in September 2014, NATO introduced a new, exclusive partnership format, the "Enhanced Opportunity Program" (EOP), and invited five privileged partners, including Sweden and Finland, to intensify their political dialogue as well as their practical military and intelligence cooperation with NATO. After 2014, due to their importance for the defense of the Baltic, Sweden and Finland have become even more important military partners than Austria and Switzerland. For the unity of WEP-5, therefore, developments since March 2014 have signified an overall negative trend for Switzerland (and Austria as well, for that matter). The existing differentiation into the military-integrated, active NATO partners Sweden and Finland and the less integrated and more passive partner countries Switzerland, Austria, and Ireland has since become more acute. In late 2014, the Swiss delegation at the NATO Parliamentary Assembly, for example, complained about the diminishing importance of the WEP-5 format due to Sweden and Finland's privileged position within the EOP (Nünlist 2015, 32ff.).[26]

In Sweden and Finland, Russia's annexation of Crimea provoked heated domestic debates about a possible accession of their countries to NATO. In Switzerland, however, the question of full NATO membership remains a political taboo. Paradoxically, however, NATO's interest in Switzerland's defense policy has grown considerably since 2014. Switzerland's defense is still focused on territorial defense forces. The Swiss Army did not follow the general European trend of the last twenty-five years of transforming the armed forces into crisis-management armies. Today, Switzerland's defense expertise has suddenly found the interest of NATO military planners, who have to think again, as during the Cold War, about rail transports of tanks, the deployment of full divisions, or defining boundary demarcations for defense sectors. Of course, NATO insiders know that neutral Switzerland will not participate in military maneuvers to exercise collective defense according to Article 5. Nevertheless, the Western military pact has an interest in maintaining an informal dialogue with Switzerland on aspects of traditional territorial defense, which have been neglected within NATO and in most NATO member states in recent decades. Interestingly, Switzerland was invited in 2015 for the first time to participate in NATO's military planning symposium held annually at the NATO School in Oberammergau to discuss NATO's defense competence.[27]

In 2016, NATO responded to the evolving fragmentation of the "Western neutrals" by again intensifying special meetings of the North Atlantic Council with the WEP-5/6. Participants at these meetings discuss notes on Russia, the impact of NATO's missile defense program, the unfinished business of the Western Balkans and the situation in North Africa and the Middle East, or the future of arms control and nonproliferation efforts. These consultations meet a strong desire by Switzerland to have a real political dialogue with NATO. In the future, this political dialogue among the WEP-5/6 could extend to regular exchanges among intelligence services, discussion of hybrid warfare and cyber vulnerabilities, and early warning indicators for evolving crises (Shea 2016).

NICHE STRATEGIES AT THE UNITED NATIONS

After the Swiss electorate had given the green light on March 3, 2002, Switzerland gave up its fifty-seven-year self-imposed outsider role at the UN and switched from an interested onlooker and "hotelier"—Geneva is the home of the European headquarters of the UN—to a full member. Swiss foreign policy at the UN in New York distinguished itself from the outset as innovative, pro-active, and self-confident.[28] With a contribution of about CHF 110 million per year, Switzerland ranks among the top twenty of all 193 UN members. However, Switzerland still does not contribute very actively to UN peace operations with military or police personnel. With currently thirty military and police officers, Switzerland is ranked in a modest 87th place among 124 donor countries[29]—even if the Swiss Federal Council since 2005 has repeatedly expressed its intention to send more Swiss Army personnel on UN peace missions (Bieri and Nünlist 2013).

Since 2002, Switzerland has skillfully introduced its innovative diplomacy into multilateral UN processes, also on the front line, even with sensitive issues. In 2007, the then Swiss ambassador to the UN Peter Maurer was named among the fifteen most influential UN ambassadors in New York by UN staffers—quite an achievement for a small, neutral country.[30]

Switzerland regularly hosts UN peace talks (e.g., on Syria, Libya, or Yemen). In addition, Switzerland chairs the Burundi Configuration of the UN Peacebuilding Commission (since 2009) and is a member of its Central African Republic Configuration.

Together with Liechtenstein, Costa Rica, Jordan, and Singapore, Switzerland is engaged in trying to reform the UN Security Council, with the aim of improving the working methods of the Council ("Small Five Group"). Since 2013, Switzerland has directed the 27-member "ACT Group" (Accountability, Coherence, Transparence), a UN group mandated to increase the transparency of the Security Council and to include participation of all UN members in the work of the most powerful decision-making body of the UN.

Switzerland—supported by Germany, Austria, Norway, Turkey, and the United States—is also actively promoting the implementation of the Global UN Counter-Terrorism Strategy, insisting on respecting human rights and the rule of law in fighting jihadist terrorists. For example, Switzerland demands that states follow constitutional criteria for placing individuals on sanctions lists. In 2009, an UN ombudsperson was created—an important successful interim result for Swiss efforts.[31] Most recently, Switzerland made the prevention of violent extremism (PVE) a priority of Swiss foreign policy. The concept of PVE, in conjunction with peace and development policies, has developed as part of a modern approach to counterterrorism, creating opportunities for Swiss foreign policy. Switzerland actively shaped the UN debate on an UN PVE Action Plan adopted in December 2015. In April 2016, the Swiss government hosted a first summit in Geneva to discuss the implementation of this UN Action Plan on a national level around the world.[32]

Switzerland is particularly proud about its leading role in the launching of the UN Human Rights Council in 2006. The Geneva-based body, despite being often criticized, in 2011 actually reacted quickly to excesses of violence in Syria and Libya by holding three special sessions. From 2016 to 2018, Switzerland is serving for the third time as a member of the Council. Together with Costa Rica and Turkey, Switzerland introduced a resolution on the protection of human rights during peaceful demonstrations, which the Human Rights Council adopted in 2013.[33]

Overall, Switzerland's full UN membership since 2002 has been a success story. Interestingly, Switzerland within the UN usually builds ad hoc alliances rather than automatically siding with its key strategic foreign policy partners. Switzerland is deliberately pursuing an independent UN policy and does not want to be limited in its choices by group memberships or loyalties. Instead, Swiss diplomats wish to build bridges between the various power blocs within the UN. Swiss UN diplomacy is mostly opportunistic, pragmatic, and solution-oriented—thus, strategic vision is somewhat lost. In the UN framework, Switzerland as a rule prefers a niche strategy acting as a facilitator and honest broker. Critics of this Swiss strategy to continue its "good offices," which compensated for Switzerland's abstinence from the UN during the Cold War, emphasize that as a full UN member, Switzerland today should actually primarily lobby for Swiss national interests (Trachsler 2010, 121).

Ahead of the 2002 vote, the UN question had caused a deep divide in Swiss domestic politics. Critics of a full Swiss UN membership warned in alarmist tones that Switzerland would lose its neutrality. Supporters of Switzerland joining the UN described future influence and opportunities for diplomatic action in rosy colors. Since 2002, however, neutral Switzerland's active participation in the world organization has become uncontroversial domestically. In 2011, the Swiss Federal Council decided to run for a non-permanent seat on the UN Security Council in 2023–2024.[34] The Swiss candidacy is widely supported among the Swiss public, which supports Switzerland's UN diplomacy wholeheartedly. A Swiss seat in the UN Security Council in 2023–2024 would be an even stronger signal than the OSCE Chairmanship in 2014 that neutral Switzerland, according to its leitmotif "security through cooperation," is prepared to take responsibility at the global level and to make a significant contribution to cooperative efforts for global security and peace.

MODERN DEVELOPMENT POLICY FOR SUSTAINABLE PEACE

The turning point of 1990 also influenced the relationship between security policy and development cooperation. The motto had always been "no security without development; no development without security," but during the Cold War, development aid had been strongly influenced by the geopolitical and ideological confrontation between East and West. For the West, development aid had been an instrument for containing communism.

After the disappearance of the communist threat after 1990, the political instrumentalization of development aid faded away, and international development cooperation gained greater autonomy. The core task of poverty reduction came to the fore. At the same time, the aid budgets of OECD donor countries fell by 22 percent to USD 60 billion between 1992 and 1997 (Trachsler and Möckli 2008).

The interdependence between security and development became apparent in the 1990s with the failed UN missions in Somalia, Rwanda, and Bosnia. In addition, the genocide in Rwanda in 1994 exposed the assumption that development per se was an instrument to prevent conflicts, or at least was conflict-neutral, as an illusion. As a result, holistic security thinking and the concept of human security prevailed. Since the terrorist attacks of September 11, 2001, the view has become more and more accepted that development aid should contribute to shaping an environment that prevents a breeding ground for radicalization and violent extremism. It is similarly acknowledged that international development cooperation is a key component for stabilizing fragile states. In the last fifteen years, states like Afghanistan, Pakistan, Iraq, and Sudan, which were perceived by the West as being crucial for fighting jihadist terrorism, have received far disproportionately large shares of Western development assistance (Trachsler and Möckli 2008).

After modest beginnings in the 1950s, Swiss development aid earnestly began with the establishment of the Service for Technical Cooperation (1960) and an official delegate of the Federal Council for technical cooperation (1961). Priorities of Swiss aid in the Cold War included Burundi, Rwanda, Tanzania, Cameroon, India, Nepal, Bolivia, and Peru. The first Swiss projects focused on dairy farming, livestock, the hotel industry, and vocational training. Swiss development aid was very popular abroad. Due to neutrality, Swiss aid workers enjoyed confidence in most countries. Switzerland had never been a colonial power, she acted impartiality, and her development aid was not politically motivated (Holenstein 2010).

In 1993, Switzerland formulated a new development policy in "North-South Guidelines," aiming at a coherent, comprehensive policy towards the global South. However, development assistance as a share of gross national income (GNI) also declined in Switzerland after 1990. In the 1990s, public development aid was 0.34 percent of Switzerland's GNI (Holenstein 2010). The quota increased to 0.5 percent in 2015, but still remains below the UN target value of 0.7 percent.

In 1999, the Federal Council in a landmark decision tied all international agreements with third countries to a clause on respect for human rights and principles of democracy. The agreements would be nullified in case of non-compliance. Absence of efforts towards good governance, serious human rights violations, or serious breaches of peace and security, as well as lack of willingness to readmit rejected asylum seekers, would trigger a suspension or cancellation of technical or financial cooperation with Switzerland. Swiss development cooperation had already been cancelled or suspended with Belarus (1996), Myanmar (1996), India and Pakistan (after their nuclear tests in 1998), and in Niger (after a coup in 1999). Despite parliamentary criticism, however, cooperation with Russia was continued after the outbreak of the second Chechen War in 1999 (Nünlist 2014b, 249f.).

As early as 2003, this practice of conditionality was relaxed again. Since then, Switzerland's focus emphasizes positive incentives rather than negative measures. Today, supporting the transition to a democratic market economy is one of five objectives of Swiss development policy (Nünlist 2014b, 250).

The influential Swiss Agency for Development and Cooperation (SDC), which accounts for two thirds of the foreign ministry budget, has been integrated into the Federal Department of Foreign Affairs (FDFA) in recent years.[35] Among the currently twenty priority countries and regions for development cooperation and eleven countries and regions receiving humanitarian aid are North Africa, the South Caucasus, Central Asia, Syria, North Korea, and Myanmar. Extraneous reasons may explain the Swiss focus on Central Asia. Since 1992, Kyrgyzstan, Tajikistan, and Uzbekistan have joined Switzerland as members of the same voting group within the World Bank and the International Monetary Fund, which is also dubbed "Helvetistan." Similarly, Switzerland's commitment to North Korea can be explained by peace policy considerations rather than any prospect of a successful process of democratization (Guldin 2011, 106; Künzli 2008, 615f.). In general, however, the external development committee of the OECD has given Switzerland good marks for international cooperation, confirming its new, more politically framed approach.[36]

Recently, Switzerland's commitment to reducing poverty and exclusion in fragile and conflict-affected contexts, where aid is seen as crucial conflict prevention work, has become increasingly important. The Swiss strategy focuses on human rights, basic, and vocational education, community development, climate change and the environment, food security, migration, health, and finance and trade.[37] Switzerland often occupies thematic niches, for example "water security." The idea behind this new approach is the following: Not only should water not contribute to conflict (Jordan's Prince Hassan Ben Talal recently declared that water was "the most important and effective weapon of mass destruction"), but on the contrary, water should be used as a driver of cooperation. In late 2015, a high-level international global panel on "water and security" was created in Geneva. Until the end of 2017, this panel is tasked with submitting proposals for the establishment of instruments and a governance structure for preventing water conflicts at the global and regional levels.[38]

CIVILIAN PEACEBUILDING: THE NEW STRENGTH OF SWISS FOREIGN POLICY

In the past twenty years, civilian peacebuilding and strengthening of human security have been at the core of the new dynamic, neutral Swiss foreign policy. A more active contribution to security and peace was first conceptually defined as a strategic aim in the Foreign Policy White Paper in 1993 and later codified in the revised Federal Constitution, which entered into force in 2000 (Trachsler 2009).[39]

Civilian peacebuilding deliberately followed Switzerland's tradition of providing "good offices" and humanitarian engagement to compensate for Swiss neutrality with acts of solidarity. On the other hand, Switzerland's peacebuilding abroad was also motivated by Swiss national interests with the aim of creating peace and stability in Switzerland's strategic environment after violent conflicts (CSS 2006, 114–137).

The enhanced importance of civilian peacebuilding in the last twenty years was also helped by the fact that neutral Switzerland, due to domestic resistance, could contribute much less to international military peacebuilding than comparable countries such as Austria, Sweden, and Finland (Bieri and Nünlist 2013, 47).

Specifically, civilian peace promotion means active mediation in political-diplomatic peace processes; development of effective programs for civilian conflict-solving; or supporting multilateral peace operations with the Swiss Expert Pool (SEF).[40] Geographically, the Western Balkans remains a clear focus. Due to the large number of immigrants and refugees from former Yugoslavia, Switzerland was directly affected. Migration prevention thus is also very much a motive of Swiss commitment in the Western Balkans. After the Balkan Wars ended, Swiss peace policy was able to contribute meaningfully to the promotion of democracy and the protection of minorities—two recognized strengths of Swiss policy. Additional key regions for Swiss peace policy include North Africa and the Middle East, Ukraine, Caucasus, the Great Lakes Region, Tajikistan, Nepal, Sri Lanka, Myanmar, Thailand, Indonesia/Aceh, Colombia, and Guatemala (CSS 2011, 118ff.).

Thematically, Switzerland's peace diplomacy focuses on preventive-diplomatic, confidence-building, and mediating action to deescalate or solve conflicts. Switzerland is facilitating peace processes (including providing mediation activities). Swiss diplomacy is engaged in defusing small arms proliferation and personnel landmines, addressing gender aspects of security and peace (UN resolution 1325), promoting human rights (the protection of civilians in armed conflicts in particular), supporting measures to prevent violent extremism, helping with constitutional issues and dealing with the past. Compared to countries like Germany, Sweden, Norway, Canada, Australia, New Zealand, which also have specialized in civil peacebuilding, Switzerland possesses comparative advantages in these areas.

The example of Sudan demonstrates that successful civilian peacebuilding requires stamina. Switzerland was approached by Sudanese diplomats because Swiss ambassador Josef Bucher, who speaks Arabic, had maintained close contacts with his Sudanese counterparts during his tenure in Libya (1994–1997). This became the basis for Sudan's later official request that Switzerland supported talks between Khartoum and the rebel movement SPLA. During yearlong talks in Switzerland, deep trust was built. Ambassador Bucher repeatedly traveled to Khartoum and Southern Sudan and elicited the historical background and possible solutions to the conflict. Bucher's diplomatic contacts later became key figures in the Sudanese government—in

2002, Swiss conflict mediation on the Bürgenstock was successful, leading to the 2005 peace agreement (Mason 2006).[41]

Other examples of successful Swiss good offices contributed to the peace agreement in Nepal (2006), which ended a ten-year civil war (Trachsler 2012), and the Zurich Protocols between Turkey and Armenia (2009). Swiss good offices have a long tradition. During Second World War, Switzerland had 219 protecting power mandates for thirty-five countries. During the Cold War, there was also high demand for Switzerland's good offices. For Switzerland, providing them was a good way to compensate for its internationally discredited neutrality (Trachsler 2004).

After 1990, Swiss good offices were initially pushed to the background. Many countries now restored their diplomatic relations. The concept of the protecting power, an instrument for interstate conflicts, did not fit the civil wars and conflicts with nongovernmental combatants of the 1990s. In addition, Switzerland shied away from new mandates due to the new, downsized neutrality concept. In 1998, when the United Kingdom and Germany asked Switzerland on the eve of the war in Kosovo to become their protecting power in Serbia, then foreign minister Flavio Cotti declined.[42]

Under President Barack Obama, US relations with decade-old archenemies such as Cuba and Iran were normalized. As a result of this reconciliation, traditional Swiss protecting power mandates were either terminated (US-Cuba) or lost much of their relevance (US-Iran).[43] In recent years, the climate of international relations has dramatically deteriorated. Thus, Swiss good offices have experienced an unexpected comeback. Swiss diplomats can now play their traditional role as mediators again, as there is once more a strong demand for neutral good offices. For example, important new protective power mandates were added in the aftermath of the 2008 war for Russia and Georgia, and in early 2016 for Iran and Saudi Arabia.[44]

In addition, in almost all of today's important conflicts and crises, Switzerland is involved as the neutral host of international peace conferences (e.g., dealing with Iran's nuclear program, the Ukraine crisis, or wars in Ukraine, Libya, or Yemen) as well as mediating in the "frozen" territorial conflict between Armenia and Azerbaijan over Nagorno Karabakh.

In the twenty-first century, Switzerland is still benefiting from its reputation as a mediator in international conflicts. Swiss diplomacy profits from Swiss neutrality, small statehood, and a Swiss humanitarian tradition that reaches back to the founding of the ICRC and the Geneva Conventions. As a country without a colonial past and with no political power ambitions, Switzerland is often approached to act as a politically cautious, discrete, independent honest broker. Switzerland has the know-how, an excellent reputation, and a very good infrastructure for providing good offices. Switzerland benefits from decades of mediating, because a good reputation as a mediator cannot be acquired overnight.[45]

In the last twenty-five years, the UN, OSCE, and EU have all played a larger role in the mediation of conflicts. This trend towards multilateral mediation, however, is not necessarily detrimental to Swiss mediation. Modern Swiss mediation activities are happening exactly within these multilateral frameworks—leading to talks in Switzerland, including on the settlement of the nuclear conflict with Iran, de-escalation of the Ukraine crisis, or the war in Syria. In the future, Switzerland would like to provide senior mediators like Heidi Tagliavini to UN and OSCE mediations more often. In the 2016 foreign policy strategy, mediation is defined as a key priority of Swiss foreign policy for the next four years.[46]

A central challenge for Swiss foreign policy still is to provide good offices credibly and independently while simultaneously displaying solidarity with the West. Switzerland defines herself clearly as part of the Western community of values; Switzerland belongs to Europe—geographically, historically, and culturally. During the Ukraine crisis, Switzerland offered the OSCE its good offices, but at the same time, the Swiss government sharply condemned the Russian violation of international law by annexing Crimea. It was also important that Switzerland avoided benefiting economically from circumventing Western sanctions against Russia. This balancing act between impartiality and an exposed position within the West is rather precarious (Nünlist and Thränert 2015; Nünlist 2015b).

In the last twenty years, Switzerland's financial and material resources for civilian peacebuilding have continuously increased. Switzerland has succeeded in raising her international profile in the arena of peace policy. Many of the Swiss activities actually took place within a multilateral framework in the UN, OSCE, or in international Geneva. In sum, Switzerland has indeed played an active role in shaping cooperative answers to global challenges—as requested in the Foreign Affairs White Paper in 1993.

CONCLUSION: FROM NEUTRALITY TO MULTIPARTIALITY

Swiss foreign policy is traditionally shaped by constant principles such as neutrality, the rule of law, universality, dialogue, solidarity, and responsibility. According to Paul Widmer, a former Swiss diplomat and author of a much-praised handbook on diplomacy, neutrality is still the most important axiom of Swiss foreign policy (Widmer 2007, 134). Neutrality has also become an essential part of Swiss identity, alongside democracy, the mountains, or Wilhelm Tell.

After 1990, however, the Swiss government qualified neutrality and emphasized that neutrality primarily is a foreign policy instrument to secure Swiss national interests, but not a foreign policy aim in itself. Switzerland's neutrality policy is therefore flexible and always dependent on the country's changing strategic environment. Swiss neutrality policy in the twenty-first century means much more than simply passively avoiding entanglement with military alliances. For an active engagement in dealing with modern challenges to global and European security, neutrality can still be an advantage for providing impartial good offices—a traditional strength of Swiss foreign policy. Switzerland stands out among other states and is able to play a special, but relevant mediating role in the international system.

In recent years, the international context has become more unstable, more insecure, and more difficult for Swiss foreign policy. But Switzerland can play an active role and display both responsibility and solidarity in the world. Her independent foreign policy enables Switzerland to provide useful, credible diplomatic services for dealing with current European and global challenges—independent of military alliances and major powers, but actively participating in international security organizations and multilateral frameworks. Swiss diplomats are well-equipped to build bridges and to come up with innovative and sustainable solutions that are based on Swiss values and that reflect Swiss interests.

Neutrality remains an important ingredient of Swiss diplomacy, together with competence and experience in international cooperation. Switzerland's emphasis on civilian peace promotion in recent years serves as a model for a modern understanding of neutrality (Gärtner 2011, 477ff.; Goetschel 2011). Rather than passive isolation from the international scene, Switzerland uses cooperative multilateral frameworks and actively engages in contributing to security and peace in Europe's neighborhood. Switzerland's domestic strengths, such as democracy, dialogue, power-sharing, and protection of minorities, have become key topics of Switzerland's foreign policy. This modern form of Swiss foreign policy should be labeled "multipartiality" rather than neutrality. Switzerland's peace policy as the core of her foreign policy tries to care for all sides and to take everybody's side rather than to pretend to be neutral of emotions, ideas, and perceptions (Wolfstein 2016, 80).

"The hottest places in Hell are reserved for those who in time of moral crisis preserve their neutrality," the Italian poet Dante Alighieri wrote in the fourteenth century. In recent years, Swiss foreign policy has successfully transformed its passive neutrality policy into an engaged, active, independent, and multipartial peace policy—providing a model for other neutral or middle powers to make meaningful contributions in countering current global security challenges.

NOTES

1. Bundesrat, 2016. *Aussenpolitische Strategie 2016–2019*, February 17: 2.
2. "Viel Lob für 'Briefträger' Burkhalter." *Die Nordwestschweiz*, February 15, 2016.
3. Bundesrat, 1990. *Schweizerische Sicherheitspolitik im Wandel: Bericht 90 über die Sicherheitspolitik der Schweiz*, October 1: 873.
4. Bundesrat, 1993. Bericht zur Neutralität: Anhang zum Bericht über die Aussenpolitik der Schweiz in den 90er Jahren, November 29.
5. "Erweiterung der aussenpolitischen Pupillen." *NZZ*, May 20, 2005.
6. See also "Botschaft über die Weiterführung von Massnahmen zur Förderung des Friedens und der menschlichen Sicherheit 2012–2016," June 29, 2011: 6326–6330.
7. Bundesrat, *Aussenpolitischer Bericht 2007*, Anhang 1: "Neutralität," June 15, 2007. See also Möckli 2007.
8. Bundesrat, *Aussenpolitische Strategie 2012–2016*, March 2, 2012.
9. "Didier Burkhalters unerwartete Offensive." *NZZ*, December 1, 2012.
10. See "Swiss to UK: You'll miss being at the EU table." *Politico Europe*, March 16, 2016.
11. "Bundesrat zieht die Zügel an." *NZZ*, August 27, 2014.
12. Bundesrat, Stellungnahme zur Interpellation "Neutralität als Chance und Notwendigkeit für die Schweiz im veränderten internationalen Umfeld." November 19, 2014; Bundesrat, 2016. Stellungnahme zur Interpellation "Massnahmen für eine glaubwürdige Neutralitätspolitik der Schweiz," February 24.
13. For example, in public speeches in Berne on March 23, 2015 and June 17, 2015.
14. "Die Schweiz hat in der Ukraine eine besondere Rolle." *NZZ*, March 18, 2014. Burkhalter said: "The OSCE Chairmanship reinforces the Swiss role as a mediator: Our impartiality is twofold." (Translated by the author)
15. See "Eklat im Bundesrat: Maurer wirft Burkhalter Neutralitätsbruch vor." *NZZ*, March 20, 2014; "Schweigen in Krim-Krise: Macht sich die Schweiz zur nützlichen Idiotin?" *Die Nordwestschweiz*, March 8, 2014.
16. "Schweizer Bevölkerung zeigt sich offener gegenüber dem Ausland." *SRF News Online*, May 29, 2015. See also "Der Welt einen Dienst erwiesen." *Tages-Anzeiger*, December 3, 2014.
17. "Schweizer des Jahres 2014: Burkhalter überaus deutlich gewählt." *NZZ*, January 11, 2015.
18. When the OSCE began to deploy military observers and military specialists in conflict areas, the organization chose yellow bonnets as headpieces to distinguish its personnel from UN units with blue helmets.
19. "Der OSZE-Vorsitz der Schweiz ist ein Glücksfall." *Tages-Anzeiger*, May 11, 2014.
20. "Viel Lob für die Schweiz am OSZE-Ministertreffen." *SRF News Online*, December 4, 2014.
21. The following paragraphs are based on Nünlist 2015.
22. Author's background interview with Swiss foreign ministry official, Berne, September 21, 2015.

23. Author's background interviews with senior director of NATO Secretariat, Brussels, September 27, 2013, and WEP-5 diplomat, Brussels, September 21, 2015. See also FDFA, 2013. *Table ronde informelle sur la situation au Mali et dans la region du Sahel à la Mission de la Suisse auprès de l'OTAN.* Brussels, February 15.

24. Bundesrat, *PfP-Jahresbericht 2013*, March 26, 2014: 5.

25. Based on author's background interviews with a WEP-5 diplomat (Brussels), an IS/NATO staff member (Brussels), and a Swiss foreign ministry official (Berne) conducted in September 2015.

26. *Bericht der Schweizer Delegation bei der Parlamentarischen Versammlung der NATO*, December 31: 13.

27. Author's background interview with Swiss defense ministry official, Berne, September 16, 2015.

28. Christian Nünlist, 2012. "Die Schweiz und die UNO: Eine Erfolgsstory." *Aargauer Zeitung*, February 22: 6.

29. UN, 2016. "Switzerland." *Troop and Police Contributors*, January 31. http://www.un.org/en/peacekeeping/resources/statistics/contributors.shtml. In early 2016, Switzerland contributed 18 military experts, 9 soldiers, and 3 police officers to UN peacekeeping.

30. "Gute Noten für fünfjährige UNO-Mitgliedschaft." *NZZ*, September 11, 2007.

31. For details, see the most recent annual reports of the Swiss foreign ministry.

32. See Owen Frazer and Christian Nünlist, 2016. "The Concept of Countering Violent Extremism." *CSS Analyses in Security Policy* 183. See also FDFA, *Switzerland's Foreign Policy Action Plan on Preventing Violent Extremism.* Berne: FDFA, published on April 8, 2016.

33. FDFA, 2015. "Schweiz ab 2016 als Mitglied im UNO-Menschenrechtsrat gewählt," October 28.

34. Bundesrat, 2015. "Die Kandidatur der Schweiz für einen nichtständigen Sitz im Sicherheitsrat der Vereinten Nationen in der Periode 2023–2024." *Bundesrat Bericht*, June 5.

35. "Ambivalente Integration der Entwicklungspolitik." *NZZ*, December 5, 2013.

36. Bundesrat, 2014. *Aussenpolitischer Bericht 2013*, January 15: 1100.

37. Bundesrat, 2016. *Aussenpolitische Strategie 2016–19*, February 17: 29.

38. EDA, 2015. "Zugang zu Wasser: Eine Priorität der Schweizer Aussenpolitik," September 11.

39. See also *Bundesverfassung*, April 18, 1999, art. 54, para. 2.

40. Bundesrat, 2002. *Botschaft über einen Rahmenkredit für Massnahmen zur zivilen Konfliktbearbeitung und Menschenrechtsförderung*, October 23.

41. See also Josef Bucher, 2004. "Innovative Ansätze für die Friedenspolitik." *NZZ*, January 16.

42. "Schlechter Start für Gute Dienste." *NZZ*, April 16, 1999.

43. "Die Schweizer Diplomatie verliert ein Prestigeobjekt." *Tages-Anzeiger,* December 9, 2014.

44. EDA, 2016. "Good Offices: A Swiss Specialty." *Ansprache von Didier Burkhalter.* Valetta, March 9.

45. "Das Comeback der Schweiz als Vermittlerin: Der zweite Frühling der Guten Dienste," *NZZ*, January 28, 2014. See also Trachsler 2012.
46. Ibid.

BIBLIOGRAPHY

Andrey, Marjorie. 2010. "Security Implications of Neutrality: Switzerland in the Partnership of Peace Framework." *The Quarterly Journal* 9(4): 83–97.

Bieri, Matthias and Christian Nünlist. 2013. "Friedensförderung à la Suisse: Schweizerische Sicherheitspolitik im 21. Jahrhundert." *International: Die Zeitschrift für internationale Politik* 4: 43–48.

Bonjour, Edgar. 1965. *Geschichte der schweizerischen Neutralität*. Basel: Helbing.

Calmy-Rey, Micheline. 2014. *Die Schweiz, die ich uns wünsche*. Zurich: Nagel & Kimche.

Center for Security Studies (CSS). 2006. *Zivile Friedensförderung als Tätigkeitsfeld der Aussenpolitik: Eine vergleichende Studie anhand von fünf Ländern*. Zürich: ETH Zürich.

Dahinden, Erwin. 1998. "Globales Personenminenverbot als humanitäres Anliegen." *Allgemeine Schweizerische Militärzeitschrift* 3: 20–21.

Fischer, Thomas. 2009. *Neutral Power in the CSCE*. Baden-Baden: Nomos.

Fuhrer, Hans Rudolf. 2005. "Das Phänomen der Verweigerung: Zur Frage der Beziehung oder Nichtbeziehung der Schweiz zur NATO 1949–1966." In *La Suisse 1945–1990 / Die Schweiz 1945–1960*, edited by Hervé de Weck, 101–138. Bern: ASHSM.

Gärtner, Heinz. 2011. "Frieden und Neutralität." In *Handbuch Frieden*, edited by Hans J. Giessmann and Bernhard Rinke, 475–485. Wiesbaden: VS Verlag.

Gerber, Marcel. 1999. "Schweizerische Rüstungskontrollpolitik in einem neuen internationalen Umfeld: Das innovative Engagement für ein Personenminen-Verbot als Modell für die Zukunft?" *Bulletin zur schweizerischen Sicherheitspolitik*: 77–98.

Goetschel, Laurent. 2011. "Neutrals as brokers of peacebuilding ideas?" *Cooperation and Conflict* 46(3): 312–333.

Goetschel, Laurent (Ed.). 1997. *Vom Statisten zum Hauptdarsteller: Die Schweiz und ihre OSZE-Präsidentschaft*. Bern: Haupt.

Grätz, Jonas. 2013. "Partnerschaft mit Russland: Bestandsaufnahme einer aussenpolitischen Akzentsetzung." *Bulletin zur schweizerischen Sicherheitspolitik*: 41–70.

Greminger, Thomas. 2011. "Die Entwicklung der zivilen Friedensförderung der Schweiz seit 2006." In *Zivile Friedensförderung der Schweiz: Bestandsaufnahme und Entwicklungspotential*, edited by Andreas Wenger, 13–68. Zürich: CSS.

Guldin, Philippe. 2011. *Kohärenz in der Schweizer Aussen- und Entwicklungspolitik*. PhD Thesis, University of Zurich.

Haltiner, Karl. 2011. "Vom schmerzlichen Verlieren alter Feindbilder: Bedrohungs- und Risikoanalysen in der Schweiz." In *Transformation der Sicherheitspolitik: Deutschland, Österreich, Schweiz im Vergleich*, edited by Thomas Jäger and Ralph Thiele, 39–58.Wiesbaden: VS Verlag.

Holenstein, René. 2010. *Wer langsam geht, kommt weit: Ein halbes Jahrhundert Schweizer Entwicklungshilfe.* Zürich: Chronos.

Kunz, Matthias and Petro Morandi. 2000. "Der Kosovo-Krieg als heimliche Epochenwende der schweizerischen Aussenpolitik." In *Schweizerische Aussenpolitik im Kosovo-Krieg,* edited by Jürg Martin Gabriel, 63–88. Zürich: Orell Füessli.

Künzli, Jörg. 2008. *Vom Umgang des Rechtsstaats mit Unrechtsregimes.* Bern: Stämpfli.

Lanteigne, Marc. 2014. "The Sino-Swiss Free Trade Agreement." *CSS Analyses in Security Policy* 147.

Liechtenstein, Stephanie. 2014. "A Permanent Swiss Chairmanship for the OSCE: A Viable Suggestion?" *Security and Human Rights Blog,* 28 July 2014. http://www.shrblog.org.

Mantovani, Mauro. 1999. *Schweizerische Sicherheitspolitik im Kalten Krieg 1947–1963.* Zurich: Orell Füessli.

Mason, Simon. 2006. "Lehren aus den Schweizer Mediations- und Fazilitationsdiensten im Sudan." *Bulletin zur schweizerischen Sicherheitspolitik*: 43–96.

Möckli, Daniel. 2000. *Neutralität, Solidarität, Sonderfall: Die Konzeptionierung der schweizerischen Aussenpolitik der Nachkriegszeit, 1943–1947.* Zurich: ETH.

———. 2007. "Swiss Neutrality: Rhetoric and Relevance." *CSS Analyses in Security Policy* 20.

———. 2011. "Swiss Foreign Policy 2012: Challenges and Perspectives." *CSS Analyses in Security Policy* 106.

Nünlist, Christian. 2014. "Testfall Ukraine-Krise: Das Konfliktmanagement der OSZE unter Schweizer Vorsitz." *Bulletin zur schweizerischen Sicherheitspolitik*: 35–61.

———. 2014b. "Umdenken der neutralen Schweiz." In *Aussenpolitik mit Autokratien,* edited by Josef Braml et al., 246–255. Berlin: De Gruyter.

———. 2015. "20 Jahre Partnerschaft für den Frieden: Die Schweiz und die Gruppe der WEP-5." *Bulletin zur schweizerischen Sicherheitspolitik*: 19–40.

———. 2015b. "Swiss Security Policy after 2014." *European Security & Defence* 3–4: 18–21.

———. 2016. "Switzerland and NATO: From Non-relationship to Cautious Partnership, 1949–2016." In *The European Neutrals and NATO: Non-alignment, Partnership, Membership?* edited by Andrew Cottey. Basingstoke, forthcoming in 2017.

Nünlist, Christian and Oliver Thränert. 2015. "Putin's Russia and European Security after 2014." *CSS Analyses in Security Policy* 172.

Riklin, Alois. 1992. "Die Neutralität der Schweiz." In *Neues Handbuch der schweizerischen Aussenpolitik,* edited by Alois Riklin et al., 191–209. Bern: Haupt.

Rosin, Philip. 2014. *Die Schweiz im KSZE-Prozess 1972–1983: Einfluss durch Neutralität.* Munich: Oldenbourg.

Schaller, André. 1987. *Schweizer Neutralität im Ost-West-Handel: Das Hotz-Linder-Agreement vom 23. Juli 1951.* Bern: Haupt.

Shea, Jamie. 2016. "Rethinking NATO's Partnership for the New Security Environment." *Politorbis* 61: 83–86.

Spillmann, Kurt R., et al. 2001. *Schweizer Sicherheitspolitik, seit 1945.* Zurich: NZZ.

Stern, Maximilian and David Svarin. 2014. "A Permanent Chairmanship for the OSCE?" *Security and Human Rights Blog*, June 25, 2014. http://www.shrblog.org.

Szvircsev Tresch, Tibor, and Andreas Wenger (Eds.). 2015. *Sicherheit 2015: Aussen-, Sicherheits- und Verteidigungspolitische Meinungsbildung im Trends.* Zurich: ETH.

Trachsler, Daniel. 2004. "Gute Dienste: Mythen, Fakten, Perspektiven." *Bulletin zur schweizerischen Sicherheitspolitik:* 33–64.

———. 2008. "Partizipation oder Alleingang? Die UNO-Beitrittsfrage aus der Sicht Max Petitpierres (1945–1961)." *Politorbis* 33: 13–20.

———. 2009. "Swiss Civilian Peace Support: Potential and Limitations." *CSS Analyses in Security Policy* 63.

———. 2010. "Die Schweiz in der UNO: Mittendrin statt nur dabei." *Bulletin zur schweizerischen Sicherheitspolitik:* 121–156.

———. 2010b. "UN Security Council Reform: A Gordian Knot?" *CSS Analyses in Security Policy* 72.

———. 2011. *Bundesrat Max Petitpierre: Schweizerische Aussenpolitik im Kalten Krieg, 1945–1961.* Zurich: NZZ.

———. 2012. "Nepal's Faltering Peace Process and Swiss Engagement." *CSS Analyses in Security Policy* 125.

———. 2012b. "Restoring Foreign Interests: Rebirth of a Swiss Tradition?" *CSS-Analysen zur Sicherheitspolitik* 108.

Trachsler, Daniel, and Daniel Möckli. 2008. "Security and Development: Convergence or Competition?" *CSS Analyses in Security Policy* 40.

Watanabe, Lisa. 2015. "Die strategische Partnerschaft der Schweiz mit der Türkei." *Bulletin zur schweizerischen Sicherheitspolitik*: 41–61.

Wenger, Andreas et al. 1997/98. "Die Partnerschaft für den Frieden: Eine Chance für die Schweiz." *Bulletin zur schweizerischen Sicherheitspolitik*: 45–102.

———. 1996/97. "Das schweizerische OSZE-Präsidialjahr 1996." *Bulletin zur schweizerischen Sicherheitspolitik*: 4–46.

Widmer, Paul. 2007. *Die Schweiz als Sonderfall: Grundlagen, Geschichte, Gestaltung.* Zurich: NZZ.

Wolfstein, Mirjam. 2016. "Negotiation for Sustainable Peace." In Handbook of Research on Transitional Justice and Pece Building in Turbulent Regions, edited by Fredy Cante and Hartmut Quehl, 76–96. Hershey, PA: IPI Global.

Chapter 8

The Common Foreign, Security, and Defense Policy of the EU

Opportunities and Limitations for Neutral Member States

Franz Leidenmühler and Sandra Grafeneder

Since 1992, the European Union has been working on the ongoing development of a Common Foreign, Security and Defense Policy. This framework facilitates the commitment to establish appropriate Rapid Reaction Forces, so-called Battle Groups, in order to conduct demanding missions. Austria's existing permanent neutrality does not hamper the country to participate in the EU's crisis management. On the contrary, a permanently neutral member state can play a vital role in enhancing the EU's CFSP and CSDP, assessing current challenges for and threats to the security of the Union more effective.

Due to the unanimity requirement, decisions concerning the Common Foreign, Security and Defense Policy frequently fail to be made. The increased use of the "Permanent Structured Cooperation" instrument by member states willing to enhance their cooperation serves as a possible relief to strengthen the EU's capacity to act in the area of the Common Security and Defense Policy. A new EU Security Strategy also needs to assess the threat posed by regional instability of failing states having a geographical proximity to the EU and to provide solutions to assure Europe's security and to prevent those refugee movements to Europe that are triggered by political instability or war.

WHAT ARE THE EU'S CFSP AND CSDP?

In her origins, the EU was an economic project with the goal of establishing a common market. Early attempts to build a European Defense Community did fail in the 1950s because of the resistance of the French parliament. It took another twenty years before the first steps of creating a Common European

Foreign Policy were successfully made in the 1970s. With the Treaty of Maastricht in 1992, the provisions on the Common Foreign and Security Policy (CFSP) of the European Union were introduced, which aimed to coordinate the EU member states foreign policy positions and to enable Europe to speak with one voice. Adjustments made by the Treaty of Amsterdam 1997 and Nice 2001, as well as a number of noncontractual decisions by the European Council[1] contributed to the development of the CFSP resulting in the establishment of the Common Security and Defense Policy (CSDP) (Hummer 2001, 147; Dietrich 2006, 663).

The tasks, which are completed by using civilian and military means, include joint disarmament operations, humanitarian and rescue tasks, military advice and assistance tasks, conflict prevention and peacekeeping tasks, tasks of combat forces in crisis management including peace-making and post-conflict stabilization. All these tasks may contribute to the fight against terrorism by supporting third countries in combating terrorism in their territories.[2]

Instruments available to the EU for reacting to certain incidents are adopting a common position[3] on particular geographic or thematic issues or—in case operational actions are required—the execution of civilian or military operations by the Union.[4]

In order to response to international crisis as fast as possible, Rapid Response Forces in the form of so-called "Battle Groups" were established with high availability. Every half year, two battalion-sized forces (about 1,500 personnel strong), formed by one or more member states, are deployable within ten days and, after another five days in the country of deployment, able to sustain operations for at least thirty days until being replaced by another unit.

As far as the decision-making process is concerned, the general rule still requires a unanimous vote for CFSP and CSDP decisions. Only a few implementing decisions that are not related to military and defense policy matters are excluded from this rule.[5] Abstention from member states does not block the adoption of the decision, and even the abstaining state is obliged to accept and apply the decision. In case a member of the Council qualifies its abstention by making a formal declaration, it shall not be obliged to apply the decision, but shall accept that the decision commits the Union. The other member states shall respect its position.[6] In return, the member state concerned shall, due to a spirit of mutual solidarity, refrain from any action likely to conflict with or impede Union action based on that decision. Such an abstaining in a vote by delivering an appropriate explanation is called "constructive abstention."[7] Such a "constructive abstention" commits the Union[8] and all twenty-eight member states. The abstaining member state, however, is not obliged to apply the decision.

AUSTRIA'S NEUTRALITY AND THE PARTICIPATION
IN THE CFSP AND CSDP OF THE EUROPEAN UNION

On October 26, 1955, Austria declared its permanent neutrality by adopting the constitutional law on permanent neutrality.[9] Later the legal text was notified to all states, which Austria then had diplomatic relations with, requesting recognition with the consequence of having a legally binding effect for Austria under international law. Austria's permanent neutrality is, just like Switzerland's, hereby vested in public international law (Rotter 1983, 306, 310 et seq.) and therefore deviating from the Swedish status (Christianson 2010).

Substantially, the rules of permanent neutrality under international law are limited to the obligation of a permanently neutral state to adopt a neutral position[10] in every war, regardless of whenever and wherever it may occur in the future. Thus, the obligations of a permanently neutral state in times of peace anticipate its legal obligations in times of war in a certain way (Christianson 2010, 311; Luif 1995, 124 et seqs.).

According to the prevailing view, Austria's status of neutrality was not affected by its accession to the European Union (Leidenmühler 2003, 204, 217 et seq.).[11] To abandon or to modify the status was and still is not necessary, as is shown in the following.

The main duty of any neutral state is the "non-participation in war," regardless of when and where the war is taking place and who is involved. Considering that, it is definitely possible for a permanently neutral Austria to participate unconditionally in humanitarian tasks, rescue operations, and peace-keeping functions, since those activities conducted by the CFSP and CSDP are not related to war. Such cases actually do not activate the duties resulting from permanent neutrality.[12]

Much more, a permanently neutral state can possibly play a more vital role in carrying out such tasks, as it is potentially less burdened by a war-prone history and past conflict involvement than other member states.

Merely participating in tasks of combat forces in crisis management and peace-making operations has to be considered as problematic on first sight. Right from the start of Austria's EU membership, the question came up whether or not Austria would be able to contribute to a combat operation decided upon by the EU without the UN's legal endorsement (Luif 1995, 240). Evidently, this leads to the fundamental question, whether a mandate of the UN Security Council is necessary for actions of the EU outside of its territory in general. The relation to the UN as a whole and especially to the UN Security Council is in fact not only important for the neutrals, but for member states overall. According to chapter VII of the UN Charter the use of military force within the territory of third states is only legal under the following circumstances: it is either justified by consent or by the exercise of the right of self-defense or by a mandate of the UN Security Council that allows the International Community to act.

In the aftermath of the Kosovo crisis 1999, intense discussions about the so-called "humanitarian intervention" (Beyerlin 1982, 211 et seqs.) outside the framework of the UN Charter were initiated (Cassese 1999, Henkin 2006; Köck, Horn and Leidenmühler 2009, 37). In these days and as a result of the Lisbon Treaty, a lot of arguments affirm the subordination of the EU in relation to the UN Charter.

First of all, every single member state of the EU is a party to the UN Charter and thereby bound as sovereign state affecting all actions (rights of third states cannot be infringed by the EU Treaty; in this particular case the rights of all other members of the UN Charter).

In addition to this, the EU as such is binding itself to the UN Charter by provisions in the EU Treaty, which have just been enlarged by the Treaty of Lisbon. Article 3 (5) TEU calls for the "strict observance and the development of international law, including respect for the principles of the United Nations Charter." The fact that Article 21 (1) TEU refers four times to the UN Charter emphasizes the importance and makes this article worth being mentioned as well. Especially the wording in para. 2 lit. c shows that the purpose of the UN matters as such since the paragraph refers explicitly to both "purposes and principles" of the UN Charter. And, without any doubt, the highest purpose of the Charter is to maintain international peace and security by taking collective measures (Article 1 UN Charter). Again, in the chapter on CSDP the missions of the UN have the intent "to strengthen international security in accordance with the principles of the United Nations Charter" (Article 42 (1) TEU). So it is safe to say that the EU subordinates itself under the UN Charter and the main responsibility of the UN Security Council for the promotion of world peace by the Treaty of Lisbon.

In addition, some states, for example, Ireland and Malta, consider UN Security Council mandate as absolutely necessary for any external action of the EU. Considering the unanimity requirement, it takes only one state to obstruct any action of the EU without a UN mandate.

Accordingly, the EU's crisis management is not a competitor to the UN, but functions much more as a servant to the world organization, and this is important due to the fact that the Security Council lacks having its own troops. Under Article 43 UN Charter

all Members of the United Nations, in order to contribute to the maintenance of international peace and security, undertake to make available to the Security Council, on its call and in accordance with a special agreement or agreements, armed forces, assistance, and facilities, including rights of passage, necessary for the purpose of maintaining international peace and security.

However, these special agreements have never been concluded. Building troops and making them available for the needs of the UN Security Council actually means the application of Article 43 UN Charter for the very first time (Leidenmühler 2008, 9 et seqs.).

As a result, all EU operations, including the deployment of combat forces in crisis management and peace-making operations, due to international law may only occur with a Security Council mandate anyways.

And, according to Article 103 UN Charter,[13] all armed activities happening within the context of a UN mandate are in general compatible with neutrality.[14] Actually, military sanctions under chapter VII of the UN Charter are not considered as a war being relevant for neutrality law, but as legal means of the Security Council acting in the name of the international community.

According to that, it does make sense to involve neutral states in this European security alliance. The fact that Ireland received affirmation from the European Council by confirming that the EU's CSDP does not affect Ireland's (military) neutrality and that Irish troops will not be deployed to any war zone without UN authorization, serves as a good example for illustration. Likewise, Malta's declaration attached to the Act of Accession in 2004 upholds the fact that participation in the European Union's Common Foreign and Security Policy does not affect or prejudice neutrality.

Even the introduction of a mutual defense clause between the EU member states in the Lisbon Treaty[15] does not contradict the existing permanent neutrality of a member state.[16] It is true that such a commitment results ultimately in at least a symbolic military alliance that obligates all member states to aid and assist by all the means in their power in case a member state becomes the victim of armed aggression on its territory. When taking a closer look at the second sentence, the situation takes some sort of a turn though. The so-called "Irish Formula" states namely, "This (meant is the obligation of assistance) shall not prejudice the specific character of the security and defense policy of certain member states." So we are faced with a curiosity now: The European Union is a defense alliance, without obligating the neutrals to assist. That means that a mutual defense obligation does exist between twenty-three States only while the five neutral states benefit from a one-sided defense obligation. As curious as it may seem, such a situation is compatible with the status of permanent neutrality. Therefore, we have no consequences for the neutrals, although the EU mutates to a defense alliance. A mutual obligation of alliance exists now only for non-neutral states whereas, because of the "Irish Formula," all neutral member states are exempted from the obligation to provide assistance. This applies to Austria's neutrality status just as well, since in this constellation the permanently neutral state has no obligations to do anything that would violate the status of neutrality.[17]

So even though the EU is initiating a military alliance (the reasonableness of it can be doubted, by the way[18]), there is still chance and maneuvering room for neutrality. On the contrary, a permanently neutral member state can play a vital role in enhancing the EU's CFSP and CSDP in order to be more effective in assessing current challenges posing a threat to the security of the Union, although the capacity of neutrality as an instrument for solving international conflicts should not be overestimated (Rotter 1973).

WEAKNESS OF THE CFSP AND CSDP

The CSDP serves as an instrument to manage international crises. Considering this definition, the term "crisis" becomes the key interest as being the cause and source to trigger CSDP missions and operations. Given the Treaty on European Union, it does not define the term "crisis." The recognition of and the appropriate reaction to such situations remain a political decision being made case by case. In other words, a crisis only exists after the member states agreed on its existence.[19]

The fact that agreements on CFSP and CSDP decisions require a unanimous vote cripples the decision-making process (Article 31 (1) TEU). An agreement on whether or not the Union should interfere is a matter of CFSP and CSDP demanding unanimity and is generally difficult to reach.

With the option of a "Permanent Structured Cooperation" introduced by the Lisbon Treaty,[20] the member states receive the opportunity to cooperate in a more dynamic and effective way.[21] This creates the opportunity for those member states, whose military capabilities fulfil higher criteria, to make more binding commitments to one another in this area. Those member states that wish to participate in the "Permanent Structured Cooperation" shall notify their intention to the Council. Within three months following the notification, the Council shall adopt a decision by qualified majority, establishing permanent structured cooperation and enabling the member states to act autonomously. Hence, the "Permanent Structured Cooperation" is the perfect way for member states willing to strengthen the cooperation in the area of Common Security and Defense Policy of the EU, while extending solidarity and cohesion within the European Union ("unity in diversity") (Bendiek 2008).

FUTURE OF THE CFSP AND CSDP

Besides improving the EU's ability to act in the field of CFSP and CSDP by providing more flexible tools, a realignment of the concept for a general reorientation deserves consideration as well. The EU's Security Strategy is still based on the Strategy Paper of 2003, which is dominated by and limited to the events of September 11, 2001 ("A Secure Europe in a Better World") and identifies terrorism, weapons of mass destruction, as well as securing (worldwide) trade and investment flows as the fundamental issues concerning the Union's security.

A new Security Strategy shall be less focused on the Union's role as a global power, but instead concentrated on prioritizing regional conflicts[22] in order to find solutions to issues coming from failing states located near the EU to prevent insecurity and refugee movements to Europe caused by these conflicts. The "EU Global Strategy on Foreign and Security Policy" presented by Federica Mogherini in summer 2016 only partially meets these requirements.

The military action against human smuggling and traffickers in the Mediterranean launched at the beginning of October 2015 provides a good example for such a context. Under "Operation Sophia," which continues the mission "EUNAVFOR MED,"[23] the Union conducts a military crisis management operation in accordance with international law to disrupt the business model of human smuggling and trafficking networks in the Southern Central Mediterranean by undertaking systematic efforts to identify, capture and dispose vessels, as well as items used or suspected to being used by migrant smugglers or traffickers. Perspectively and under the assumption an appropriate mandate of the UN Security Council does exist, it is possible to extend military action under the "Operation Sophia," which is currently conducted by Germany, Belgium, Italy, Spain, France, and Great Britain, to traffickers operating on Libyan territory as well. However, if this action really pictures the claimed paradigm shift making the EU to realign its Security Strategy remains to be seen.

NOTES

1. Compare with: Conclusion of the (Cologne) European Council (June 3–4, 1999) and the (Helsinki) European Council (December 10–12, 1999); as well as: the previous Anglo-French summit in Saint-Malo (December 4, 1998); see also Kathrin Blanck, 2005. *Europäische Sicherheits- und Verteidigungspolitik im Rahmen der europäischen Sicherheitsarchitektur.* Wien: Springer: 110 et seq.

2. The so-called Petersberg tasks in Article 43 (1) TEU (Treaty on European Union): "The tasks referred to in Article 42 (1), in the course of which the Union may use civilian and military means, shall include joint disarmament operations, humanitarian and rescue tasks, military advice and assistance tasks, conflict prevention and peace-keeping tasks, tasks of combat forces in crisis management, including peace-making and post-conflict stabilisation. All these tasks may contribute to the

fight against terrorism, including by supporting third countries in combating terrorism in their territories."

3. According to Article 29 TEU "the Council shall adopt decisions which shall define the approach of the Union to a particular matter of a geographical or thematic nature. Member states shall ensure that their national policies conform to the Union positions."

4. According to Article 28 TEU "where the international situation requires operational action by the Union, the Council shall adopt the necessary decisions. They shall lay down their objectives, scope, the means to be made available to the Union, if necessary their duration, and the conditions for their implementation."

5. Article 31 (2) TEU.

6. The second subparagraph of Article 31 (1): "When abstaining in a vote, any member of the Council may qualify its abstention by making a formal declaration under the present subparagraph. In that case, it shall not be obliged to apply the decision, but shall accept that the decision commits the Union. In a spirit of mutual solidarity, the Member State concerned shall refrain from any action likely to conflict with or impede Union action based on that decision and the other Member States shall respect its position. If the members of the Council qualifying their abstention in this way represent at least one third of the Member States comprising at least one third of the population of the Union, the decision shall not be adopted."

7. See more extensively Franz Leidenmühler, 2000. "Österreichs dauernde Neutralität und die Gemeinsame Außen- und Sicherheitspolitik der Europäischen Union— Eine völker- bzw. gemeinschaftsrechtliche Bestandsaufnahme zur Jahrtausendwende." In *Neutralität oder Verteidigungsbündnis. Rechtsexperten und Spitzenpolitiker über die sicherheitspolitische Zukunft Österreichs*, edited by Michael F. Strohmer and Günter H. Lutzenberger: 37, 48 et seq.

8. Second sentence of the second subparagraph of Article 31 (1) TEU.

9. Federal Law Gazette Austria 1955/211.

10. Meant in a strictly military sense. The obligations of a permanently neutral State do not cover so-called economic neutrality, let alone acting within a policy of neutrality; see Magnus Christianson, 2010. *Solidarity and Sovereignty—The Two-Dimensional Game of Swedish Security Policy.* Tartu: Baltic Deffene College, 311 et seq.

11. See also Paul Luif, 1995. *On the Road to Brussels.* West Lafayette: Purdue University Press: 238 et seqs.

12. Aside of political considerations these tasks are not problematic in a legal sense, as they base per definition on the consent of the concerned third countries.

13. Article 103 states that members' obligations under the UN Charter override their obligations under any other treaty.

14. See on this Franz Leidenmühler, 2008. "From Common Market to Common Defense." *EUWatch* 1: 9, 10 et seq.

15. Article 42 (7) TEU: "If a Member State is the victim of armed aggression on its territory, the other Member States shall have towards it an obligation of aid and assistance by all the means in their power, in accordance with Article 51 of the United Nations Charter. This shall not prejudice the specific character of the security and defence policy of certain Member States."

16. For another opinion see Gerhard Jandl, 2015. "Österreich zwischen Können, Müssen, Wollen." *Die Presse*, April 16.

17. See also Peter Hilpold, 2015. "Die österreichische Neutralität und die GASP—Stationen einer dynamischen Entwicklung." *Wiener Blätter zur Friedensforschung* 164: 41.

18. Alliances of collective defense make sense in a situation of menace, as their function is deterrence. And the addressee of this deterrent function is a potential enemy state. This deterrence function versus enemy states is the only sense of a defense alliance. But today, threats are much more resulting from terrorism or from instability in other regions of the world. And terrorists, for example, cannot be deterred by a mutual defense clause, as can be enemy states. So there exists no rational cause for establishing a defense alliance at the moment. Much more, transforming the EU into a defense alliance at the moment would not produce more security, but create more insecurity. Because a defense alliance, built without necessity, is making neighbors nervous, because they have to think that they are potential addressees of the deterrence function of the alliance. So, in the result, this clause of mutual defense in the Treaty of Lisbon is not only senseless, it is even more creating insecurity and has thereby a destabilizing function.

19. How difficult it is to identify common interests of the EU—see Thomas Gimesi, Anja Opitz, Alexander Siedschlag and Jodok Troy, 2006. *Theoretische Ableitung europäischer Sicherheitsinteressen*: 9 et seq.

20. Article 42 (6) in conjunction with Article 46 TEU.

21. Article 42 (6) TEU now is the legal base for a kind of differentiated integration ("Europe of different speeds") in the field of CFSP and CSDP. In the result, with the Treaty of Lisbon for the first time the concept of differentiated integration is extended to the field of Foreign and Security Policy. Previously we only know it in the so-called first pillar of the EU, the internal market; as an example can serve the Monetary Union.

22. Annegret Bendiek and Markus Kaim, 2014. "Die neue Europäische Sicherheitsstrategie—der transatlantische Faktor." *SWP-Aktuell* 2015/A 55.

23. Compare Council Decision (CFSP) 2015/778 of May 18, 2015, on a European Union military operation in the Southern Central Mediterranean (EUNAVFOR MED); http://eur-lex.europa.eu/search.html?DTN=0778&SUBDOM_INIT=ALL_ALL&DTS_DOM=ALL&CASE_LAW_SUMMARY=false&type=advanced&DTS_SUBDOM=ALL_ALL&excConsLeg=true&typeOfActStatus=DECISION&qid=145 0639034530&DB_TYPE_OF_ACT=decision&DTA=2015&locale=en.

BIBLIOGRAPHY

Bendiek, Annegret. 2008. "Perspektiven der EU-Außenpolitik." *SWP-Aktuell*, June.

Bendiek, Annegret and Markus Kaim. 2014. "Die neue Europäische Sicherheitsstrategie—der transatlantische Faktor." *SWP-Aktuell* 2015/A 55.

Beyerlin, Ulrich. 1982. "Humanitarian Intervention." In *Encyclopedia of Public International Law,* edited by Bernhardt, Instalment 3, 211 et seqs.

Blanck, Kathrin. 2005. *Europäische Sicherheits- und Verteidigungspolitik im Rahmen der europäischen Sicherheitsarchitektur.* Wien: Springer.

Cassese, Antonio. 1999. "Ex iniuria ius oritur: Are We Moving Towards International Legitimation of Forcible Humanitarian Countermeasures in the World Community?" *EJIL*: 23–30.

Christianson, Magnus. 2010. *Solidarity and Sovereignty—The Two-Dimensional Game of Swedish Security Policy.* Tartu: Baltic Deffene College.

Dietrich, Sascha. 2006. "Die rechtlichen Grundlagen der Verteidigungspolitik der Europäischen Union." *ZaöRV* 66: 663–696.

Gimesi, Thomas, Anja Opitz, Alexander Siedschlag, and Jodok Troy. 2006. *Theoretische Ableitung europäischer Sicherheitsinteressen.*

Henkin, Louis. 2006. "Kosovo and the Law of 'Humanitarian Intervention.'" *AJIL* 93(4): 824–828

Hilpold, Peter. 2015. "Die österreichische Neutralität und die GASP—Stationen einer dynamischen Entwicklung." *Wiener Blätter zur Friedensforschung* 164: 41.

Hummer, Waldemar. 2001. "Solidarität versus Neutralität: Das immerwährend neutrale Österreich in der GASP vor und nach Nizza." *Österreichische Militärische Zeitschrift* 2: 147–166.

Jandl, Gerhard. 2015. "Österreich zwischen Können, Müssen, Wollen." *Die Presse*, April 16.

Köck, Heribert, Daniela Horn, and Franz Leidenmühler. 2009. *From Protectorate to Statehood: Self-Determination v. Territorial Integrity in the Case of Kosovo and the Position of the European Union.* Wien: NWV Verlag.

Leidenmühler, Franz. 2000. "Österreichs dauernde Neutralität und die Gemeinsame Außen- und Sicherheitspolitik der Europäischen Union—Eine völker- bzw. gemeinschaftsrechtliche Bestandsaufnahme zur Jahrtausendwende." In *Neutralität oder Verteidigungsbündnis. Rechtsexperten und Spitzenpolitiker über die sicherheitspolitische Zukunft Österreichs,* edited by Michael F. Strohmer and Günter H. Lutzenberger, 37–61. Innsbruck: Studienverlag.

———. 2003. "Loyalität im Verbund der GASP bzw. GESVP der Europäischen Union und Pflichten der Mitgliedstaaten aus dem allgemeinen Völkerrecht." In: *Europa—Macht—Friede: Die Rolle Österreichs,* edited by ÖSFK, 204 et seqs. Münster: agenda Münster.

———. 2008. "From Common Market to Common Defense." *EUWatch* 11: 8–11.

———. 2015. "Neutralität und EU: Spagat oder Symbiose?" *Die Presse*, June 25.

Luif, Paul. 1995. *On the Road to Brussels.* West Lafayette: Purdue University Press.

Rotter, Manfred. 1973. "Neutralization, an Instrument for Solving International Conflicts?" *Österreichische Zeitschrift für Politikwissenschaft* 2(1): 49–64.

———. 1983. "Austria's Permanent Neutrality and the Free Trade Agreement with the EEC: Strategies to Reduce Dependences?" In Small States in Europe and Dependence, edited by Otmar Höll, 306–328. West Lafayette: Purdue University Press.

Conclusions

Heinz Gärtner

The notion that the concept of neutrality is a phenomenon and a part of the Cold War is false in many ways. First, the history of neutrality is much older; the Swiss idea of neutrality dates back to the fifteenth and sixteenth century. It got its legal basis at the Hague Convention of 1907. Second, neutrality was not constitutive for the Cold War but its anomaly. The Cold War was about building blocks, neutrality about staying out of them. When the Cold War was the norm, neutrality was the exception. Michael Gehler finds that Austria's neutrality played an important role in the debate in the fifties as a model for Germany and other Central European states to stay out of the two military blocs. He also makes clear why this model case could not be achieved. It was the German chancellor Adenauer, who played a key role in the final decision-making process by the Western Powers in 1952 as well as 1955. He disliked neutrality as a model for Germany and did everything to prevent it in order to keep the Federal Republic fully Western integrated.

After the end of the Cold War, neutral states became active in peace operations outside of military alliances. In many ways, small neutral states have more room for maneuver than members of alliances or big powers. They receive more acceptance and hold less geopolitical interests. Johanna Rainio-Niemi observes that neutrality has been declared obsolete many times in its long and layered history. Yet a close companion to wars and conflicts throughout documented human history, and an inherently flexible concept, it has also made many comebacks in varying forms and contexts. She concludes, that, considering the Cold War experiences, in the most successful neutral countries of the Cold War, neutrality was—and could be—made use of as an instrument of state- and nation-building. Austria is a success case yet Finland—exactly because of the more pronounced fragility of its Cold War neutrality—offers equally important lessons to be learned. Practically forgotten for a few decades, the idea of neutrality—embedded in the debates about the "Finland Option" and the "Austrian model"—made a comeback especially in connection with the escalation of the Ukrainian question in the spring of 2014.

More specific, Liliane Stadler asks why neutral European states have remained neutral since the end of the Cold War. She finds that neutral states respond to critical moments in their environment by pursuing reversible, rather than irreversible foreign policy options.

Neutrality in the twenty-first century does not mean to keep out but to engage. Adrian Hyde-Price sees a wide spectrum for neutrality. For him it comes in "57 varieties." It stretches from a passive and isolationist stance at one end of the spectrum, to an engaged and interventionist approach at the other. It goes without saying that there always has to be a balance between engagement and disengagement. When and how much should a state be involved in or keep distance from a conflict? What is too much and what is too little? These questions are always difficult to address in a complex and volatile security environment. It has to be said, however, that the issue of engagement is not unique to neutral states per se, but rather relates to deeper philosophical and moral questions about issues such as state sovereignty and the use of force (Cottey 2015).

More specifically, Laurent Götschel attributes the role of middle powers to neutral states. Middle powers have two meanings: a power of medium size (medium) or a power "in-between" (mediation). Through their activities as an "in-between" of conflict parties, neutral states can become more relevant to the international system (a traditional factor of power), and they can also strengthen their own networks and groups of friends (network-power). Götschel argues that this element of power is not limited to neutral states. A country like Norway has been very active in this field. Turkey would also like to be seen as a "friend of mediation." However, neutral states might have a comparative advantage to be mediators.

Terrence Hopmann attributes normative power to neutral states contingent on organizations. Thus, while NATO, the European Union (EU) and the Collective Security Treaty Organization have generally been dominated by the major states of Europe and North America, the OSCE—for Hopmann—remains a vehicle in which the concerns of the neutral and nonaligned states may be addressed, and in which their normative power may be advanced in contrast to the military and economic powers that otherwise dominate the interstate relations of Europe.

As to the EU, for Franz Leidenmühler and Sandra Grafeneder Austria's permanent neutrality does not only hamper the country's participation in the EU's crisis management. On the contrary, a permanently neutral member state can play a vital role in enhancing the EU's CFSP and CSDP making the assessment of current challenges and threats to the security of the Union more effective.

Crisis management and conflict prevention can be conducted within the framework of the EU, NATO Partnerships or the OSCE. Neutral states actively participate in the EU crisis-management tasks, as provided for by the Lisbon Treaty and the Security Strategy of the European Union (Shared Vision, 2016). Neutrality is no obstacle to the EU crisis-management operations, whatsoever. Neutral states also cooperate closely with NATO in important and necessary areas, such as crisis management, humanitarian operations or peacekeeping. Cooperative security and the concept of partners offer the possibility of co-decision for every operation with neutral states. Rather than passive isolation from the international scene, Switzerland for example uses cooperative multilateral frameworks and actively engages in contributing to security and peace in Europe's neighborhood. Based on Switzerland's domestic strengths, Christian Nünlist labels the modern form of Swiss foreign policy "multipartiality" rather than neutrality. In recent years, Swiss foreign policy has successfully transformed its passive neutrality policy into an engaged, active, independent, and multipartial peace policy—providing a model for other neutral or middle powers to make meaningful contributions in countering current global security challenges.

In contrast to disengagement and staying out, "engaged neutrality" means active participation in the international security policy in general and in international peace operations in particular. Engaged neutrality means involvement whenever possible and staying out if necessary; it does not mean staying out when possible and engagement only if necessary. It goes without saying that there can be no neutrality between democracy and dictatorship, between a constitutional state and despotism, between the adherence to human rights and their violation. Nonetheless, neutrality allows for a crucial advantage in the debate on these values. It releases from geopolitical and alliance-related considerations. Neutrality cannot mean standing outside, but rather demands an intense involvement in international crisis management.

Diplomacy and conflict prevention are traditionally fields in which neutral states can be active. Of course, neutrality must not be interpreted as "sitting still" in the integral sense of sitting on the sidelines. This definition would support economic neutrality and an equidistance between the blocks and would be incompatible with a membership in the United Nations. Neutrality has never oriented itself along these lines discussed in literature on neutrality, allowing it to prove its flexibility. Flexibility of the understanding of neutrality and its adaptability to modern requirements cannot be interpreted as a loss of significance. Multilateralism, readiness to talk, and global partnership have priority for the neutrals.

ANNEX: NEUTRALITY AS A PROBLEM-SOLVING MODEL?

Under some circumstances, the concept of neutrality could serve as a model. It did so already in the fifties during the Cold War. As the Cold War was about building blocks in Europe and military alliances, neutrality represented the anomaly. Neutral states managed to stay out of the spheres of influence created by the two military superpowers, the United States and the Soviet Union. On several occasions during the Cold War, there have been suggestions to create a "neutral belt" in Central Europe. Austria and Finland can serve as classic examples here. In Central Europe, such a solution was only possible for Austria after 1955.

The question is whether neutrality is a phase-out model of a former policy between military blocks, or if it is a sustainable conceptual option also for the future. Indeed, there are indications for the latter.

The Example of Georgia

The conflict between Russia and Georgia in 2008–2009 provoked a new debate, particularly within NATO, regarding the range and future of military obligations of alliance. Officially, NATO stands by its decision to continue its expansion into the East and South of Europe. However, the precarious role of Georgia before and in the first days of clashes, and the open political pressure onto NATO to choose sides, applied by Georgian president Saakashvili, led to barely concealed irritations and worries regarding further accession commitments from NATO's side. The transatlantic alliance, which wanted to support Georgia politically and militarily, and at the same time did not want to damage the cooperative relationship with Russia, is trying to please both sides if possible and itself—squaring the circle, so to speak. Yet the dilemma is obvious. If Georgia joined NATO and a further military conflict between Georgia and Russia should erupt or be provoked, NATO could even, in an extreme scenario, be dragged into a conflict with nuclear Russia, due to the commitment of assistance in Article V of its Treaty. If NATO did not act, its commitments of assistance would seem unreliable both internally and externally, which could also have fatal consequences. Under these circumstances, an at first glance strange solution becomes a viable political option: neutrality for Georgia and security guarantees from NATO and Russia.

Austria's status of neutrality was reached when all occupying forces agreed after the Second World War that they all would withdraw their troops from the Austrian territory. The same model of neutrality could be an interesting solution for Georgia. Following the status of neutrality's logic, it would have to include the withdrawal of all Russian troops from Georgia, including those rogue provinces which declared themselves independent

(South Ossetia and Abkhazia). The price for the withdrawal—the waiving of a Georgian membership in NATO—would not be so much a concession to Russia, but rather a requirement for a sovereign Georgia, free of foreign troops and with territorial integrity. This step would in no way exclude the possibility of close cooperation with NATO—such as the one practiced by Austria and Sweden.

The Austrian Independence Treaty supporting neutrality demanded wide-ranging guarantees from Austria concerning ethnic minorities. A demand, which would of course be of essential importance for Georgia and its treatment of minorities. The chances of neutrality being accepted are currently looking bleak, in Georgia as well as in Abkhazia, South Ossetia and, of course, Moscow. Certainly though, it is an interesting political option for all involved parties.

Neutrality for Ukraine?

When it comes to Ukraine, there is no military solution in sight. Sanctions will do little to stop Russia's aggressive behavior. As a diplomatic solution the Austrian model could be an interesting alternative for Ukraine. In its neutrality law of 1955, Austria agreed not to join a military alliance and not to allow any foreign military bases on its territory. The foreign soldiers finally retreated and Austria regained its independence. A guarantee that Ukraine will not join a military alliance based on international law might be acceptable for Russia. In addition to its neutrality, the State Treaty also guaranteed that Austria would not join a new union with Germany (Anschluss), as it had happened in 1938. In the case of Ukraine, such a prohibition for the Ukraine or parts of it together with neutrality could guarantee its unity.

In addition, in a separate Austrian State Treaty, the minority rights were regulated and certain capabilities of Austria's military were limited. In the case of Ukraine, such a State Treaty could expressly detail the Russian minorities within the country's borders, as well as clarify the future status of Crimea, whereby the unity of Ukraine should be guaranteed.

The alternative for the Ukraine would be a partition similar to the one in Germany. Austria quickly adopted the Western values and started a process of integration in the market economy, which eventually led to the accession to the European Union in the nineties. This development was accepted by the Soviet Union, mainly because Austria did not become a member of NATO.

The principles of the EU's neighborhood policy, the promotion of democracy, the rule of law and market economy are essential for Ukraine. However, a solution without Russia will not be possible, as EU politicians and officials continue to indicate. Moreover, they also emphasize that becoming a NATO member is not on the Ukrainian agenda.

Diplomacy is not just talking to each other. There has to be an offer that can save face for Ukraine, the West and Russia. Sanctions will not solve the problem. It becomes somewhat clear that Austria's model could provide such an offer. Austria is a member of the European Union but not a NATO member. In the immediate aftermath of Second World War, Austria was divided into four major zones and jointly occupied by the United States, Britain, France in the West and South and the Soviet Union in the East of the country. Therefore, there was a danger of partition similar to the one in Germany.

All in all, a democratic and economically developed Ukraine could in the long run represent a valuable advantage for the Kremlin. European and American economic aid packages, similar to the post–Second World War Marshall Plan, are now essential for Ukraine. Similar to the situation in Austria, the aid packages should also target the Eastern part of the country. The combination of neutrality and the Marshall Plan was a definite success for Austria. Moreover, one could argue that Austria's neutrality law was the beginning of the détente policy between East and West. The directions outlined above advocate that the Austrian model delivers a diplomatic solution that should be taken into consideration.

BIBLIOGRAPHY

Cottey, Andrew. 2015. At the Conference "Neutrality from the Cold War to Engaged Neutrality," Austrian Defense Academy, Vienna, October 2.

European External Action Service (EEAS). 2016. Shared Vision, Common Action: A Stronger Europe, A Global Strategy for the European Union's Foreign and Security Policy, June.

Index

About the Contributors

Prof. Dr. Heinz Gärtner lectures at the department of political science at the University of Vienna and at the Diplomatic Academy of Vienna. He is former academic director of the Austrian Institute for International Affairs (oiip). He held a Fulbright Fellowship as well as the visiting Austrian chair at the "Freeman Spogli Institute for International Studies" at Stanford University, where he had further visiting fellowships. He was also visiting professor at the King's College, London; Johns Hopkins Institute for East-West Security Studies, New York; University of Erlangen, Germany; St. Hugh's College, Oxford; University of British Columbia; World Policy Institute, New York; University of New Haven. He lectures often at other American, European, and Asian universities and research institutes. Heinz Gärtner is "senior external expert of the RAND-Corporation Europe." He chairs the advisory board "Strategy and Security" of the Science Commission of the Austrian Armed Forces. His research areas are among others European, international security, arms control, and International Relations Theory. Heinz Gärtner received the Bruno Kreisky (legendary former Austrian Chancellor) Award for most outstanding Political Books.

Prof. Dr. Michael Gehler studied history and German studies, Mag. and Dr.phil. habil. He was a research fellow of the Austrian Science Fond (FWF) in Vienna 1992–1996, associate professor for modern history and contemporary history at the Institute of Contemporary History at Leopold-Franzens-University Innsbruck 1999–2006, receiver of a Alexander Humboldt-scholarship 2001–2002 and permanent senior fellow at the Center for European Integration Studies (ZEI) of University Bonn, associated member of the research group at the Institute for Advanced Study in the Humanities in Essen under Wilfried Loth 2001–2002, visiting professor at University

Rostock in 2004, at University Salzburg 2004–2005 and the Catholic University (KU) Leuven in 2005, member of the Historic Commission at the Austrian Academy of Science (ÖAW) in Vienna, professor and leader of the Institute of History at the University in Hildesheim, receiver of a "Jean-Monnet Chairs" for European history through the European Commission in 2006 and member of the Liaison Committee. He was voted chairman of the Historic Commission at the Austrian Academy of Science (ÖAW) and received a second "Jean-Monnet Chairs" from the European Commission in 2011. He published a lot on Austrian, German, and European contemporary history.

Prof. Dr. Laurent Goetschel is professor of political science at the Europe Institute, University of Basel and director of the Swiss Peace Foundation (swisspeace) in Bern. He worked as director of a research module "Research Partnerships for Mitigating Syndromes of Global Change (NCCR North-South)." He is a researcher in the fields of international relations, European politics, (Swiss) foreign policy, as well as international conflicts and peace-building. Götschel received his BA and MA (1985–1991) in international relations from IUHEI, University of Geneva and his PhD (1993) in international relations also from IUHEI, University of Geneva. He is head of a program at the International Graduate School North-South and the Faculty of Humanities at the University of Basel.

Mag. Sandra Grafeneder LLB, was born on February 2, 1990, in Linz/Austria. She studied legal studies at Paris Lodron University of Salzburg, Johannes Kepler University of Linz, Georgia Southern University (Statesboro, Georgia) and Lewis and Clark Law School (Portland, Oregon). She is a lecturer and research fellow at the Institute of European Law, Johannes Kepler University, Linz/Austria. Her research centers on international and European environmental law and the substantive law of the EU.

Prof. Dr. Terrence Hopmann is professor of international relations at the Johns Hopkins School of Advanced International Studies. He is a former professor and chair of the Political Science Department at Brown University, where he was director of the Global Security Program of the Thomas J. Watson Jr. Institute of International Studies, the Centre for Foreign Policy Development and the International Relations Program; was professor of political science at the University of Minnesota and director of its Centre for International Studies. Hopmann served as vice president of the International Studies Association and program chair of three ISA international meetings; was editor of the *International Studies Quarterly*, was a Fulbright Fellow in Belgium and Austria, and a senior fellow at the United States Institute of Peace and the Woodrow Wilson International Centre for Scholars. His main research focuses on the Organization for Security and Co-operation in Europe; PhD, political science, Stanford University.

Prof. Dr. Adrian Hyde-Price is professor of political science at the University of Gothenburg, Sweden. He has previously held academic appointments at the universities of Bath, Leicester, Birmingham, Southampton and Manchester, and has been a research fellow at the Royal Institute of International Affairs (Chatham House) in London, working on the International Security Programme. He has also been a visiting research fellow at the Swedish Institute of International Affairs; Lund University; the Friedrich Ebert Stiftung, Bonn; Konrad Adenauer Stiftung, Bonn; and the Humboldt University. His research focuses on European security, and he specializes on the EU and NATO, German foreign and security policy, and security in Eastern Europe and the Baltic Sea region. His main publications include *The Challenge of Multipolarity: European Security in the Twenty-First Century* (2007); *Germany and European Order* (2000); *The International Politics of East Central Europe* (1996); *European Security Beyond the Cold War: Four Scenarios for the Year 2010* (1991); and *British Foreign Policy and the Anglican Church: Christian Engagement with the Contemporary World* (co-edited 2008).

Prof. Dr. Franz Leidenmühler was born on April 10, 1973, in Linz/Austria. He studied legal studies in Linz, Florence, and Thessaloniki. Leidenmühler is head of the Institute of European Law, Johannes Kepler University, Linz/Austria, guest lecturer at the Non-Commissioned Officers Academy (HUAK) of the Austrian Federal Armed Forces (Enns) and the former European Peace University (Stadtschlaining). He made numerous publications dealing with public international law (especially state-building, collapsed states, law of neutrality), law of international organizations (especially UN law), European Union law (especially CFSP and Internal Market), humanitarian law, and constitutional law. He was a member of numerous scientific associations at home and abroad.

Dr. Christian Nünlist is senior researcher at the Center for Security Studies (CSS) at ETH Zurich. At the CSS, he directs the think tank team "Swiss and Euro-Atlantic Security." He is the coeditor of both the monthly policy brief series "CSS Analyses in Security Policy" and the annual yearbook "Bulletin zur schweizerischen Sicherheitspolitik." His research focuses on Swiss multilateral diplomacy, with a focus on the OSCE and NATO partnerships.

Prof. Dr. Johanna Rainio-Niemi (PhD December 2008, University of Helsinki) works as a senior lecturer in international history at the University of

Tampere and is, since 2014, associate professor in contemporary and political history at the University of Helsinki. Her research interests include state- and nation-building, welfare state traditions, histories of neutrality and the Cold War. She specializes in transnational and comparative historical perspectives into European history. Her recent publications include *The Ideological Cold War. Politics of Neutrality in Austria and Finland* (Routledge 2014).

Liliane Stadler is currently pursuing a DPhil in History at the University of Oxford. In 2016, she completed the MPhil in International Relations at the Department of Politics and International Relations (DPIR) at the University of Oxford, after having read International Relations and Modern History at the University of St. Andrews. She currently serves as deputy editor of OxPol, the departmental blog of the DPIR.